CLEP

College Level Examination Program

Military

XAMonline, Inc.
21 Orient Avenue
Melrose, MA 02176
Toll Free 1-800-301-4647
Email: info@xamonline.com
Web: www.xamonline.com
Fax: 1-617-583-5552

Library of Congress Cataloging-in-Publication Data

Wynne, Sharon A.

CLEP Military Favorites/ Sharon Wynne.
  ISBN: 978-1-60787-551-2

1. CLEP 2. Study Guides.

Disclaimer:
The opinions expressed in this publication are the sole works of XAMonline and were created independently from The College Board or other testing affiliates. Between the time of publication and printing, test standards as well as testing formats and website information may change that are not included in part or in whole within this product. XAMonline develops sample test questions, and they reflect similar content as on real tests; however, they are not former tests. XAMonline assembles content that aligns with test standards but makes no claims nor guarantees candidates a passing score. Numerical scores are determined by testing companies such as The College Board.

Cover photo provided by ©iStock.com/LifeJourneys

Printed in the United States of America   œ-1
CLEP Military Favorites
ISBN: 978-1-60787-551-2

TABLE OF CONTENTS

I. The College-Level Examination Program

How the Program Works

CLEP exams are administered at over 1,800 institutions nationwide, and 2,900 colleges and universities award college credit to those who perform well on them. This rigorous program allows many self-directed students of a wide range of ages and backgrounds to demonstrate their mastery of introductory college-level material and pursue greater academic success. Students can earn credit for what they already know by getting qualifying scores on any of the 33 examinations.

The CLEP exams cover material that is taught in introductory-level courses at many colleges and universities. Faculty at individual colleges review the exams to ensure that they cover the important material currently taught in their courses.

Although CLEP is sponsored by the College Board, only colleges may grant credit toward a degree. To learn about a particular college's CLEP policy, contact the college directly. When you take a CLEP exam, you can request that a copy of your score report be sent to the college you are attending or planning to attend. After evaluating your score, the college will decide whether or not to award you credit for a certain course or courses, or to exempt you from them.

If the college decides to give you credit, it will record the number of credits on your permanent record, thereby indicating that you have completed work equivalent to a course in that subject. If the college decides to grant exemption without giving you credit for a course, you will be permitted to omit a course that would normally be required of you and to take a course of your choice instead.

The CLEP program has a long-standing policy that an exam may not be taken within the specified wait period. This waiting period provides you with an opportunity to spend additional time preparing for the exam or the option of taking a classroom course. If you violate the CLEP retest policy, the administration will be considered invalid, the score canceled, and any test fees will be forfeited. If you are a military service member, please note that DANTES will not fund retesting on a previously funded CLEP exam. However, you may personally fund a retest after the specified wait period.

The CLEP Examinations

CLEP exams cover material directly related to specific undergraduate courses taught during a student's first two years in college. The courses may be offered for three, four, six or eight semester hours in general areas such as mathematics, history, social sciences, English composition, natural sciences and humanities. Institutions will either grant credit for a specific course based on a satisfactory score on the related exam, or in the general area in which a satisfactory is earned. The credit is equal to the credit awarded to students who successfully complete the courses. See the Table of Contents for a complete list of all exam titles.

What the Examinations Are Like

CLEP exams are administered on computer and are approximately 90 minutes long, with the exception of College Composition, which is approximately 120 minutes long. Most questions are multiple-choice; other types of questions require you to fill in a numeric answer, to shade areas of an object, or to put items in the correct order. Questions using these kinds of skills are called zone, shade, grid, scale, fraction, numeric entry, histogram and order match questions.

CLEP College Composition includes a mandatory essay section, responses to which must be typed into the computer.

Some of the examinations have optional essays. You should check with the individual college or university where you are sending your score to see whether an optional essay is required for those exams. These essays are administered on paper and are scored by faculty at the institution that receives your score.

Where to Take the Examinations and How to Register

CLEP exams are administered throughout the year at over 1,800 test centers in the United States and select international sites. Once you have decided to take a CLEP examination, you can log into My Account at https://clepportal.collegeboard.org/myaccount to create and manage your own personal accounts, pay for CLEP exams and purchase study materials. You can self-register at any time by completing the online registration form.

Through My Account you can also access a list of institutions that administer CLEP and locate a test center in your area. **After paying for your exam through My Account, you must still contact the test center to schedule your CLEP exam.**

If you are unable to locate a test center near you, call 800-257-9558 for more information.

ACE's College Credit Recommendation Service

The College Credit Recommendation Service (CREDIT) of the American Council on Education (ACE) enables you to put all of your educational achievements on a secure and universally accepted ACE transcript. All of your ACE-evaluated courses and examinations, including CLEP, appear in an easy-to-read format that includes ACE credit recommendations, descriptions and suggested transfer areas. The service is perfect for candidates who have acquired college credit at multiple ACE-evaluated organizations or credit-by-examination programs. You may have your transcript released at any time to the college of your choice. There is a one-time setup fee of $40 (includes the cost of your first transcript) and a fee of $15 for each transcript requested after release of the first. ACE has an additional transcript service for organizations offering continuing education units.

The College Credit Recommendation Service is offered through ACE's Center for Lifelong Learning. For more than 50 years, ACE has been at the forefront of the evaluation of education and training attained outside the classroom. For more information about ACE CREDIT, contact:

ACE CREDIT
One Dupont Circle, NW
Suite 250
Washington, DC 20036

ACE's Call Center is open Monday to Friday, 8:45 a.m. to 4:45 p.m., and can be reached at 866-205-6267 or CREDIT@ace.nche.edu. Staff are able to assist you with courses and certifications that carry ACE recommendations for both civilian organizations and training obtained through the military.

If you are already registered for an ACE transcript, you can access your records and order transcripts using the ACE Online Transcript System: https://www.acenet.edu/transcripts/.

ACE's Center for Lifelong Learning can be found on the Internet at: http://www.acenet.edu/ higher-education.

How Your Score Is Reported

You have the option of seeing your CLEP score immediately after you complete the exam, except in the case of College Composition, for which scores are available four to six weeks after the exam date. Once you choose to see your score, it will be sent automatically to the institution you have designated as a score recipient; it cannot be canceled. You will receive a candidate copy of your score before you leave the test center. If you have tested at the institution that you have designated as a score recipient, it will have immediate access to your test results.

If you do not want your score reported, you may select that as an option at the end of the examination *before the exam is scored*. Once you have selected the option to not view your score, the score is canceled.

The score will not be reported to the institution you have designated, and you will not receive a candidate copy of your score report. You will have to wait the specified wait period before you can take the exam again.

CLEP scores are kept on file for 20 years. During this period, for a small fee, you may have your transcript sent to another college or to anyone else you specify. Your score(s) will never be sent to anyone without your approval.

II. Approaching a College about CLEP

The following sections provide a step-by-step guide to learning about the CLEP policy at a particular college or university. The person or office that can best assist you may have a different title at each institution, but the following guidelines will lead you to information about CLEP at any institution.

Adults and other nontraditional students returning to college often benefit from special assistance when they approach a college. Opportunities for adults to return to formal learning in the classroom are now widespread, and colleges and universities have worked hard to make this a smooth process for older students. Many colleges have established special offices that are staffed with trained professionals who understand the kinds of problems facing adults returning to college. If you think you might benefit from such assistance, be sure to find out whether these services are available at your college.

How to Apply for College Credit

Step 1. *Obtain, or access online, the general information catalog and a copy of the CLEP policy from each college you are considering.*

Information about admission and CLEP policies can be obtained on the college's website at clep.collegeboard.org/search/colleges, or by contacting or visiting the admissions office. Ask for a copy of the publication in which the college's complete CLEP policy is explained. Also, get the name and the telephone number of the person to contact in case you have further questions about CLEP.

Step 2. If you have not already been admitted to a college that you are considering, look at its admission requirements for undergraduate students to see whether you qualify.

Whether you're applying for college admission as a high school student, transfer student or as an adult resuming a college career or going to college for the first time, you should be familiar with the requirements for admission at the schools you are considering. If you are a nontraditional student, be sure to check whether the school has separate admissions requirements that might apply to you. Some schools are very selective, while others are "open admission."

It might be helpful for you to contact the admissions office for an interview with a counselor. State why you want the interview and ask what documents you should bring with you or send in advance. (These materials may include a high school transcript, transcript of previous college work or completed application for admission.) Make an extra effort to have all the information requested in time for the interview.

During the interview, relax and be yourself. Be prepared to state honestly why you think you are ready and able to do college work. If you have already taken CLEP exams and scored high enough to earn credit, you have shown that you are able to do college work. Mention this achievement to the admissions counselor because it may increase your chances of being accepted. If you have not taken a CLEP exam, you can still improve your chances of being accepted by describing how your job training or independent study has helped prepare you for college-level work. Discuss with the counselor what you have learned from your work and personal experiences.

Step 3. *Evaluate the college's CLEP policy.*

Typically, a college lists all its academic policies, including CLEP policies, in its general catalog or on its website. You will probably find the CLEP policy statement under a heading such as Credit-by-Examination, Advanced Standing, Advanced Placement or External Degree Program. These sections can usually be found in the front of the catalog. You can also check out the institution's CLEP Policy by visiting clep.collegeboard.org/search/colleges.

Many colleges publish their credit-by-examination policies in separate brochures, which are distributed through the campus testing office, counseling center, admissions office or registrar's office. If you find a very general policy statement in the college catalog, seek clarification from one of these offices.

Review the material in the section of this chapter entitled "Questions to Ask about a College's CLEP Policy." Use these guidelines to evaluate the college's CLEP policy. If you have not yet taken a CLEP exam, this evaluation will help you decide which exams to take. Because individual colleges have different CLEP policies, a review of several policies may help you decide which college to attend.

Step 4. *If you have not yet applied for admission, do so as early as possible.*

Most colleges expect you to apply for admission several months before you enroll, and it is essential that you meet the published application deadlines. It takes time to process your application for admission. If you have yet to take a CLEP exam, you may want to take one or more CLEP exams while you are waiting for your application to be processed. Be sure to check the college's CLEP policy beforehand so that you are taking exams your college will accept for credit. You should also find out from the college when to submit your CLEP score(s).

Complete all forms and include all documents requested with your application(s) for admission.

Normally, an admission decision cannot be reached until all documents have been submitted and evaluated. Unless told to do so, do not send your CLEP score(s) until you have been officially admitted.

Step 5. *Arrange to take CLEP exam(s) or to submit your CLEP score(s).*

CLEP exams can be taken at any of the 1,800 test centers world-wide. To locate a test center near you. clep.collegeboard.org/search/test-centers.

If you have already taken a CLEP exam, but did not have your score sent to your college, you can have an official transcript sent at any time for a small fee. Fill out the Transcript Request Form included on the same page as your exam score. If you do not have the form, visit clep.collegeboard.org/about/score to download a copy, or call 800-257-9558 to order a transcript using a major credit card. Completed forms should be faxed to 610-628-3726 or sent to the following address, along with a check or money order made payable to CLEP for $20 (this fee is subject to change).

CLEP Transcript Service
P.O. Box 6600
Princeton, NJ 08541-6600

Transcripts will only include CLEP scores for the past 20 years; scores more than 20 years old are not kept on file.

Your CLEP scores will be evaluated, probably by someone in the admissions office, and sent to the registrar's office to be posted on your permanent record once you are enrolled. Procedures vary from college to college, but the process usually begins in the admissions office.

Step 6. *Ask to receive a written notice of the credit you receive for your CLEP score(s).*

A written notice may save you problems later, when you submit your degree plan or file for graduation. In the event that there is a question about whether or not you earned CLEP credit, you will have an official record of what credit was awarded. You may also need this verification of course credit if you meet with an academic adviser before the credit is posted on your permanent record.

Step 7. *Before you register for courses, seek academic advising.*

A discussion with your academic adviser can help you to avoid taking unnecessary courses and can tell you specifically what your CLEP credit will mean to you. This step may be accomplished at the time you enroll. Most colleges have orientation sessions for new students prior to each enrollment period. During orientation, students are usually assigned academic advisers who then give them individual help in developing long-range plans and course schedules for the next semester. In conjunction with this counseling, you may be asked to take some additional tests so that you can be placed at the proper course level.

Questions to Ask about a College's CLEP Policy

Before taking CLEP exams for the purpose of earning college credit, try to find the answers to these questions:

1. *Which CLEP exams are accepted by the college?*

   A college may accept some CLEP exams for credit and not others — possibly not the exams you are considering. For this reason, it is important that you know the specific CLEP exams for which you can receive credit.

2. *Does the college require the optional free-response (essay) section for exams in composition and literature as well as the multiple-choice portion of the CLEP exam you are considering? Will you be required to pass a departmental test such as an essay, laboratory or oral exam in addition to the CLEP multiple-choice exam?*

Knowing the answers to these questions ahead of time will permit you to schedule the optional free-response or departmental exam when you register to take your CLEP exam.

3. *Is CLEP credit granted for specific courses at the college? If so, which ones?*

You are likely to find that credit is granted for specific courses and that the course titles are designated in the college's CLEP policy. It is not necessary, however, that credit be granted for a specific course for you to benefit from your CLEP credit. For instance, at many liberal arts colleges, all students must take certain types of courses; these courses may be labeled the core curriculum, general education requirements, distribution requirements or liberal arts requirements. The requirements are often expressed in terms of credit hours. For example, all students may be required to take at least six hours of humanities, six hours of English, three hours of mathematics, six hours of natural science and six hours of social science, with no particular courses in these disciplines specified. In these instances, CLEP credit may be given as "6 hrs. English Credit" or "3 hrs. Math Credit" without specifying for which English or mathematics courses credit has been awarded. To avoid possible disappointment, you should know before taking a CLEP exam what type of credit you can receive or whether you will be exempted from a required course but receive no credit.

4. *How much credit is granted for each exam you are considering, and does the college place a limit On the total amount of CLEP credit you can earn toward your degree?*

Not all colleges that grant CLEP credit award the same amount for individual exams. Furthermore, some colleges place a limit on the total amount of credit you can earn through CLEP or other exams. Other colleges may grant you exemption but no credit toward your degree. Knowing several colleges' policies concerning these issues may help you decide which college to attend. If you think you are capable of passing a number of CLEP exams, you may want to attend a college that will allow you to earn credit for all or most of them. Check out if your institution grants CLEP policy by visiting clep.collegeboard.org/search/colleges.

5. *What is the required score for earning CLEP credit for each exam you are considering?*

   Most colleges publish the required scores for earning CLEP credit in their general catalogs or in brochures. The required score may vary from exam to exam, so find out the required score for each exam you are considering.

6. *What is the college's policy regarding prior course work in the subject in which you are considering taking a CLEP exam?*

   Some colleges will not grant credit for a CLEP exam if the candidate has already attempted a college-level course closely aligned with that exam. For example, if you successfully completed English 101 or a comparable course on another campus, you will probably not be permitted to also receive CLEP credit in that subject. Some colleges will not permit you to earn CLEP credit for a course that you failed.

7. *Does the college make additional stipulations before credit will be granted?*

   It is common practice for colleges to award CLEP credit only to their enrolled students. There are other stipulations, however, that vary from college to college. For example, does the college require you to formally apply for or to accept CLEP credit by completing and signing a form? Or does the college require you to "validate" your CLEP score by successfully completing a more advanced course in the subject? Getting answers to these and other questions will help to smooth the process of earning college credit through CLEP.

III. Preparing to Take CLEP Examinations

Test Preparation Tips

1. Familiarize yourself as much as possible with the test and the test situation before the day of the exam. It will be helpful for you to know ahead of time:

   a. how much time will be allowed for the test and whether there are timed subsections. (This information is included in the examination guides and in the CLEP Tutorial video.)

   b. what types of questions and directions appear on the exam. (See the examination guides.)

c. how your test score will be computed.

d. in which building and room the exam will be administered.

e. the time of the test administration.

f. direction, transit and parking information to the test center.

2. Register and pay your exam fee through My Account at https://clepportal.collegeboard.org/myaccount and print your registration ticket. Contact your preferred test center to schedule your appointment to test. Your test center may require an additional administration fee. Check with your test center and confirm the amount required and acceptable method of payment.

3. On the day of the exam, remember to do the following.

   a. Arrive early enough so that you can find a parking place, locate the test center, and get settled comfortably before testing begins.

   b. Bring the following with you:

      o completed registration ticket
      o any registration forms or printouts required by the test center. Make sure you have filled out all necessary paperwork in advance of your testing date.
      o a form of valid and acceptable identification. Acceptable identification must:

         ▪ Be government-issued
         ▪ Be an original document — photocopied documents are not acceptable
         ▪ Be valid and current — expired documents (bearing expiration dates that have passed) are not acceptable, no matter how recently they may have expired
         ▪ Bear the test-taker's full name, in English language characters, exactly as it appears on the
         ▪ Registration Ticket, including the order of the names.
         ▪ Middle initials are optional and only need to match the first letter of the middle name when present on both the ticket and the identification.
         ▪ Bear a recent recognizable photograph that clearly matches the test-taker

- Include the test-taker's signature
- Be in good condition, with clearly legible text and a clearly visible photograph

Refer to the Exam Day Info page on the CLEP website (http://clep.collegeboard.org/exam-day-info) for more details on acceptable and unacceptable forms of identification.

- o military test-takers, bring your Geneva Convention Identification Card. Refer to clep.collegeboard.org/military for additional information on IDs for active duty members, spouses, and civil service civilian employees.
- o two number 2 pencils with good erasers. Mechanical pencils are prohibited in the testing room.

c. Leave all books, papers and notes outside the test center. You will not be permitted to use your own scratch paper; it will be provided by the test center.

d. Do not take a calculator to the exam. If a calculator is required, it will be built into the testing software and available to you on the computer. The CLEP Tutorial video will have a demonstration on how to use online calculators.

e. Do not bring a cell phone or other electronic devices into the testing room.

4. When you enter the test room:

a. You will be assigned to a computer testing station. If you have special needs, be sure to communicate them to the test center administrator *before* the day you test.

b. Be relaxed while you are taking the exam. Read directions carefully and listen to all instructions given by the test administrator. If you don't understand the directions, ask for help before the test begins. If you must ask a question that is not related to the exam after testing has begun, raise your hand and a proctor will assist you. The proctor cannot answer questions related to the exam.

c. Know your rights as a test-taker. You can expect to be given the full working time allowed for taking the exam and a reasonably quiet and comfortable place in which to work. If a poor testing situation is preventing you from doing your best, ask whether the situation can be remedied. If it can't, ask the test administrator to report the problem on a Center Problem Report that will be submitted with your test results. You may also wish to immediately write a letter to CLEP, P.O. Box 6656, Princeton, NJ 08541-6656. Describe the exact circumstances as completely as you can. Be sure to include the name of the test center, the test date and the name(s) of the exam(s) you took.

Accommodations for Students with Disabilities

If you have a disability, such as a learning or physical disability, that would prevent you from taking a CLEP exam under standard conditions, you may request accommodations at your preferred test center. Contact your preferred test center well in advance of the test date to make the necessary arrangements and to find out its deadline for submission of documentation and approval of accommodations. Each test center sets its own guidelines in terms of deadlines for submission of documentation and approval of accommodations.

Accommodations that can be arranged directly with test centers include:

- ZoomText (screen magnification)
- Modifiable screen colors
- Use of a reader, amanuensis, or sign language interpreter
- Extended time
- Untimed rest breaks

If the above accommodations do not meet your needs, contact CLEP Services at clep@info.collegeboard.org for information about other accommodations.

IV. Interpreting Your Scores

CLEP score requirements for awarding credit vary from institution to institution. The College Board, however, recommends that colleges refer to the standards set by the American Council on Education (ACE). All ACE recommendations are the result of careful and periodic review by evaluation teams made up of faculty who are subject-matter experts and technical experts in testing and measurement. To determine whether you are eligible for credit for your CLEP scores, you should refer to the policy of the college you will be attending. The policy will state the score that is required to earn credit at that institution. Many colleges award credit at the score levels recommended by ACE. However, some require scores that are higher or lower than these.

Your exam score will be printed for you at the test center immediately upon completion of the examination, unless you took College Composition. For this exam, you will receive your score four to six weeks after the exam date. Your CLEP exam scores are reported only to you, unless you ask to have them sent elsewhere. If you want your scores sent to a college, employer or certifying agency, you must select this option through My Account. This service is free only if you select your score recipient at the time you register to take your exam. A fee will be charged for each score recipient you select at a later date. Your scores are kept on file for 20 years. For a fee, you can request a transcript at a later date.

The pamphlet *What Your CLEP Score Means*, which you will receive with your exam score, gives detailed information about interpreting your scores. A copy of the pamphlet is in the appendix of this Guide. A brief explanation appears below.

How CLEP Scores Are Computed

In order to reach a total score on your exam, two calculations are performed.

First, your "raw score" is calculated. This is the number of questions you answer correctly. Your raw score is increased by one point for each question you answer correctly, and no points are gained or lost when you do not answer a question or answer it incorrectly.

Second, your raw score is converted into a "scaled score" by a statistical process called *equating*. Equating maintains the consistency of standards for test scores over time by adjusting for slight differences in difficulty between test forms. This ensures that your score does not depend on the specific test form you took or how well others did on the same form. Your raw score is converted to a scaled score that ranges from 20, the lowest, to 80, the highest. The final scaled score is the score that appears on your score report.

How Essays Are Scored

The College Board arranges for college English professors to score the essays written for the College Composition exam. These carefully selected college faculty members teach at two- and four-year institutions nationwide. The faculty members receive extensive training and thoroughly review the College Board scoring policies and procedures before grading the essays. Each essay is read and scored by two professors, the sum of the two scores for each essay is combined with the multiple-choice score, and the result is reported as a scaled score between 20 and 80. Although the format of the two sections is very different, both measure skills required for expository writing. Knowledge of formal grammar, sentence structure and organizational skills are necessary for the multiple-choice section, but the emphasis in the free-response section is on writing skills rather than grammar.

Optional essays for CLEP Composition Modular and the literature examinations are evaluated and scored by the colleges that require them, rather than by the College Board. If you take an optional essay, it will be sent to the institution you designate when you take the test. If you did not designate a score recipient institution when you took an optional essay, you may still select one as long as you notify CLEP within 18 months of taking the exam. Copies of essays are not held beyond 18 months or after they have been sent to an institution.

V. Information for the Military

DANTES

DANTES stands for **D**efense **A**ctivity for **N**on-**T**raditional **E**ducation **S**upport. The DANTES program offers a wide range of programs that is intended to help service members and veterans with career planning and be a one stop shop location for all military sponsored education programs. For example, under their administration is the GI Bill, Troops to Teachers program, SAT testing at some military locations, GED completion programs, etc. DANTES also generates a Joint Service Transcript for the student, which the student can use in applying to other colleges

For more information, visit their website at http://www.dantes.doded.mil

Financial Assistance

Tuition assistance (TA) is reimbursement for taking CLEP single area tests. All branches of the military are eligible for 100% tuition and fees for courses taken by active duty personnel. The College Board test is currently an $80 charge and there is a $20 university fee, all covered by DANTES for all authorized military personnel which excludes spouses. 33 exams are included in this program, each of which may be funded collectively. In the event that you fail, DANTES will not fund a second round to that same test. Both the U.S. Air Force and the U.S. Army policies provide 100% tuition and fees as described above. There are no requirements for re-enlisting. By contrast, tuition assistance for the US Navy and US Marines Officers must agree to remain on active duty for two years.

Department of Defense Virtual Education Fair

2015 was the first time the DoD had held this fair. The purpose of the fair was to connect students with universities, so they could ask questions about their interest areas and see what prerequisites they would need to apply to a specific college. DoD reps and college reps were also available for online chats.

The education fair had a few archived videos that participants could watch – an introduction from a DoD official and some career search and university application process videos. The fair was open to active duty military, veterans, and spouses.

The fair was geared towards informing potential students about how to apply to a university or college, what prerequisites might be needed, how to apply for DoD funding for the courses, and basically to see what programs DoD had and how to decide between them. About 30 colleges and universities had counselors available on chat, to help the student with questions about the college or a program of study.

For more information, visit their website at www.dodeducationfair.com

Participating Schools

- Armstrong State University
- Ashford University
- Bellevue University
- Campbell University
- Central Texas College
- Chaminade University
- Coastal Carolina Community College
- Coastline Community College
- Drury University
- ECPI University
- El Paso Community College
- Embry-Riddle Aeronautical University - Worldwide
- Empire State College, SUNY
- Everett Community College
- Excelsior College
- Fayetteville Technical Community College
- Florida Institute of Technology
- Fort Hays State University - Virtual College
- Grand Canyon University
- Hawaii Pacific University
- Hopkinsville Community College
- Jefferson Community College
- Liberty University - Online
- National American University
- National University
- Old Dominion University
- Park University
- Pensacola State College
- Pikes Peak Community College
- Post University - Online
- Regis University
- Roger Williams University
- Saint Leo University
- Southern New Hampshire University
- Southwest Tennessee Community College
- Sullivan University
- Thomas Edison State College
- Tidewater Community College
- Trident University International
- Troy University
- University of Maryland University College
- University of the Incarnate Word
- Upper Iowa University

DoD & Federal Partners

- Air Force Voluntary Education
- Army Voluntary Education
- Marine Corps Voluntary Education
- Navy Voluntary Education
- DANTES
- Dept. of Education Federal Student Aid
- Dept. of Veterans Affairs GI Bill & Education Services

CLEP Military Statistics

About 55,000 students take the various CLEP exams, and the passing rate is about 59%. The table below lists all 33 CLEP exams with 2015 military test takers. Over 20,000 candidates failed therefore it behooves the candidate to obtain full study guides. XAMonline is proud to offer full study guides for Analyzing and Interpreting Literature, College Composition/Modular, College Mathematics, Spanish Language and College Algebra. Additionally, each of the 33 titles are available as full length practice tests with detailed explanations from XAMonline as ebooks.

CLEP title	2015 # test takers (military)	2015 Passing rate (%)
Analyzing & Interpreting Literature	12,938	76
College Composition Modular	6,296	83
Principles of Management	5,257	35
College Mathematics	4,204	61
Introductory Psychology	2,628	55
College composition	2,626	72
Spanish	2,494	87
College Algebra	2,308	24
Introductory Sociology	2,197	54
History of the United States I	1,578	38
Information Systems	1,574	66
American Government	1,530	22
Humanities	1,285	39
Social Sciences & History	1,213	48
History of the United States II	1,155	37
Natural Sciences	1,078	45

Description of the Examination

The Analyzing and Interpreting Literature examination covers material usually taught in a general undergraduate course in literature. Although the examination does not require familiarity with specific works, it does assume that candidates have read widely and perceptively in poetry, drama, fiction and nonfiction. The questions are based on passages supplied in the test. These passages have been selected so that no previous experience with them is required to answer questions. The passages are taken primarily from American and British literature.

The examination contains approximately 80 multiple-choice questions to be answered in 98 minutes. Some of these are pretest questions that will not be scored. Any time candidates spend taking tutorials and providing personal information is additional to actual testing time.

An optional essay section can be taken in addition to the multiple-choice test. The essay section requires that two essays be written during a total time of 90 minutes. For the first essay, candidates are asked to analyze a short poem. For the second essay, candidates are asked to apply a generalization about literature (such as the function of a theme or a technique) to a novel, short story, or play that they have read.

Knowledge and Skills Required

Questions on the Analyzing and Interpreting Literature examination require candidates to demonstrate the following abilities.

- Ability to read prose, poetry, and drama with understanding
- Ability to analyze the elements of a literary passage and to respond to nuances of meaning, tone, imagery and style
- Ability to interpret metaphors, to recognize rhetorical and stylistics devices, to perceive relationships between parts and wholes, and to grasp a speaker's or author's attitudes
- Familiarity with the basic terminology used to discuss literary texts

The examination emphasizes comprehensions, interpretation and analysis of literary works. A specific knowledge of historical context (authors and movements) is not required, but a broad knowledge of literature gained through reading widely and a familiarity of basic literary terminology is assumed. The following outline indicates the relative emphasis given to the various types of literature and the periods from which the passages are taken. The approximate percentage of exam questions per classification is noted within each main category.

Genre
35% - 45% Poetry
35% - 45% Prose (fiction & nonfiction)
15% - 30% Drama

National Tradition
50% - 65% British Literature
30% - 45% American Literature
5% - 15% Works in Translation

Period
3% - 7%   Classical & pre-Renaissance
20% - 30% Renaissance & 17th Century
35% - 45% 18th & 19th Centuries
25% - 35% 20th & 21st Centuries

CLEP Practice Exam: Analyzing and Interpreting Literature

INSTRUCTIONS

This exam gives passages from known writings (fiction, poems, non-fiction/history, biographies, drama and more) over the past five hundred years. While the student taking the exam is not expected to have read the material or have familiarity with the passage prior to the exam, the test taker is expected to have the knowledge of an undergraduate English and writing class.

TIP: As the writing changes and the time periods change, it's important for a student to note the author and time period as that may assist in answering questions by either eliminating unlikely answers or allow the student to recall items about the author.

At the end of the test passages and answers, there is an answer key and a "rationale" key for each question. Take the test without referencing these guides. For questions that you guess the answers or get wrong, the rationale is provided to help you see how test makers frame answers to questions or explain pieces of information with which you are unfamiliar.

There are 80 questions on this particular practice test, and the CLEP also uses around 80 for the credit exam. As with the CLEP exam, the passages are taken primarily from American and British Literature - though at least once question, just as in the actual exam, is taken from another area of literature. Within the questions of the CLEP, the mixture of genre types falls typically almost 80-90% between poetry and prose (both fiction and non-fiction within the prose selections) and the remaining on drama. The entire test is balanced between three main eras - Renaissance/17th Century, 18th/19th Century, as well as 10th/21st Century; in the past, there is a slightly heavier emphasis on 18th/19th work, and usually there is one passage from the Classical/pre-Renaissance period.

The CLEP allows 98 minutes to take the exam of approximately 80 questions. Time yourself during the exam, but as you practice, focus more attention on accurately answering questions as the total number of correct answers impacts your score, not how many you skip or get wrong. If you skip any questions, make sure that you also skip that line on the answer sheet - or you may spend a lot of time erasing and redoing your answer key.

These passages do not actually appear on the CLEP exam, but are meant to show how the exam is written and the various range of questions, answers,

3

and key knowledge points required in order to pass the CLEP exam. Read each question carefully and provide the best answer choice. Good luck.

PASSAGE 1
(Prose fiction, American, 21st century)

Mornings, he likes to sit in his new leather chair by his new living room window, looking out across the rooftops and chimney pots, the clotheslines and telegraph lines and office towers. It's the first time Manhattan, from high above, hasn't crushed him with desire. On the contrary the view makes him feel smug. All those people down there, striving, hustling, pushing, shoving, busting to get what Willie's already got. In spades. He lights a cigarette, blows a jet of smoke against the window. Suckers.

~J.R. Moehriger, 2012 p120

1. The subject in this passage is:

   A. a character, and seems to be the lead of the story

   B. a supporting character

   C. someone with an attitude of a criminal

   D. female

   E. has been poor his whole life

2. What kind of description is the author providing of this scene?

   A. Backstory of the character

   B. A characterization of what the character is like

   C. A narrative, with the end of the selection giving thoughts in the first person

   D. The unreliable narrative about a character

   E. The author is using a persuasive argument

3. What types of words are "striving, hustling, pushing, shoving, bustling"?

   A. Adjectives

   B. Adverbs

   C. Nouns

   D. Gerunds

   E. Verbs

4. If you had to explain the phrase "crushed him" in the paragraph above and context of the paragraph, what would be the best appropriate explanation?

   A. The city sustained him with all the opportunity available.

   B. The city called to him to be part of its life.

   C. The city complimented him for everything he has achieved.

   D. The city had energized him to get what he felt he deserved.

   E. The city smothered him with all its offerings.

5. The author portrays the attitude of the character toward the people on the street below as:

   A. condescending

   B. sarcastic

   C. affectionate

   D. tolerant

   E. encouraged

PASSAGE 2
(Poetry, American, 19th century)

There is no frigate like a book
To take us lands away,
Nor any coursers like a page
Of prancing poetry;
This traverse may the poorest take
Without oppress of toll;
How frugal is the chariot
That bears the human soul!
~Emily Dickinson (1830-1886)

6. Authors use particular literary structures for descriptions. What best explains the one that Emily Dickinson employs in this poem?

   A. A literary allegory

   B. Personification

   C. Idioms

   D. Similes

   E. Flashbacks

7. How many types of transport types does the author incorporate?

A. Two

B. Three

C. Four

D. Five

E. None

8. If the words 'frigate, coursers, and chariot' were replaced with synonyms, what would the best choice of the following options include?

A. Train, car, carriage

B. Train, horse, carriage

C. Ship, car, carriage

D. Ship, car, train

E. Ship, horse, carriage

9. Which of the following descriptions more closely describes the author's intended meaning of poem?

A. Difficulties at work

B. The importance of books

C. Confessions for the soul

D. Poverty makes things difficult

E. Describing modes of transportation

10. There are very descriptive and strong feelings conveyed by the poet. Which of the following is not a feeling that this poem expresses?

A. Enjoyment of reading

B. Excitement of where reading can take you

C. Encouragement to get others to read

D. Fascination with topics in books

E. Discouragement for new readers

11. What is a good paraphrase of "To take us lands away" that Ms. Dickinson writes in this poem?

   A. War makes it unsafe to travel, so we can just read about places.

   B. Poems will drive us to save our souls.

   C. Books can engage us to see new things.

   D. Authors can show us how to go on vacation.

   E. It shows poems are short and fun.

PASSAGE 3
(Poetry, British, 17th century)

Since brass, nor stone, nor earth,
nor boundless sea,
But sad mortality o'ersways their
power,
How with this rage shall beauty
hold a plea,
Whose action is no stronger than
a flower? (line 4)
O how shall summer's honey
breath hold out
Against the wrackful siege of
batt'ring days,
When rocks impregnable are not
so stout,
Nor gates of steel so strong, but
Time decays? (line 8)
O fearful meditation! where,
alack,

Shall Time's best jewel from
Time's chest lie hid?
Or what strong hand can hold
his swift foot back?
Or who his spoil of beauty can
forbid? (line 12)
O none, unless this miracle have
might,
That in black ink my love may
still shine bright.
           ~William Shakespeare,
                    1609

12. In line four, what is the strength of a flower describing?

   A. Beauty (beauty line above)

   B. Time

   C. Summer's honey breath

   D. Strong hand

   E. Meditation

13. The first line of the poem tries to explain _____.

   A. that there are a lot of things discussed in the poem.

   B. that the strongest natural things are no match for beauty.

   C. where you can find love.

   D. what the author went through to write this poem.

   E. that prayer can solve any problems.

14. "Black ink" references what in the last line?

   A. Written poems

   B. Street signs

   C. Black diamonds

   D. Summer flowers dying

   E. Graffiti

15. The main idea of this poem is describing all of the following except:

   A. hope

   B. time, aging and death overthrow beauty

   C. marriage

   D. things that time cannot destroy

   E. the author's victory

16. Shakespeare creates emotions in this poem, and expresses all of the following except:

   A. rage

   B. defeat

   C. love

   D. devotion

   E. mortality

PASSAGE 4
(Prose non-fiction, American, 20th century)

When rays of light pass through a prism, they undergo a change of direction: they are always deflected away from the refractive edge. It is possible to conceive an assembly of prisms whose refractive surfaces progressively become more nearly parallel to each other towards the middle: light rays passing through the outer prisms will undergo the greatest amount of refraction, with consequent deflection of their path towards the center, whereas the middle prism with its two parallel surfaces causes no deflection at all. When a beam of parallel rays passes through these prisms, the rays are all deflected towards the axis and converge at one point. Rays emerging from a point are also deflected by the prisms that they converge. A lens can be conceived as consisting of a large number of such prisms placed close up against one another, so that their surfaces merge into a continuous spherical surface. A lens of this kind, which collects the rays and concentrates them at one point, is called a convergent lens. Since it is thicker in the middle than at the edge, it is known as a convex lens.

In the case of a concave lens, which is thinner in the middle than at the edge, similar considerations show that all rays diverge from the center. Hence such a lens is called a divergent lens. After undergoing refraction, parallel rays appear to come from one point, while rays remerging from a point will, after passing through the lens, appear to emerge from another point. Lenses have surfaces in the same direction but having a different radii of curvature, these are known as meniscus lenses and are used more particularly in spectacles.

~The Way Things Work, ©1963

17. According to the passage above, light rays hit convex mirror and:

A. the rays pass straight through

B. the rays bounce only straight back to the light source

C. bend together to cross at a single point on the other side

D. are refracted to open outward on the other side

E. are reflected outward at angles back toward the light source

18. Light rays hit a concave surface. As the passage explains, light:

   A. travels through the prism's surface, angling together to a point

   B. moves in the same direction but has a different radii of curvature

   C. the light merges to a point on the continuous spherical surface

   D. is always reflected away from the refractive edge

   E. experiences no deflection

19. Spectacles use meniscus lenses, which are explained by the author that these lenses are:

   A. flat

   B. concave lenses

   C. convex lenses

   D. round on both sides of the lens, meaning they have double refraction

   E. always convergent lenses

PASSAGE 5
(Prose fiction, British, 18th century)

There is likewise another diversion, which is only shown before the Emperor and Empress, and first minister, upon particular occasions. The Emperor lays on a table three fine silken threads of six inches long. One is blue, the other red, and the third green. These threads are proposed as prizes for those persons whom the Emperor hath a mind to distinguish by a peculiar mark of his favor. The ceremony is performed in his Majesty's great chamber of state; where the candidates are to undergo a trial of dexterity very different from the former, and such as I have not observed the least resemblance of in any other country of the old or the new world. The Emperor holds a stick in his hands, both ends parallel to the horizon, while the candidates, advancing one by one, sometimes leap over the stick, sometimes creep under it backwards and forwards several times, according as the stick is advanced or depressed. Sometimes the Emperor holds one end of the stick, and his first minister holds the other; sometimes the minister has it entirely to himself. Whoever performs his part with most agility, and holds out the longest in *leaping* and

11

creeping, is rewarded with the blue-colored silk; the red is given to the next, and the green is given to the third, which they all wear girt twice round the middle; and you see few great persons about this court who are not adorned with one of these girdles.

~Jonathan Swift, 1704

20. **The stick game described by the author in this passage is an allusion to what?**

   A. Jumping to the tune of the Emperor's (his boss') direction

   B. Baseball

   C. War games

   D. A circus

   E. Tennis

21. **Why are the silk threads highly valued?**

   A. Silk is a common material.

   B. Green is the Empress' favorite color.

   C. People don't give gifts very often.

   D. Silk was very expensive in the 1700s, when the story was written.

   E. All great persons wear silk.

22. **Using the information only in the passage, are the colors of the silk threads significant?**

   A. Yes, because they are royal colors.

   B. Yes, because they represent places of winners.

   C. No, because everyone has them.

   D. No, because hardly everyone has them.

   E. You cannot determine from the passage if the colors are important.

PASSAGE 6
(Prose non-fiction, 20th century)

On the other hand, however, we have no intention whatever of maintaining such a foolish and doctrinaire thesis as that the spirit of capitalism could only have arisen as the result of certain effects of Reformation, or even that of capitalism as an economic system is a creation of the Reformation. In itself, the fact that certain important forms of capitalistic business organizations are known to be considerably older than the Reformation is a sufficient refutation of such a claim. On the contrary, we only wish to ascertain whether and to what extent religious forces have taken part in the qualitative formation and the quantitative expansion of that spirit over the world. Furthermore, what concrete aspects of our capitalistic culture can be traced to them. In the view of the tremendous confusion of interdependent influences between the material basis, the forms of social and political organization, and the ideas current in the time of Reformation, we can only proceed by investigating whether and at what points certain correlations between forms of religious belief and practical ethics can be worked out. At the same time, we shall as far as possible clarify the manner and the general direction which, by virtue of those relationships, the religious movements have influenced development of material culture. Only when this has been determined with reasonable accuracy can the attempt be made to estimate to what extent the historical development of modern culture can be attributed to those religious forces and to what extent others.

~Max Weber, 1904

23. Capitalism is what type of system according to this passage?

A. Democratic

B. Economic

C. Religious

D. Cultural

E. Expansionist

13

24. When the author compares capitalism to the Reformation, what were the main ideas of the Reformation?

   A. Democratic

   B. Economic

   C. Religious

   D. Cultural

   E. Expansionist

25. What word or phrase originating at least in part in the above passage best describes the goal or target of capitalism?

   A. Ethics based

   B. Culture driven

   C. Historical application

   D. Material accumulation

   E. Force of nature

26. From the passage above, which of the following phrases best describes the author's attitude toward capitalism?

   A. The author approves of capitalism if it involves religion.

   B. The author approves of capitalism when it is driven by "qualification expansion of spirit".

   C. The author disapproves of capitalism when it involves modern culture.

   D. The author disapproves of capitalism when Reformation is involved.

   E. The author disapproves of capitalism but wants to investigate why it is wrong.

PASSAGE 7
(Prose non-fiction, 20th century)

I'd like to say here, that I wasn't the only important one. I was part of a family, just like all of my brothers and sisters. The whole community was important. We used to discuss

14

many of the community's problems together, especially when someone was ill and we couldn't buy medicine, because we were getting poorer and poorer. We'd start discussing and heaping insults on the rich who'd made us suffer for so long. It was about then I began learning about politics. I tried to talk to people who could help me sort my ideas out. I wanted to know what the world was like on the other side. I knew the *finca*, I knew the *Altiplano*. But what I didn't know was about the other problems of the Indians in Guatemala. I didn't know the problems the other groups had to holding onto their land. I knew there were lots of other Indians in other parts of the country, because I'd been meeting them in the *finca* since I was a child, but though we all worked together, we didn't know any of the names of the towns they came from, or how they lived, or what they ate. We just imagined that they were like us.
~Rigoberta Menchu, Nobel Peace Prize Winner 1992

27. From the context of the passage, what is a *finca*?

A. A farm

B. A village or town

C. A mountain range

D. A house

E. It cannot be determined

28. The author is telling a story about her own life. What is this kind of document called?

A. Autobiography

B. Mystery

C. Biography

D. Narrative

E. Romance

15

29. Given the information in the passage, the author most likely worked as:

 A. a washer woman

 B. a seamstress

 C. a farmer

 D. a teacher

 E. it cannot be determined from the passage

30. The author describes who is the most important. She defines it as:

 A. herself

 B. her family

 C. her community

 D. the rich people that employed them

 E. the *finca*

PASSAGE 8
(Poetry, British, 18th century)

Tyger! Tyger! burning bright
In the forests of the night,
What immortal hand or eye
Could frame thy fearful symmetry?

In what distant deeps or skies
Burnt the fire of thine eyes?
On what wings dare he aspire?

What the hand dare seize the flame?

And what shoulder, & what art,
Could twist the sinews of they heart?
And when thy heart began to beat,
What dread hand? & what dread feet?
 ~Excerpt, William Blake, 1794

31. Which of the topics below is this best description of the poem's main idea?

 A. Strength, as sinews of the heart are strong.

 B. Creationism, and the author asks what immortal being created the tiger.

 C. Flying, because it talks about wings.

 D. Fire, with references to flames and burning forests.

 E. Love, describing the heart and how it beats.

16

32. Sinews, in the third stanza, can be best compared to:

    A. thread

    B. a cage

    C. rope

    D. heart strings or emotions

    E. burnt fire, from the second stanza

33. Another phrase for "deeps or skies" that would fit in this poem could be:

    A. caves or planes

    B. trees or forests

    C. seas or air

    D. waves or wind

    E. oceans or lakes

34. What is personified in the poem?

    A. A lion

    B. Birds

    C. Candle

    D. A tiger

    E. The sky

35. In line 7 of this poem, what word below most nearly means "aspire"?

    A. Soar

    B. Plunge

    C. Scheme

    D. Travel

    E. Admire

36. The poet, William Blake, uses all of the following literary tools to convey his message, except:

    A. metaphors

    B. rhymed couplets

    C. personification

    D. symbols

    E. lyrics

PASSAGE 9
(Prose fiction, British, 19th century)

"Without their visits you cannot hope to shun the path I tread. Expect the first tomorrow night, when the bell tolls One. Expect the second on the next night at the same hour. The third, upon the next night, when the last stroke of Twelve has ceased to vibrate Look to see me no more; and look that, for your own sake, you remember what has passed between us!"

It walked backward from him; and at every step it took, the window raised itself a little, so that, when the apparition reached it, it was wide open.

Scrooge closed the window, and examined the door by which the Ghost had entered. It was double-locked, as he had locked it with his own hands, and the bolts were undisturbed. Scrooge tried to say "Humbug!" but stopped at the first syllable. And being, from the emotion he had undergone, or the fatigues of the day, or his glimpse of the invisible world, or the dull conversation of the Ghost, or the lateness of the hour, much in need of repose, he went straight to bed, without undressing, and fell asleep on the instant.

~Charles Dickens, 1843

37. What quality of the Ghost is the most likely trait that Scrooge dislikes the most?

A. The Ghost's old fashioned speech bothers Scrooge the most.

B. The authoritative nature the Ghost takes with Scrooge is the quality disliked the most.

C. The fact that the Ghost could break into his house is the trait that Scrooge dislikes.

D. The Ghost is taller than Scrooge, and that bothers him.

E. Scrooge dislikes that his bedtime was later than usual.

38. The way Scrooge's reaction to the Ghost is portrayed could mean that according to this passage that Scrooge is:

    A. tired

    B. angry

    C. looking for excuses

    D. forgetful

    E. planning to ignore the Ghost

39. The Ghost's remarks listed in the passage can most likely be inferred as:

    A. a warning to Scrooge

    B. the Ghost is talking to the wrong person

    C. Scrooge is hallucinating

    D. a friend was playing a joke on Scrooge

    E. no inference can be made

40. Scrooge's reaction to the Ghost in this passage leads a reader to conclude:

    A. that Scrooge was just conducting a normal nighttime house-check

    B. when the Ghost comes back for him, Scrooge will go along willingly

    C. even wealthy people like Scrooge lock their houses

    D. that Scrooge does not believe in the supernatural

    E. Scrooge is likely overcome with exhaustion

41. The tone of the passage is intended to:

A. serve as a warning to Scrooge about things he will be shown

B. serve as a reminder that Scrooge has forgotten appointments

C. describe how disconcerted Scrooge felt after the warning was given by the Ghost

D. provide backstory

E. explain why Scrooge is so stingy

PASSAGE 10
(Prose, non-fiction, American, 20th century)

Using the Constitution to protect the minorities, James Madison's system of government is largely an attempt to divide and frustrate the majority. Madison envisioned a political system with the broadest possible power base. For example, he rejected the common belief that a democracy could work only in a very small area, arguing that it could succeed in a large country like the United States. A large population spread over a huge area would make it very difficult to force a permanent majority. Such a society would probably divide into varied and fluctuating minorities, making a long lasting majority unlikely. Instead, majorities would be created out of combinations of competing minorities. Thus, any majority would be temporary, and new ones would be elusive. This system, political scientists now term *pluralism*.

~Leon Baradat, 1973

42. According to the passage, what is pluralism?

A. Majorities created out of combinations of competing minorities

B. A new division of political science

C. A political system with the smallest possible power base

D. A new name for a permanent majority

E. The system for democracy to work in a very small area

43. The Constitution mentioned in the first line, in context to this passage, is:

A. James Madison's document to create a permanent majority

B. the document creating the United States

C. the personality of James Madison

D. the health of the majority

E. instructions on how to create combinations of competing minorities

44. The passage talks about democracy. Another phrase for a democracy is:

A. the rule of a few over the many

B. the welfare state

C. a laissez-faire economy

D. an elected government system

E. an appointed government by a monarch

PASSAGE 11
(Prose non-fiction, British, 21st century)

American black music was going along like an express train. But white cats, after Buddy Holly died and Eddie Cochran died, and Elvis was in the army gone wonky, white American music when I arrived was the Beach Boys and Bobby Vee. They were still stuck in the past. The past was six months ago; it wasn't a long time. But things changed. The Beatles were the milestone. And then they got stuck inside their own cage. "The Fab Four." Hence, eventually, you got the Monkees, all this ersatz stuff. But I think there was a vacuum somewhere in white American music at the time.

When we first got to America and to LA, there was a lot of Beach Boys on the radio, which was pretty funny to us - it was before *Pet Sounds* - it was hot rod songs and surfing songs, pretty lousily played, familiar Chuck Berry licks going on. "Round, round get around / I get around," I thought that was brilliant. It was later on, but Brian Wilson had something. "In My Room," "Don't Worry Baby." I was more interested in their B-sides, the ones he slipped in. There was no particular correlation with what we were doing so I could just listen to it on another level. I thought these

21

are very well-constructed songs. I took easily to the pop song idiom. I'd always listened to everything, and America opened it all out - we were hearing records there that were regional hits. We'd get to know local labels and local acts, which is how we came across "Time Is on My Side," in LA, sung by Irma Thomas. It was a B-side of a record on Imperial Records, a label we'd have been aware of because it was independent and successful and based on Sunset Strip.

~Keith Richards, 2010

45. How many unique singers versus unique bands, respectively, are named in the passage above?

A. Seven and Four

B. Six and Three

C. Eight and Three

D. Seven and Three

E. Six and Four

46. How many songs are referenced in the passage above?

A. Two

B. Three

C. Four

D. Five

E. Six

47. In the context of the selection's first paragraph, how many white singers or groups are named by the author?

A. Four

B. Five

C. Three

D. Seven

E. One

22

48. Given what the author says about the B-side of a record, which of the following sentences is closest to the author's opinion?

   A. The B-side had more creativity and outlets for artists, making it unique.

   B. It was called the B-side because the songs were generally not as good.

   C. Only regional labels took the time to press B-sides.

   D. The B-side was where all the surfing songs were recorded.

   E. Labels were strict about the contents of the B-sides.

49. When the author talks about the Beatles and says "they got stuck inside their own cage," the author most likely means:

   A. that the Beatles always had to hide in hotels because they were so famous

   B. that successful musical groups could never enjoy the publicity

   C. that the Beatles were trapped on planes all the time

   D. that the Beatles couldn't perform with anyone outside of their four members

   E. the Beatles outgrew the standard previously set for successful musicians, and were trapped in their own famous sensation

50. Given the descriptions in the passage, the author's profession is likely:

A. a roadie

B. a writer

C. a singer

D. a photographer

E. a teacher

PASSAGE 12
(Prose fiction, British, pre-Ren/Classic)

A marvelous case is it to hear, either the warnings of that he should have voided, or the tokens of that he could not void. For the self night next before his death, the lord Stanley sent a trusty secret messenger unto him at midnight in all the haste, requiring him to rise and ride away with him, for he was disposed utterly no longer to bide; he had so fearful a dream, in which him thought that a boar with his tusks so raced them both by the heads, that the blood ran about both their shoulders. And forasmuch as the protector gave the boar for his cognizance, this dream made so fearful an impression in his heart, that he was thoroughly determined no longer to tarry, but had his horse ready, if the lord Hastings would go with him to ride so far yet the same night, that they should be out of danger ere day. Ay, good lord, quoth the lord Hastings to this messenger, leaneth my lord thy master so much to such trifles, and hath such faith in dreams, which either his own fear fantasieth or do rise in the night's rest by reason of his day thoughts? Tell him it is plain witchcraft to believe in such dreams; which if they were tokens of things to come, why thinketh he not that we might be as likely to make them true by our going if we were caught and brought back (as friends fail fleers), for then had the boar a cause likely to race us with his tusks, as folk that fled for some falsehood, wherefore either is there no peril (nor none there is indeed), or if any be, it is rather in going than biding. And if we should, needs cost, fall in peril one way or other, yet had I livelier that men should see it were by other men's falsehood, than think it were either our own fault or faint heart. And therefore go to thy master, man, and commend me to him, and pray him be merry and have no fear: for I ensure him I am as sure of the man that he wotteth of, as I am of my own hand. God send grace, sir, quoth the messenger, and went his way.
~Sir Thomas More, 1513

51. The beginning of the passage is describing what?

    A. An injury sustained by the main character

    B. A rider that is trying to escape injury

    C. The main character's dream

    D. A witch's story

    E. The boar that the character will grill for dinner

52. What is the cautionary message that the rider gets when he reaches his destination?

    A. Dreams are witchcraft if you believe in them.

    B. Dreams can come true if you believe in them.

    C. God sends His grace.

    D. Those faint of heart do not have dreams.

    E. Men cannot fall for other men's falsehoods.

53. Did the main character in this passage believe he could out run bad visions?

    A. No, the passage makes it clear you always get what's coming in a dream.

    B. No, dreams mean nothing, so the main character didn't pay any attention to it.

    C. Yes, it was possible to escape bad visions on horseback.

    D. Yes, the main character thought dancing would rid himself of bad dreams.

    E. There is nothing in the passage that assists in answering this question.

PASSAGE 13
(Prose fiction, British, 19th century)

To go into solitude, a man needs to retire as much from his chamber as from society. I am not solitary whilst I read and write, though nobody is with me. But if a man would be alone, let him look at the stars. The rays that come from those heavenly worlds, will separate between him and what he touches. One might think the atmosphere was made transparent with this design, to give man, in the heavenly bodies, the perpetual presence of the sublime. Seen in the streets of cities, how great they are! If the stars should appear one night in a thousand years, how would men believe and adore; and preserve for many generations the remembrance of the city of God which had been shown! But every night come out these envoys of beauty, and light the universe with their admonishing smile.

~Ralph Waldo Emerson, 1836

54. **The first two lines of this passage imply what?**

   A. A man is never alone.

   B. A man is always alone.

   C. A man can be alone if he turns his back on people.

   D. A man can be alone if he makes his mind focus.

   E. A man who is lonely is considered alone.

55. **Given the whole passage, which of the following is the best match for the author's opinion about nature?**

   A. The author prefers to seek to retire in his chamber.

   B. The author sees wonder in the sky and beauty at night.

   C. The author does not like trees.

   D. The author can only see stars one night in a thousand years.

   E. You cannot tell the author's opinion from this passage.

56. **The phrase "light the universe with their admonishing smile" is an example of:**

   A. personification

   B. a simile

   C. a metaphor

   D. irony

   E. satire

PASSAGE 14
(Poetry, American, 20th century)

Two roads diverged in a yellow
wood,
And sorry I could not travel
both
And be one traveler, long I
stood
And looked down one as far as I
could
To where it bent in the
undergrowth;

Then took the other, as just as
fair,
And having perhaps the better
claim,
Because it was grassy and
wanted wear;
Though as for that the passing
there
Had worn them really about the
same,

And both that morning equally
lay
In leaves no step had trodden
black.
Oh, I kept the first for another
day!
Yet knowing how way leads on
to way,
I doubted if I should ever come
back.

I shall be telling this with a
sigh
Somewhere ages and ages
hence:
Two roads diverged in a wood,
and I—
I took the one less traveled by,

And that has made all the
difference.

~Robert Frost, 1920

57.   When the author uses the
      phrase "wanted wear" in
      the third stanza, what
      does that mean?

      A.   It looked just as fair as
           the other path.

      B.   It was not as inviting.

      C.   The path didn't go the
           same way as the other
           one.

      D.   The path was less
           traveled than the other
           one.

      E.   You cannot determine
           what the author
           means.

58. The author says that he "took the one less traveled by"; what does that mean?

   A. The other path looked like it was used more.

   B. He did the right thing when others chose the wrong one.

   C. He took the one on the left.

   D. He took the one on the right.

   E. It cannot be determined what the author meant by this short selection.

59. What is another way the author states his path was the "one less traveled by"?

   A. "both that morning equally lay"

   B. "no step had trodden black"

   C. "Somewhere ages and ages hence"

   D. "bent in the undergrowth"

   E. "having perhaps the better claim"

60. What does the author imply since he took the path less traveled?

   A. He has run into fewer people that try to bully him into doing what they want.

   B. Life is tougher getting to see the light.

   C. He was sorry he didn't chose to go the more well-trod path.

   D. He didn't make as much money as the people that took the other path.

   E. His life is better for choosing to go his own path.

PASSAGE 15
(Prose fiction, American, 20th century)

His memories of the Boston Society Contralto were nebulous and musical. She was a lady who sang, sang, sang in the music room on their house on Washington Square - sometimes with guests all about her, the men with their arms folded, balanced breathlessly on the edges of sofas, the women with their hands in their laps, occasionally making little whispers to the men and always clapping very briskly and

28

uttering cooing cries after each song - and she often sang to Anthony alone, in Italian or French or in a strange and terrible dialect...

Oblivious to the social system, he lived for a while alone and unsought in a high room in Beck Hall - a slim dark boy of medium height with a shy sensitive mouth. His allowance was more than liberal. He laid the foundations for a library by purchasing from a wandering bibliophile first editions of Swinburne, Meredith, and Hardy, and a yellowed illegible autograph letter of Keats', finding later he had been amazingly overcharged. He became an exquisite dandy, amassed a rather pathetic collection of silk pajamas, brocaded dressing-gowns, and neckties too flamboyant to wear; in this secret finery he would parade before a mirror in his room or lie stretched in satin along the window-seat looking down on the yard and realizing this clamor, breathless and immediate, in which it seemed he was to never have a part.

~F. Scott Fitzgerald, 1922

61. Based on the information in the passage, what is a "contralto"?

A. A Boston slang term for a high class man

B. A female singer

C. A female dancer

D. A writer

E. A bibliophile

62. Based on the information in the passage, an "exquisite dandy" refers to:

A. the first editions of the books listed in the passage

B. anyone who wears silk pajamas

C. a gentleman who has money to spend extravagantly on fancy things

D. someone who likes to parade before a mirror

E. someone who likes candy

63. Why would the social system be important in this reading selection?

    A. Richer classes don't have dandies, so the main character can't be dandy.

    B. A rich man with no female friends is called a dandy, and it helps explain the story.

    C. The character seems ostracized and that can't happen in certain social classes.

    D. If the main character was of a lower class, he could not live the life described.

    E. No one lives the luxurious life described in the passage.

PASSAGE 16
(Prose fiction, American, 20th century)

These are morning matters,
pictures you dream as the final
wave heaves you up on the sand
in the bright light and drying
air. You remember pressure, and
a curved sleep you rested
against, soft, like a scallop in its
shell. But the air hardens your
skin; you stand; you leave the
lighted shore to explore some
dim headland, and soon you're
lost in the leafy interior, intent,
remembering nothing.

I still think of that old tomcat,
mornings, when I wake. Things
are tamer now; I sleep with the
window shut. The cats and our
rites are gone and my life is
changed, but the memory
remains of something powerful
playing over me. I wake
expectant, hoping to see a new
thing. If I'm lucky I might be
jogged awake by a strange bird
call. I dress in a hurry,
imagining the yard flapping
with auks, or flamingos. This
morning it was a wood duck,
down at the creek. It flew away.
    ~Annie Dillard, 1975 Pulitzer
                  Prize

64. The tone of the selection is:

    A. reflective

    B. indulgent

    C. indifferent

    D. dishonest

    E. ironic

65. The author uses _____ to describe the setting.

  A. personification

  B. ambivalence

  C. satire

  D. allusion

  E. clichés

66. The phrase, "like a scallop in its shell" is an example of:

  A. irony

  B. a simile

  C. a metaphor

  D. personification

  E. euphemism

67. The author describes many of her feelings and situations by focusing the conversation on animals. Based on the information in the passage, one reason could be:

  A. animals are comforting and relax the reader

  B. birds are flighty and the center of her story

  C. the setting of this story is a farm

  D. the lead character doesn't have many human friends

  E. it is the backstory of how animals and nature are always present in the character's life

68. The phrase "the air hardens your skin" within the context of the passage most likely refers to what?

A. The morning air woke the character up from dreaming.

B. The scallop shell bed the character sleeps in has opened.

C. The air dries out the character's skin.

D. The coldness of the room turns off the brain of the character.

E. The air turns the character's skin cold when the cat leaves the bed.

PASSAGE 17
(Drama, British, 16th century/classical)

Bernardo : Welcome, Horatio: welcome, good Marcellus.
Marcellus : What, has this thing appear'd again to-night?
Bernardo : I have seen nothing.
Marcellus : Horatio says 'tis but our fantasy,
And will not let belief take hold of him
Touching this dreaded sight, twice seen of us:
Therefore I have entreated him along

With us to watch the minutes of this night;
That if again this apparition come,
He may approve our eyes and speak to it.
Horatio : Tush, tush, 'twill not appear.
Bernardo : Sit down awhile;
And let us once again assail your ears,
That are so fortified against our story
What we have two nights seen.
~William Shakespeare, 1599-1602

69. The three men in the play can be said, in this passage:

A. to disagree about a ghost that was seen

B. to disagree that two days ago they saw people meeting "twice seen of us"

C. that Horatio and Bernardo are trying to persuade Marcellus they saw something

D. that Horatio and Marcellus are trying to persuade Bernardo they saw something

E. to meet for a drink for "fortification"

70. When Marcellus speaks of "approving our eyes", what is he saying?

A. Marcellus and Bernardo need glasses.

B. Bernardo didn't believe what Marcellus saw.

C. Horatio believes what Marcellus saw.

D. Horatio should see what Bernardo and Marcellus saw.

E. Marcellus should believe what Bernardo saw.

71. When Bernardo says "once again assail your ears", what does he mean?

A. He wants to repeat himself to Marcellus to make him believe him.

B. He wants to repeat himself to Horatio to make him believe him.

C. He wants to repeat himself to help all three of them believe the story.

D. He wants Marcellus and Horatio to poke holes in the story.

E. None of these are the meaning of that phrase in the passage.

72. In the context of the passage, entreated means:

A. invited

B. engaged

C. demanded

D. refused

E. ignored

PASSAGE 18
(Drama, American, 20th century)

Edmund : That's foolishness. You know it's only a bad cold.
Mary : Yes, of course, I know that!
Edmund : But listen, Mama. I want you to promise me that even if it turns out to be something worse, you'll know I'll soon be alright again, anyway, and don't worry yourself sick, and you'll keep on taking care of yourself -
Mary : I won't listen when you talk so silly! There's absolutely no reason to talk as if you expect something dreadful! Of course, I promise you I give you my sacred word of honor! But I suppose you're remembering I've promised before on my word of honor.
Edmund : No!
Mary : I'm not blaming you, dear. How can you help it? How can any one of us forget? That's what makes it so hard - for all of us. We can't forget.
Edmund : Mama! Stop it!
Mary : All right, dear. I didn't beam to be so gloomy. Don't mind me. Here. Let me feel your head. Why, it's nice and cool. You certainly don't have any fever now.

~Eugene O'Neill, 1955

73. It can be said that this passage of the drama:

A. puts American dream against American nightmare

B. describes the normal American family

C. portrays Americans in a very resilient fashion

D. was likely written during a war so obviously has negative overtones

E. has the mother remembering the death of another child

74. Mary changes the direction of the conversation by:

A. stopping Edmund from talking by taking his temperature

B. making Edmund feel badly about the death of his brother

C. walking out of the room

D. tucking the covers up to his chin

E. ignoring him

75. This portion of the play is a:

   A. monologue

   B. dialogue

   C. soliloquy

   D. entendre

   E. stichomythia

76. Mary talks about Edmund expecting something dreadful. What's a literary term for that action?

   A. Oxymoron

   B. Dissonance

   C. Foreshadowing

   D. Stream of consciousness

   E. Understatement

PASSAGE 19
(Prose fiction, British, 18th century)

But though thus largely indebted to fortune, to nature she had yet greater obligation: her form was elegant, her heart was liberal. Her countenance announced the intelligence of her mind, her complexion varied with every emotion of her foul, and her eyes, the heralds of her speech, now beamed with understanding and now glistened with sensibility.

For the short period of her minority, the management of her fortune and the care of her person, had by the Dean been entrusted to three guardians, among whom her own choice was to settle to her residence: but her mind, saddened by the lots of all her natural friends, coveted to regain its serenity in the quietness of the country, and in the bosom of an aged and maternal counsellor, whom she loved as her mother, and to whom she had been known from her childhood.
Fanny Burney, 1782

77. From the context of this passage, which of the following statements is the most likely to be true?

   A. The main character is poor.

   B. The main character is an orphan.

   C. The setting of the story is in England.

   D. The main character is going to live with her aunt.

   E. The main character doesn't like to live in town.

35

78. In the quote, "her heart was liberal", what is the author trying to express?

   A. The author implies that the main character is of loose morals.

   B. The author implies that while ladylike, she has a wild streak.

   C. The author alludes that the woman is more open than her demeanor.

   D. The author makes it clear that she is alone.

   E. The author shows how she was older than her natural friends.

79. What does the word "minority" mean in the context of the passage?

   A. The woman in the passage is a Native American.

   B. The character is not yet an adult.

   C. The group of people in the story are members of the minority political party.

   D. The character has less money than her friends.

   E. None of the given options explain "minority" in this passage.

80. What is another word for serenity in this passage?

   A. Peacefulness

   B. Counsellor

   C. Bosom

   D. Rambunctiousness

   E. Prayerful

ANSWER KEY

Question Number	Correct Answer	Your Answer	Question Number	Correct Answer	Your Answer	Question Number	Correct Answer	Your Answer
1	A		28	A		55	B	
2	C		29	C		56	A	
3	E		30	C		57	D	
4	D		31	B		58	A	
5	A		32	D		59	B	
6	A		33	C		60	E	
7	B		34	D		61	B	
8	E		35	A		62	C	
9	B		36	C		63	D	
10	E		37	B		64	A	
11	C		38	C		65	D	
12	A		39	A		66	C	
13	B		40	D		67	E	
14	A		41	C		68	A	
15	C		42	A		69	A	
16	B		43	B		70	D	
17	E		44	D		71	B	
18	A		45	D		72	A	
19	B		46	C		73	E	
20	A		47	D		74	A	
21	D		48	A		75	B	
22	B		49	E		76	C	
23	B		50	C		77	B	
24	C		51	C		78	C	
25	D		52	A		79	B	
26	E		53	C		80	A	
27	B		54	D				

RATIONALES

If there are words that are options for answers that you do not know, now is the time to look them up and prepare yourself for the CLEP exam! Many answer options includes words or phrases used in literary discussions, and some may not be familiar. It is possible they will be on the actual exam, so you should familiarize yourself with them now.

PASSAGE 1
(Prose fiction, American, 21ˢᵗ century)

Mornings, he likes to sit in his new leather chair by his new living room window, looking out across the rooftops and chimney pots, the clotheslines and telegraph lines and office towers. It's the first time Manhattan, from high above, hasn't crushed him with desire. On the contrary the view makes him feel smug. All those people down there, striving, hustling, pushing, shoving, busting to get what Willie's already got. In spades. He lights a cigarette, blows a jet of smoke against the window. Suckers.

J.R. Moehriger, 2012 p120

1.   The subject in this passage is:

   A.   a character, and seems to be the lead of the story

   B.   a supporting character

   C.   someone with an attitude of a criminal

   D.   female

   E.   has been poor his whole life

The answer is A.
The story being explained is about the main character. B is wrong because there are no other characters explained by the author, to have a main and a supporting character. You cannot tell if the person is a criminal or poor from this excerpt, so it is presumptuous to guess C or E could be the answers. D is also incorrect because the pronoun "he" is used so it is clearly wrong.

2.   **What kind of description is the author providing of this scene?**

    A.   Backstory of the character

    B.   A characterization of what the character is like

    C.   A narrative, with the end of the selection giving thoughts in the first person

    D.   The unreliable narrative about a character

    E.   The author is using a persuasive argument

The answer is C.
The backstory of a character tells about some time in the past, and since this scene is of the present, that choice A is wrong. B is also incorrect as there is no descriptions about the main character, only the current scene he is observing. There is no basis to assume D is correct and in the option E, there is no argument for or against a topic. Therefore, the correct answer is C.

3.   **What types of words are "striving, hustling, pushing, shoving, bustling"?**

    A.   Adjectives

    B.   Adverbs

    C.   Nouns

    D.   Gerunds

    E.   Verbs

The answer is E.
This is a simple definition of words. Verbs are listed for choice E.

4. If you had to explain the phrase "crushed him" in the paragraph above and context of the paragraph, what would be the best appropriate explanation?

    A. The city sustained him with all the opportunity available.

    B. The city called to him to be part of its life.

    C. The city complimented him for everything he has achieved.

    D. The city had energized him to get what he felt he deserved.

    E. The city smothered him with all its offerings.

The answer is D.
When looking at the context of the paragraph, there are no leading clues that the city has sustained the character, complimented him or smothered him. Of the options B and D, the better answer is D, as the city didn't call the character to join in the opportunity directly. D offers a description back to the excerpt - that he "deserved" what he has achieved.

5. The author portrays the attitude of the character toward the people on the street below as:

    A. condescending

    B. sarcastic

    C. affectionate

    D. tolerant

    E. encouraged

The answer is A.
Knowing what these words mean, the only choice that is close is A.

PASSAGE 2
(Poetry, American, 19th century)

There is no frigate like a book
To take us lands away,
Nor any coursers like a page
Of prancing poetry;
This traverse may the poorest take
Without oppress of toll;
How frugal is the chariot
That bears the human soul!
            ~Emily Dickinson (1830-1886)

6.   Authors use particular literary structures for descriptions. What best
      explains the one that Emily Dickinson employs in this poem?

      A.   A literary allegory

      B.   Personification

      C.   Idioms

      D.   Similes

      E.   Flashbacks

The answer is A.
This is another definition type of question, and the correct choice is A.

7.   How many types of transport types does the author incorporate?

      A.   Two

      B.   Three

      C.   Four

      D.   Five

      E.   None

The answer is B.
This is a counting exercise - B, for three, as listed in the next question.

8. If the words 'frigate, coursers, and chariot' were replaced with synonyms, what would the best choice of the following options include?

    A. Train, car, carriage

    B. Train, horse, carriage

    C. Ship, car, carriage

    D. Ship, car, train

    E. Ship, horse, carriage

The answer is E.
Defining frigate (ship), coursers (horses) and chariots (similar to a carriage drawn by a horse), the best choice is E.

9. Which of the following descriptions more closely describes the author's intended meaning of poem?

    A. Difficulties at work

    B. The importance of books

    C. Confessions for the soul

    D. Poverty makes things difficult

    E. Describing modes of transportation

The answer is B.
This poem is about the journeys available through stories and books. From the first sentence, the author lays forth the meaning of the poem is B.

10. There are very descriptive and strong feelings conveyed by the poet. Which of the following is not a feeling that this poem expresses?

   A. Enjoyment of reading

   B. Excitement of where reading can take you

   C. Encouragement to get others to read

   D. Fascination with topics in books

   E. Discouragement for new readers

The answer is E.
It is important to read the questions carefully. This is a reverse question, asking which is not something that is mentioned or implied in the poem. Therefore, the correct answer is E. If you don't know the answer, you can try to look at all five options to select the one that doesn't fit with the others.

11. What is a good paraphrase of "To take us lands away" that Ms. Dickinson writes in this poem?

   A. War makes it unsafe to travel, so we can just read about places.

   B. Poems will drive us to save our souls.

   C. Books can engage us to see new things.

   D. Authors can show us how to go on vacation.

   E. It shows poems are short and fun.

The answer is C.
Option A is very abrupt and makes too many assumptions; Option E is not relevant to the subject of the poem - both of these are obviously out. Of the choices remaining, using the references with the different ways people traveled in her earlier lines, the best answer is C.

43

PASSAGE 3
(Poetry, British, 17th century)

Since brass, nor stone, nor earth, nor boundless sea,
But sad mortality o'ersways their power,
How with this rage shall beauty hold a plea,
Whose action is no stronger than a flower? (line 4)
O how shall summer's honey breath hold out
Against the wrackful siege of batt'ring days,
When rocks impregnable are not so stout,
Nor gates of steel so strong, but Time decays? (line 8)
O fearful meditation! where, alack,
Shall Time's best jewel from Time's chest lie hid?
Or what strong hand can hold his swift foot back?
Or who his spoil of beauty can forbid? (line 12)
O none, unless this miracle have might,
That in black ink my love may still shine bright.
~William Shakespeare, 1609

12.   In line four, what is the strength of a flower describing?

A.   Beauty   (beauty line above)

B.   Time

C.   Summer's honey breath

D.   Strong hand

E.   Meditation

The answer is A.
This is a direct answer from line three - A.

13. The first line of the poem tries to explain _____.

    A. that there are a lot of things discussed in the poem.

    B. that the strongest natural things are no match for beauty.

    C. where you can find love.

    D. what the author went through to write this poem.

    E. that prayer can solve any problems.

The answer is B.
The author does not mention love, personal struggles, or prayer in this poem. Of the remaining answers, A is too general and B is the correct answer (using many of the lines about strength that cannot compare to beauty).

14. "Black ink" references what in the last line?

    A. Written poems

    B. Street signs

    C. Black diamonds

    D. Summer flowers dying

    E. Graffiti

The answer is A.
A is the best answer, as all others are not pertaining to the time period or not mentioned even indirectly with the poem.

15.   The main idea of this poem is describing all of the following except:

    A.   hope

    B.   time, aging and death overthrow beauty

    C.   marriage

    D.   things that time cannot destroy

    E.   the author's victory

The answer is C.
This is another question where you must read carefully. All of the items are mentioned or alluded to with the exception of C; therefore, that is the answer that is NOT in the poem.

16.   Shakespeare creates emotions in this poem, and expresses all of the following except:

    A.   rage

    B.   defeat

    C.   love

    D.   devotion

    E.   mortality

The answer is B.
Again, another question to make sure you are reading and not just going with the first answer that matches a word in the passage, making B the correct answer.

PASSAGE 4
(Prose non-fiction, American, 20th century)

When rays of light pass through a prism, they undergo a change of direction: they are always deflected away from the refractive edge. It is possible to conceive an assembly of prisms whose refractive surfaces progressively become more nearly parallel to each other towards the middle: light rays passing through the outer prisms will undergo the greatest amount of refraction, with consequent deflection of their path towards the center, whereas the middle prism with its two parallel surfaces causes no deflection at all. When a beam of parallel rays passes through these prisms, the rays are all deflected towards the axis and converge at one point. Rays emerging from a point are also deflected by the prisms that they converge. A lens can be conceived as consisting of a large number of such prisms placed close up against one another, so that their surfaces merge into a continuous spherical surface. A lens of this kind, which collects the rays and concentrates them at one point, is called a convergent lens. Since it is thicker in the middle than at the edge, it is known as a convex lens.

In the case of a concave lens, which is thinner in the middle than at the edge, similar considerations show that all rays diverge from the center. Hence such a lens is called a divergent lens. After undergoing refraction, parallel rays appear to come from one point, while rays remerging from a point will, after passing through the lens, appear to emerge from another point. Lenses have surfaces in the same direction but having a different radii of curvature, these are known as meniscus lenses and are used more particularly in spectacles.

~ The Way Things Work, ©1963

17.   According to the passage above, light rays hit convex mirror and:

A.   the rays pass straight through

B.   the rays bounce only straight back to the light source

C.   bend together to cross at a single point on the other side

D.   are refracted to open outward on the other side

E.   are reflected outward at angles back toward the light source

The answer is E.
The passage explains that a convex mirror "is thicker in the middle than at the edge" in the last line of the first paragraph. Thus, both A and B are wrong as the surface isn't flat (without curve). C describes a concave lens and D describes a lens not explained in the passage. Therefore, the correct answer is E.

18.   **Light rays hit a concave surface. As the passage explains, light:**

A.   travels through the prism's surface, angling together to a point

B.   moves in the same direction but has a different radii of curvature

C.   the light merges to a point on the continuous spherical surface

D.   is always reflected away from the refractive edge

E.   experiences no deflection

The answer is A.
Similar to 4.1, the definition is in the passage that matches A. The other four options are wrong or nonsensical as explained in the paragraphs.

19.   Spectacles use meniscus lenses, which are explained by the author
       that these lenses are:

    A. flat

    B. concave lenses

    C. convex lenses

    D. round on both sides of the lens, meaning they have double
        refraction

    E. always convergent lenses

The answer is B.
Think about a pair of glasses. They aren't flat, so A is wrong. If they were D,
round on both sides, then they wouldn't work. Within E, an extreme
modifier is used - always - and when words are extreme - such as always,
never, every - that is usually an indicator of a wrong answer (unless it's a
quote). Thus, the correct choice is B.

PASSAGE 5
(Prose fiction, British, 18th century)

There is likewise another diversion, which is only shown before the
Emperor and Empress, and first minister, upon particular occasions. The
Emperor lays on a table three fine silken threads of six inches long. One is
blue, the other red, and the third green. These threads are proposed as
prizes for those persons whom the Emperor hath a mind to distinguish by
a peculiar mark of his favor. The ceremony is performed in his Majesty's
great chamber of state; where the candidates are to undergo a trial of
dexterity very different from the former, and such as I have not observed
the least resemblance of in any other country of the old or the new
world. The Emperor holds a stick in his hands, both ends parallel to the
horizon, while the candidates, advancing one by one, sometimes leap over
the stick, sometimes creep under it backwards and forwards several times,
according as the stick is advanced or depressed. Sometimes the Emperor
holds one end of the stick, and his first minister holds the other; sometimes
the minister has it entirely to himself. Whoever performs his part with
most agility, and holds out the longest in *leaping* and *creeping*, is rewarded
with the blue-colored silk; the red is given to the next, and the green is
given to the third, which they all wear girt twice round the middle; and you

see few great persons about this court who are not adorned with one of these girdles.

~ Jonathan Swift, 1704

20. **The stick game described by the author in this passage is an allusion to what?**

A. Jumping to the tune of the Emperor's (his boss') direction

B. Baseball

C. War games

D. A circus

E. Tennis

The answer is A.
This is another passage where it makes sense to check the year the item was written. Baseball was not yet invented, and tennis as we know it today was not yet played - so both B and E are wrong. A circus doesn't have anything to do with a straight line, so D is also wrong. While A and C are both possible, only A is probable and directly connects to the passage.

21. **Why are the silk threads highly valued?**

A. Silk is a common material.

B. Green is the Empress' favorite color.

C. People don't give gifts very often.

D. Silk was very expensive in the 1700s, when the story was written.

E. All great persons wear silk.

The answer is D.
A is not true, so it can be eliminated. B has no basis of support in the passage, so it is not true. E has some reference in the passage, but it uses one of those extreme words, so it can be eliminated. Between C and D, C has no mention in the passage whereas D references the time period of the story and is the best answer.

22. Using the information only in the passage, are the colors of the silk threads significant?

   A. Yes, because they are royal colors.

   B. Yes, because they represent places of winners.

   C. No, because everyone has them.

   D. No, because hardly everyone has them.

   E. You cannot determine from the passage if the colors are important.

The answer is B.
This question is straight from the passage and is explained in the third sentence. The correct answer is B.

PASSAGE 6
(Prose non-fiction, 20th century)

On the other hand, however, we have no intention whatever of maintaining such a foolish and doctrinaire thesis as that the spirit of capitalism could only have arisen as the result of certain effects of Reformation, or even that of capitalism as an economic system is a creation of the Reformation. In itself, the fact that certain important forms of capitalistic business organizations are known to be considerably older than the Reformation is a sufficient refutation of such a claim. On the contrary, we only wish to ascertain whether and to what extent religious forces have taken part in the qualitative formation and the quantitative expansion of that spirit over the world. Furthermore, what concrete aspects of our capitalistic culture can be traced to them. In the view of the tremendous confusion of interdependent influences between the material basis, the forms of social and political organization, and the ideas current in the time of Reformation, we can only proceed by investigating whether and at what points certain correlations between forms of religious belief and practical ethics can be worked out. At the same time, we shall as far as possible clarify the manner and the general direction which, by virtue of those relationships, the religious movements have influenced development of material culture. Only when this has been determined with reasonable accuracy can the attempt be made to estimate to what extent the historical development of modern culture can be attributed to those religious forces and to what extent others.

~ Max Weber, 1904

23. Capitalism is what type of system according to this passage?

   A. Democratic

   B. Economic

   C. Religious

   D. Cultural

   E. Expansionist

The answer is B.
This is a question where you have to understand that the passage discusses business organizations and actually refutes the religious forces interference. C is wrong, as per the passage. D is mentioned in capitalistic culture, but as you should not answer a question with the same word as is being asked, the choice C is wrong. Democracy is a governmental system, so it does not define the capitalism. Expansionist is not relevant to the passage, therefore B is the correct answer.

24. When the author compares capitalism to the Reformation, what were the main ideas of the Reformation?

   A. Democratic

   B. Economic

   C. Religious

   D. Cultural

   E. Expansionist

The answer is C.
The passage describes the reformation as a religious movement; C is the correct answer.

25. **What word or phrase originating at least in part in the above passage best describes the goal or target of capitalism?**

   A. Ethics based

   B. Culture driven

   C. Historical application

   D. Material accumulation

   E. Force of nature

The answer is D.
Items A, B and C are talked about differently in the passage, and not about the goal of capitalism. D and E are the only possible remaining choices. There is nothing about nature in the paragraph, so D is the correct answer.

26. **From the passage above, which of the following phrases best describes the author's attitude toward capitalism?**

   A. The author approves of capitalism if it involves religion.

   B. The author approves of capitalism when it is driven by "qualification expansion of spirit".

   C. The author disapproves of capitalism when it involves modern culture.

   D. The author disapproves of capitalism when Reformation is involved.

   E. The author disapproves of capitalism but wants to investigate why it is wrong.

The answer is E.
The tone of the passage is disapproval, so A and B are automatically incorrect. D is also incorrect as the author does not describe the interaction with religion so this applies. Between C and E, culture is used to describe different components within the passage but not in this manner; therefore, E is the best answer.

PASSAGE 7
(Prose non-fiction, 20ᵗʰ century)

I'd like to say here, that I wasn't the only important one. I was part of a family, just like all of my brothers and sisters. The whole community was important. We used to discuss many of the community's problems together, especially when someone was ill and we couldn't buy medicine, because we were getting poorer and poorer. We'd start discussing and heaping insults on the rich who'd made us suffer for so long. It was about then I began learning about politics. I tried to talk to people who could help me sort my ideas out. I wanted to know what the world was like on the other side. I knew the *finca*, I knew the *Altiplano*. But what I didn't know was about the other problems of the Indians in Guatemala. I didn't know the problems the other groups had to holding onto their land. I knew there were lots of other Indians in other parts of the country, because I'd been meeting them in the *finca* since I was a child, but though we all worked together, we didn't know any of the names of the towns they came from, or how they lived, or what they ate. We just imagined that they were like us.

~ Rigoberta Menchu, Nobel Peace Prize Winner 1992

27. From the context of the passage, what is a *finca*?

A. A farm

B. A village or town

C. A mountain range

D. A house

E. It cannot be determined

The answer is B.
In the passage, only two Spanish words are used. Since the author describes a group of unrelated people The answer is not D. When offered an option like E, typically that is not the correct choice in a reading comprehension exam. Of the three remaining choices, since it talks about a gathering at this location, C is not an appropriate choice. Either A or B could apply, but A is a workplace not a gathering place. Choose B as the best answer - note that it is also mentioned at the end of the paragraph about people living in towns, another clue that this is the best answer.

28.   The author is telling a story about her own life. What is this kind of document called?

    A.   Autobiography

    B.   Mystery

    C.   Biography

    D.   Narrative

    E.   Romance

The answer is A.
A is the type of story where someone talks about their own life. While narrative could be another possible answer, the best answer is A.

29.   Given the information in the passage, the author most likely worked as:

    A.   a washer woman

    B.   a seamstress

    C.   a farmer

    D.   a teacher

    E.   it cannot be determined from the passage

The answer is C.
There are no indications that the woman washed clothes, worked as a seamstress or a teacher. Thus, A, B and D are eliminated. Between choices C and E, you must decide. If you read the book in full, C is the correct answer. But because this is about this passage, you do not have enough information to decide and E is the best selection - a rare occurrence in this exam, but it does happen.

30. The author describes who is the most important. She defines it as:

   A. herself

   B. her family

   C. her community

   D. the rich people that employed them

   E. the *finca*

The answer is C.
It is clear that the author says the community is important. It is literally part of the passage. She denounces A (herself) and even to an extent her family (option B); she goes on to talk about the community together, so the best answer is C. D is opposite of the intent of the passage and E is incongruous, though the translation is town that is just a physical location. Community has stronger meaning and is the best answer.

PASSAGE 8
(Poetry, British, 18th century)

Tyger! Tyger! burning bright
In the forests of the night,
What immortal hand or eye
Could frame thy fearful symmetry? (line 4)

In what distant deeps or skies
Burnt the fire of thine eyes?
On what wings dare he aspire?
What the hand dare seize the flame? (line 8)

And what shoulder, & what art,
Could twist the sinews of they heart?
And when thy heart began to beat,
What dread hand? & what dread feet? (line 12)
                    ~Excerpt, William Blake, 1794

31. **Which of the topics below is this best description of the poem's main idea?**

    A. Strength, as sinews of the heart are strong.

    B. Creationism, and the author asks what immortal being created the tiger.

    C. Flying, because it talks about wings.

    D. Fire, with references to flames and burning forests.

    E. Love, describing the heart and how it beats.

The answer is B.
This passage references the first word of each answer, but only one explanation for the excerpt can be correct. Remember this is about the main idea, not just one idea of the passage. If all of these were right, you need to find the option that is the best choice of all the options - one that can be seen in all of the other options. B represents the best choice.

32. **Sinews, in the third stanza, can be best compared to:**

    A. thread

    B. a cage

    C. rope

    D. heart strings or emotions

    E. burnt fire, from the second stanza

The answer is D.
Sinews are like tendons. They are strong binding fibers. So, A is not correct, nor is E. The closest two options are C and D; however, since this is poetry, sinews are figurative and the meaning is emotions, choice D.

33. Another phrase for "deeps or skies" that would fit in this poem could be:

   A. caves or planes

   B. trees or forests

   C. seas or air

   D. waves or wind

   E. oceans or lakes

The answer is C.
In this selection, synonyms - or similar words - need to be used in the same order as the original passage. Knowing this, C is the best option. While D could be considered, the original words do not describe movement, so it is not the best selection.

34. What is personified in the poem?

   A. A lion

   B. Birds

   C. Candle

   D. A tiger

   E. The sky

The answer is D.
This should be a fairly straightforward question, with the correct answer being D.

35. In line 7 of this poem, what word below most nearly means "aspire"?

A. Soar

B. Plunge

C. Scheme

D. Travel

E. Admire

The answer is A.
Again, look for synonym in the list. Plunge is an antonym. A is the right choice.

36. The poet, William Blake, uses all of the following literary tools to convey his message, except:

A. metaphors

B. rhymed couplets

C. personification

D. symbols

E. lyrics

The answer is C.
For this question, you need to know your literary terms. Look them up if there are any unfamiliar to you. C - personification - is the right answer... it was also hinted in question four for this passage.

PASSAGE 9
(Prose fiction, British, 19ᵗʰ century)

"Without their visits you cannot hope to shun the path I tread. Expect the first tomorrow night, when the bell tolls One. Expect the second on the next night at the same hour. The third, upon the next night, when the last stroke of Twelve has ceased to vibrate Look to see me no more; and look that, for your own sake, you remember what has passed between us!"

It walked backward from him; and at every step it took, the window raised itself a little, so that, when the apparition reached it, it was wide open.

Scrooge closed the window, and examined the door by which the Ghost had entered. It was double-locked, as he had locked it with his own hands, and the bolts were undisturbed. Scrooge tried to say "Humbug!" but stopped at the first syllable. And being, from the emotion he had undergone, or the fatigues of the day, or his glimpse of the invisible world, or the dull conversation of the Ghost, or the lateness of the hour, much in need of repose, he went straight to bed, without undressing, and fell asleep on the instant.

~Charles Dickens, 1843

37.   What quality of the Ghost is the most likely trait that Scrooge dislikes the most?

A.   The Ghost's old fashioned speech bothers Scrooge the most.

B.   The authoritative nature the Ghost takes with Scrooge is the quality disliked the most.

C.   The fact that the Ghost could break into his house is the trait that Scrooge dislikes.

D.   The Ghost is taller than Scrooge, and that bothers him.

E.   Scrooge dislikes that his bedtime was later than usual.

The answer is B.
You should eliminate wrong answers. C is wrong because Scrooge checks his house and it is secure. D is wrong as there is no indication about a height difference. E is also not appropriate, though the passage notes he went straight to bed, it mentions no discomfort caused by the ghost for this reason. Between choices A and B, either could be true but the stronger dislike would be B, so that makes it the correct answer.

38. The way Scrooge's reaction to the Ghost is portrayed could mean that according to this passage that Scrooge is:

   A. tired

   B. angry

   C. looking for excuses

   D. forgetful

   E. planning to ignore the Ghost

The answer is C.
Again, by eliminating the wrong choices, there is nothing that suggests Scrooge is forgetful so it isn't D. While any of the rest are possible, the fact that Scrooge checks around the house and looks for things that could be explanations leads to the most reasonable answer as C.

39. The Ghost's remarks listed in the passage can most likely be inferred as:

   A. a warning to Scrooge

   B. the Ghost is talking to the wrong person

   C. Scrooge is hallucinating

   D. a friend was playing a joke on Scrooge

   E. no inference can be made

The answer is A.
Of the five options, the middle choices - B, C and D - have no support in the passage. As E is not a typical choice for the exam, A is the correct answer.

40. **Scrooge's reaction to the Ghost in this passage leads a reader to conclude:**

   A. that Scrooge was just conducting a normal nighttime house-check

   B. when the Ghost comes back for him, Scrooge will go along willingly

   C. even wealthy people like Scrooge lock their houses

   D. that Scrooge does not believe in the supernatural

   E. Scrooge is likely overcome with exhaustion

The answer is D.
The first answer is not accurate, as it was not a normal nighttime house check with the ghost. Also, there is no indication that Scrooge will willingly go anywhere with the ghost, so B is wrong. The generalization about wealthy people doesn't apply to the whole passage making that assumption, so C is incorrect. While Scrooge is admittedly tired, the better answer is D, given the extent of reaction to the ghost's presence in his home.

41. **The tone of the passage is intended to:**

   A. serve as a warning to Scrooge about things he will be shown

   B. serve as a reminder that Scrooge has forgotten appointments

   C. describe how disconcerted Scrooge felt after the warning was given by the Ghost

   D. provide backstory

   E. explain why Scrooge is so stingy

The answer is C.
Since the answers must be given based on the passage, A is more in line with the full story. B is not what the ghost was saying. A backstory is something that happened to the character in the past, and the ghost talks about the future, so D is incorrect. Nothing explains why Scrooge is stingy, or even that he is (other than the meaning of his name), so C is the correct answer.

PASSAGE 10
(Prose, non-fiction, American, 20th century)

Using the Constitution to protect the minorities, James Madison's system of government is largely an attempt to divide and frustrate the majority. Madison envisioned a political system with the broadest possible power base. For example, he rejected the common belief that a democracy could work only in a very small area, arguing that it could succeed in a large country like the United States. A large population spread over a huge area would make it very difficult to force a permanent majority. Such a society would probably divide into varied and fluctuating minorities, making a long lasting majority unlikely. Instead, majorities would be created out of combinations of competing minorities. Thus, any majority would be temporary, and new ones would be elusive. This system, political scientists now term *pluralism*.

~ Leon Baradat, 1973

42.   According to the passage, what is pluralism?

A.   Majorities created out of combinations of competing minorities

B.   A new division of political science

C.   A political system with the smallest possible power base

D.   A new name for a permanent majority

E.   The system for democracy to work in a very small area

The answer is A.
This is a simple reference to the passage and the correct answer is A.

43. **The Constitution mentioned in the first line, in context to this passage, is:**

   A. James Madison's document to create a permanent majority

   B. the document creating the United States

   C. the personality of James Madison

   D. the health of the majority

   E. instructions on how to create combinations of competing minorities

The answer is B.
This question discusses something that should be known outside of context, especially when referencing a President of the United States, and the correct answer is B.

44. **The passage talks about democracy. Another phrase for a democracy is:**

   A. the rule of a few over the many

   B. the welfare state

   C. a laissez-faire economy

   D. an elected government system

   E. an appointed government by a monarch

The answer is D.
Using definitions of words, the answer should be obvious. A defines a monarchy or dictatorship; a welfare state could be socialist in B. A democracy doesn't describe economy, or an appointed government with monarchy, so the correct answer is D.

PASSAGE 11
(Prose non-fiction, British, 21ˢᵗ century)

American black music was going along like an express train. But white cats, after Buddy Holly died and Eddie Cochran died, and Elvis was in the army gone wonky, white American music when I arrived was the Beach Boys and Bobby Vee. They were still stuck in the past. The past was six months ago; it wasn't a long time. But things changed. The Beatles were the milestone. And then they got stuck inside their own cage. "The Fab Four." Hence, eventually, you got the Monkees, all this ersatz stuff. But I think there was a vacuum somewhere in white American music at the time.

When we first got to America and to LA, there was a lot of Beach Boys on the radio, which was pretty funny to us - it was before *Pet Sounds* - it was hot rod songs and surfing songs, pretty lousily played, familiar Chuck Berry licks going on. "Round, round get around / I get around," I though that was brilliant. It was later on, but Brian Wilson had something. "In My Room," "Don't Worry Baby." I was more interested in their B-sides, the ones he slipped in. There was no particular correlation with what we were doing so I could just listen to it on another level. I thought these are very well-constructed songs. I took easily to the pop song idiom. I'd always listened to everything, and America opened it all out - we were hearing records there that were regional hits. We'd get to know local labels and local acts, which is how we came across "Time Is on My Side," in LA, sung by Irma Thomas. It was a B-side of a record on Imperial Records, a label we'd have been aware of because it was independent and successful and based on Sunset Strip.

~Keith Richards, 2010

45.   How many unique singers versus unique bands, respectively, are named in the passage above?

    A. Seven and Four

    B. Six and Three

    C. Eight and Three

    D. Seven and Three

    E. Six and Four

The answer is D.
This is merely counting. There are Seven singers (Buddy Holly, Eddie Cochran, Elivs, Bobby Vee, Chuck Berry, Brian Wilson, Irma Thomas) and three bands (Beatles, Monkeys, Beach Boys). D The "Fab Four" is referring to the Beatles. (Note the author's group is not named in the passage, and neither is he.)

46.   How many songs are referenced in the passage above?

A. Two

B. Three

C. Four

D. Five

E. Six

The answer is C.
Count them - In My Room, Don't Worry Baby and Time Is On My Side. B
(note "Round, round get around/I get around" are lyrics and not the name of
a song.)

47.   In the context of the selection's first paragraph, how many white
        singers or groups are named by the author?

A. Four

B. Five

C. Three

D. Seven

E. One

The answer is D.
The whole passage is about white male singers except Irma Thomas, but her
name is in the second paragraph. This question is limited to the first
paragraph. Seven singers or bands are named after the author's "white cats"
comment. D

48.	Given what the author says about the B-side of a record, which of the following sentences is closest to the author's opinion?

A.	The B-side had more creativity and outlets for artists, making it unique.

B.	It was called the B-side because the songs were generally not as good.

C.	Only regional labels took the time to press B-sides.

D.	The B-side was where all the surfing songs were recorded.

E.	Labels were strict about the contents of the B-sides.

The answer is A.
You need to read the passage to understand which is the most appropriate. A is the best answer. The others are wrong because B is opposite of what he expresses as his opinion, C is factually not what the author writes, D is the opposite of what he says about the Beach Boys, and E is also the opposite of what the author writes.

49.	When the author talks about the Beatles and says "they got stuck inside their own cage," the author most likely means:

A.	that the Beatles always had to hide in hotels because they were so famous

B.	that successful musical groups could never enjoy the publicity

C.	that the Beatles were trapped on planes all the time

D.	that the Beatles couldn't perform with anyone outside of their four members

E.	the Beatles outgrew the standard previously set for successful musicians, and were trapped in their own famous sensation

The answer is E.
For this answer, you need to interpret the author's intention from the context of the passage. The first four options are not supported by the passage at all; E is the best interpretation of the author's phrase.

50. Given the descriptions in the passage, the author's profession is likely:

   A. a roadie

   B. a writer

   C. a singer

   D. a photographer

   E. a teacher

The answer is C.
Understanding the author's voice is important. Even if you didn't know that author's name (though you could save time if you did), given the descriptions of what he writes, C is the best and right answer.

PASSAGE 12
(Prose fiction, British, pre-Ren/Classic)

A marvelous case is it to hear, either the warnings of that he should have voided, or the tokens of that he could not void. For the self night next before his death, the lord Stanley sent a trusty secret messenger unto him at midnight in all the haste, requiring him to rise and ride away with him, for he was disposed utterly no longer to bide; he had so fearful a dream, in which him thought that a boar with his tusks so raced them both by the heads, that the blood ran about both their shoulders. And forasmuch as the protector gave the boar for his cognizance, this dream made so fearful an impression in his heart, that he was thoroughly determined no longer to tarry, but had his horse ready, if the lord Hastings would go with him to ride so far yet the same night, that they should be out of danger ere day. Ay, good lord, quoth the lord Hastings to this messenger, leaneth my lord thy master so much to such trifles, and hath such faith in dreams, which either his own fear fantasieth or do rise in the night's rest by reason of his day thoughts? Tell him it is plain witchcraft to believe in such dreams; which if they were tokens of things to come, why thinketh he not that we might be as likely to make them true by our going if we were caught and brought back (as friends fail fleers), for then had the boar a cause likely to race us with his tusks, as folk that fled for some falsehood, wherefore either is there no peril (nor none there is indeed), or if any be, it is rather in going than biding. And if we should, needs cost, fall in peril one way or other, yet had I livelier that men should see it were by other men's falsehood, than think it were either our own fault or faint heart. And therefore go to thy master, man, and commend me to him, and pray him be merry and have no fear: for I ensure him I am as sure of the man that he wotteth of, as I am of my own hand. God send grace, sir, quoth the messenger, and went his way.

~Sir Thomas More, 1513

51. **The beginning of the passage is describing what?**

    A. An injury sustained by the main character

    B. A rider that is trying to escape injury

    C. The main character's dream

    D. A witch's story

    E. The boar that the character will grill for dinner

The answer is C.
Discounting the incorrect description of what's in the passage (such as in option E and A as well as B), that leaves options C and D. There is no reference to a witch, so the best choice is C. He even states that it is a dream.

52. **What is the cautionary message that the rider gets when he reaches his destination?**

    A. Dreams are witchcraft if you believe in them.

    B. Dreams can come true if you believe in them.

    C. God sends His grace.

    D. Those faint of heart do not have dreams.

    E. Men cannot fall for other men's falsehoods.

The answer is A.
The rider warns the statement included in A.

53.   Did the main character in this passage believe he could out run bad visions?

   A.   No, the passage makes it clear you always get what's coming in a dream.

   B.   No, dreams mean nothing, so the main character didn't pay any attention to it.

   C.   Yes, it was possible to escape bad visions on horseback.

   D.   Yes, the main character thought dancing would rid himself of bad dreams.

   E.   There is nothing in the passage that assists in answering this question.

The answer is C.
Again, the main character gives indications that the correct answer is C. The other options of No are wrong, as is the answer given in E. Answer D can be discounted because dancing is not discussed in the passage.

PASSAGE 13
(Prose fiction, British, 19th century)

To go into solitude, a man needs to retire as much from his chamber as from society. I am not solitary whilst I read and write, though nobody is with me. But if a man would be alone, let him look at the stars. The rays that come from those heavenly worlds, will separate between him and what he touches. One might think the atmosphere was made transparent with this design, to give man, in the heavenly bodies, the perpetual presence of the sublime. Seen in the streets of cities, how great they are! If the stars should appear one night in a thousand years, how would men believe and adore; and preserve for many generations the remembrance of the city of God which had been shown! But every night come out these envoys of beauty, and light the universe with their admonishing smile.

~Ralph Waldo Emerson, 1836

54. **The first two lines of this passage imply what?**

    A. A man is never alone.

    B. A man is always alone.

    C. A man can be alone if he turns his back on people.

    D. A man can be alone if he makes his mind focus.

    E. A man who is lonely is considered alone.

The answer is D.
Given this is fiction and nearly a poem, you need to interpret what the author intends. The first two options use those extreme words, so they are not the best choices. The literal description of turning a back on people is not discussed. The difference between lonely and being alone is not discussed, either. So, D is the answer you should choose.

55. **Given the whole passage, which of the following is the best match for the author's opinion about nature?**

    A. The author prefers to seek to retire in his chamber.

    B. The author sees wonder in the sky and beauty at night.

    C. The author does not like trees.

    D. The author can only see stars one night in a thousand years.

    E. You cannot tell the author's opinion from this passage.

The answer is B.
You should realize by now - especially when understanding poems - that it would be extremely rare to select option E as the right answer. Option D is a misstatement of a phrase in the passage. There is no mention of the author even hinting that he does not like trees, so C is incorrect. When considering A or B, A does not resound as strongly as B, which is the right answer.

56.   The phrase "light the universe with their admonishing smile" is an
       example of:

A.   personification

B.   a simile

C.   a metaphor

D.   irony

E.   satire

The answer is A.
Remember, the definition of personification is to give an inanimate object the
attributes of a human, so A is correct. If you are unfamiliar with the other
options in this example, it would be a good idea to look them up and learn
them, as at least one of these five will be included on the exam.

PASSAGE 14
(Poetry, American, 20th century)

Two roads diverged in a yellow wood,
And sorry I could not travel both
And be one traveler, long I stood
And looked down one as far as I could
To where it bent in the undergrowth;

Then took the other, as just as fair,
And having perhaps the better claim,
Because it was grassy and wanted wear;
Though as for that the passing there
Had worn them really about the same,

And both that morning equally lay
In leaves no step had trodden black.
Oh, I kept the first for another day!
Yet knowing how way leads on to way,
I doubted if I should ever come back.

I shall be telling this with a sigh
Somewhere ages and ages hence:

Two roads diverged in a wood, and I—
I took the one less traveled by,
And that has made all the difference.
~Robert Frost, 1920

57.   When the author uses the phrase "wanted wear" in the third stanza, what does that mean?

   A.   It looked just as fair as the other path.

   B.   It was not as inviting.

   C.   The path didn't go the same way as the other one.

   D.   The path was less traveled than the other one.

   E.   You cannot determine what the author means.

The answer is D.
There are two possible correct answers. Both B and D are viable options; however, you are looking for the best answer. In the context of the whole poem, the explanation of B does not ring as true since that is the one that the author actually selected. D is the best answer.

58. **The author says that he "took the one less traveled by"; what does that mean?**

   A. The other path looked like it was used more.

   B. He did the right thing when others chose the wrong one.

   C. He took the one on the left.

   D. He took the one on the right.

   E. It cannot be determined what the author meant by this short selection.

The answer is A.
This is another example of how a question is phrased to make sure you read it accurately. There is no statement about right or left direction, so both C and D are wrong. E is also eliminated as least probable answer because comprehension very rarely provides no correct answer. While B may bear some truth, in particular for the author as given in the end of the poem, A is the best answer.

59. **What is another way the author states his path was the "one less traveled by"?**

   A. "both that morning equally lay"

   B. "no step had trodden black"

   C. "Somewhere ages and ages hence"

   D. "bent in the undergrowth"

   E. "having perhaps the better claim"

The answer is B.
This is another way to look for a synonym, but using a whole phrase. You should be able to narrow it down to D and B; however, B describes what happens when you walk on leaves that haven't been disturbed in a while. It is a parallel description to the straightforward "less traveled" statement, in that it describes the actions and ensuing results. Therefore, B is correct.

60. What does the author imply since he took the path less traveled?

    A. He has run into fewer people that try to bully him into doing what they want.

    B. Life is tougher getting to see the light.

    C. He was sorry he didn't chose to go the more well-trod path.

    D. He didn't make as much money as the people that took the other path.

    E. His life is better for choosing to go his own path.

The answer is E.
Running through the list of options, there is no mention of the author having people force him to make a decision (so A is wrong). B is also not applicable to this passage. There is no expression of remorse as provided in option C anywhere in the passage, so C is not correct. Monetary considerations - making money - are not mentioned either (as in D), so the only option left, which is correct, is E.

PASSAGE 15
(Prose fiction, American, 20th century)

His memories of the Boston Society Contralto were nebulous and musical. She was a lady who sang, sang, sang in the music room on their house on Washington Square - sometimes with guests all about her, the men with their arms folded, balanced breathlessly on the edges of sofas, the women with their hands in their laps, occasionally making little whispers to the men and always clapping very briskly and uttering cooing cries after each song - and she often sang to Anthony alone, in Italian or French or in a strange and terrible dialect...

Oblivious to the social system, he lived for a while alone and unsought in a high room in Beck Hall - a slim dark boy of medium height with a shy sensitive mouth. His allowance was more than liberal. He laid the foundations for a library by purchasing from a wandering bibliophile first editions of Swinburne, Meredith, and Hardy, and a yellowed illegible autograph letter of Keats', finding later he had been amazingly overcharged. He became an exquisite dandy, amassed a rather pathetic collection of silk pajamas, brocaded dressing-gowns, and neckties too flamboyant to wear; in this secret finery he would parade before a mirror in his room or lie stretched in satin along the window-seat looking down on the yard and realizing this clamor, breathless and immediate, in which it seemed he was to never have a part.

~ F. Scott Fitzgerald, 1922

61.   Based on the information in the passage, what is a "contralto"?

A.   A Boston slang term for a high class man

B.   A female singer

C.   A female dancer

D.   A writer

E.   A bibliophile

The Answer B.
Using the pronouns in the passage, contralto is a female - so A is obviously wrong. While any of the remaining options may be true, in the passage it talks about the woman singing, so B is the correct choice.

62.   Based on the information in the passage, an "exquisite dandy" refers to:

A.   the first editions of the books listed in the passage

B.   anyone who wears silk pajamas

C.   a gentleman who has money to spend extravagantly on fancy things

D.   someone who likes to parade before a mirror

E.   someone who likes candy

The answer is C.
The term "dandy" references a person, so A is out. E is also out because candy is not mentioned in the passage; it is merely a rhyme for dandy. B is mentioned in the passage that the man like to wear silk pajamas and so is D, when it talks about the mirror. However, you have to look at the whole passage and the thing the man does, so C is the best answer if you do not know what "dandy" means.

63. Why would the social system be important in this reading selection?

   A. Richer classes don't have dandies, so the main character can't be dandy.

   B. A rich man with no female friends is called a dandy, and it helps explain the story.

   C. The character seems ostracized and that can't happen in certain social classes.

   D. If the main character was of a lower class, he could not live the life described.

   E. No one lives the luxurious life described in the passage.

The answer is D.
In this question, it helps to know the meaning of dandy, which you may use from the previous answer if you do not know it. Since the man described in the passage seems to have a lot of money, A cannot be the right answer. E also is not a choice because it uses an extreme phrase - "no one". D is not correct because anyone can be excluded from a group (it also has an extreme contraction of "can't"). Between B and D, there are two reasons why B isn't a good choice. First, no female friends could be read as an extreme description, using "no". Another tip that this may not be the right choice is that if you removed the part of the passage about dandy, the story still works. Therefore, if you don't know that dandies are rarely lower classes, you can reason your way that D is correct.

PASSAGE 16
(Prose fiction, American, 20th century)

These are morning matters, pictures you dream as the final wave heaves you up on the sand in the bright light and drying air. You remember pressure, and a curved sleep you rested against, soft, like a scallop in its shell. But the air hardens your skin; you stand; you leave the lighted shore to explore some dim headland, and soon you're lost in the leafy interior, intent, remembering nothing.

I still think of that old tomcat, mornings, when I wake. Things are tamer now; I sleep with the window shut. The cats and our rites are gone and my life is changed, but the memory remains of something powerful playing over me. I wake expectant, hoping to see a new thing. If I'm lucky I might be jogged awake by a strange bird call. I dress in a hurry, imagining the yard flapping with auks, or flamingos. This morning it was a wood duck, down at the creek. It flew away.

~Annie Dillard, 1975 Pulitzer Prize

64.　The tone of the selection is:

    A.　reflective

    B.　indulgent

    C.　indifferent

    D.　dishonest

    E.　ironic

The answer is A.
This is knowing what the different words mean. A is the correct answer. Review the definitions of these words if you don't know them, to make sure they won't trip you up on the exam.

65.　The author uses _____ to describe the setting.

    A.　personification

    B.　ambivalence

    C.　satire

    D.　allusion

    E.　clichés

The answer is D.
Definitions are a large part of reading comprehension answer possibilities, as they like to know that you understand more than just what the passage says. D is the correct answer.

66.   The phrase, "like a scallop in its shell" is an example of:

A. irony

B. a simile

C. a metaphor

D. personification

E. euphemism

The answer is C.
Again, this is about definitions. When you use the word "like" in a comparison, which is one hint that the phrase is a metaphor. The answer is C.

67.   The author describes many of her feelings and situations by focusing the conversation on animals. Based on the information in the passage, one reason could be:

A. animals are comforting and relax the reader

B. birds are flighty and the center of her story

C. the setting of this story is a farm

D. the lead character doesn't have many human friends

E. it is the backstory of how animals and nature are always present in the character's life

The answer is E.
There are some weigh out options for these answers! A, B, C and D make great leaps if you were to make those conclusions. E is the correct option.

68.   The phrase "the air hardens your skin" within the context of the
      passage most likely refers to what?

A.   The morning air woke the character up from dreaming.

B.   The scallop shell bed the character sleeps in has opened.

C.   The air dries out the character's skin.

D.   The coldness of the room turns off the brain of the character.

E.   The air turns the character's skin cold when the cat leaves the bed.

The answer is A.
This question looks at ensuring you understand the suggestions made by the
author. B is totally made up. D is a bit far-fetched, to turn off her brain (what
does that have to do with skin?) E gives the impression cats are extremely
warm and somehow leaving the bed is related with her description, slightly
implausible. A and C remain; but in the context of fiction, A is the better
choice.

PASSAGE 17
(Drama, British, 16th century/classical)

Bernardo : Welcome, Horatio: welcome, good Marcellus.
Marcellus : What, has this thing appear'd again to-night?
Bernardo : I have seen nothing.
Marcellus : Horatio says 'tis but our fantasy,
And will not let belief take hold of him
Touching this dreaded sight, twice seen of us:
Therefore I have entreated him along
With us to watch the minutes of this night;
That if again this apparition come,
He may approve our eyes and speak to it.
Horatio : Tush, tush, 'twill not appear.
Bernardo : Sit down awhile;
And let us once again assail your ears,
That are so fortified against our story
What we have two nights seen.
                    ~William Shakespeare, 1599-1602

69.   The three men in the play can be said, in this passage:

A.   to disagree about a ghost that was seen

B.   to disagree that two days ago they saw people meeting "twice seen of us"

C.   that Horatio and Bernardo are trying to persuade Marcellus they saw something

D.   that Horatio and Marcellus are trying to persuade Bernardo they saw something

E.   to meet for a drink for "fortification"

The answer is A.
Drama selections need you to pay close attention to the characters and who says what. B is not true - the two men don't disagree about what they saw. C and D do not list the characters correctly about who sees what. E isn't correct at all, so A is the correct answer.

70.   When Marcellus speaks of "approving our eyes", what is he saying?

A.   Marcellus and Bernardo need glasses.

B.   Bernardo didn't believe what Marcellus saw.

C.   Horatio believes what Marcellus saw.

D.   Horatio should see what Bernardo and Marcellus saw.

E.   Marcellus should believe what Bernardo saw.

The answer is D.
You need to review the members of the scene if you got this inaccurate. The only correct choice about who saw what and who needs to see what they saw is D.

71.   When Bernardo says "once again assail your ears", what does he mean?

   A.   He wants to repeat himself to Marcellus to make him believe him.

   B.   He wants to repeat himself to Horatio to make him believe him.

   C.   He wants to repeat himself to help all three of them believe the story.

   D.   He wants Marcellus and Horatio to poke holes in the story.

   E.   None of these are the meaning of that phrase in the passage.

The answer is B.
Pay attention to the characters. That's how these answer choices can be confusing. B is the correct answer.

72.   In the context of the passage, entreated means:

   A.   invited

   B.   engaged

   C.   demanded

   D.   refused

   E.   ignored

The answer is A.
Picking the best synonym should get easier at the end of the exam. A is correct.

PASSAGE 18
(Drama, American, 20th century)

Edmund : That's foolishness. You know it's only a bad cold.
Mary : Yes, of course, I know that!
Edmund : But listen, Mama. I want you to promise me that even if it turns out to be something worse, you'll know I'll soon be alright again, anyway, and don't worry yourself sick, and you'll keep on taking care of yourself -

Mary : I won't listen when you talk so silly! There's absolutely no reason to talk as if you expect something dreadful! Of course, I promise you I give you my sacred word of honor! But I suppose you're remembering I've promised before on my word of honor.

Edmund : No!

Mary : I'm not blaming you, dear. How can you help it? How can any one of us forget? That's what makes it so hard - for all of us. We can't forget.

Edmund : Mama! Stop it!

Mary : All right, dear. I didn't beam to be so gloomy. Don't mind me. Here. Let me feel your head. Why, it's nice and cool. You certainly don't have any fever now.

~Eugene O'Neill, 1955

73.   It can be said that this passage of the drama:

A.   puts American dream against American nightmare

B.   describes the normal American family

C.   portrays Americans in a very resilient fashion

D.   was likely written during a war so obviously has negative overtones

E.   has the mother remembering the death of another child

The answer is E.

You may have read this play, but you have to limit your answers to the passage; therefore, A is not correct. B invites the reader to make assumptions about normal, and that does not usually happen in the exam. There is not enough information in the passage to presume C is correct. The passage is not overly negative, so E is the best answer.

74.   **Mary changes the direction of the conversation by:**

A.   stopping Edmund from talking by taking his temperature

B.   making Edmund feel badly about the death of his brother

C.   walking out of the room

D.   tucking the covers up to his chin

E.   ignoring him

The answer is A.
You need to read the scene to make sure to pick the right answer. A is correct.

75.   **This portion of the play is a:**

A.   monologue

B.   dialogue

C.   soliloquy

D.   entendre

E.   stichomythia

The answer is B.
By definition, since there are two people, A and C are incorrect. While D is possible, E is wrong; B is the best choice. Look up the words if you are unfamiliar with them.

76.   Mary talks about Edmund expecting something dreadful. What's a
      literary term for that action?

   A.   Oxymoron

   B.   Dissonance

   C.   Foreshadowing

   D.   Stream of consciousness

   E.   Understatement

The answer is C.
Definitions again! The correct choice is C and by now you should
automatically look up any definitions for words that are unfamiliar to you.

PASSAGE 19
(Prose fiction, British, 18th century)

But though thus largely indebted to fortune, to nature she had yet greater
obligation: her form was elegant, her heart was liberal. Her countenance
announced the intelligence of her mind, her complexion varied with every
emotion of her foul, and her eyes, the heralds of her speech, now beamed
with understanding and now glistened with sensibility.

For the short period of her minority, the management of her fortune and
the care of her person, had by the Dean been entrusted to three guardians,
among whom her own choice was to settle to her residence: but her mind,
saddened by the lots of all her natural friends, coveted to regain its serenity
in the quietness of the country, and in the bosom of an aged and maternal
counsellor, whom she loved as her mother, and to to whom she had been
known from her childhood.
Fanny Burney, 1782

85

77. **From the context of this passage, which of the following statements is the most likely to be true?**

   A. The main character is poor.

   B. The main character is an orphan.

   C. The setting of the story is in England.

   D. The main character is going to live with her aunt.

   E. The main character doesn't like to live in town.

The answer is B.
The female character seems to have inherited money, so A is not correct. There is no way to know in what country the setting takes place, and remember that all answers are dependent on the passage; so C is incorrect. D is also incorrect because the passage explicitly talks about her wanting to set up her own house. B is the right answer.

78. **In the quote, "her heart was liberal", what is the author trying to express?**

    A.   The author implies that the main character is of loose morals.

    B.   The author implies that while ladylike, she has a wild streak.

    C.   The author alludes that the woman is more open than her demeanor.

    D.   The author makes it clear that she is alone.

    E.   The author shows how she was older than her natural friends.

The answer is C.
While this one may seem difficult, if you take each statement apart, the answer comes quickly. A is wrong because nowhere does the author talk about morals being questionable. B implies an overly outward exuberance by the main character, and that is overstating what is written. D is simply not accurate, and while there seems to be a difference between her and her friends, nowhere does the passage indicate she is older. C is correct. Also, when the author describes her "heart", it can mean that her inward thoughts, and since her demeanor is so proper, the outward indications of her character, C again is shown to be the right answer.

79. **What does the word "minority" mean in the context of the passage?**

    A.   The woman in the passage is a Native American.

    B.   The character is not yet an adult.

    C.   The group of people in the story are members of the minority political party.

    D.   The character has less money than her friends.

    E.   None of the given options explain "minority" in this passage.

The answer is B.
This passage does not talk about race or ethnicity or religion; A is wrong. C talks about politics and that is not within the passage, so it, too, is wrong. D is the opposite of what is implied by the author about the main character; and as you have learned, E is likely the wrong choice. Choose B.

80.   What is another word for serenity in this passage?

    A.   Peacefulness

    B.   Counsellor

    C.   Bosom

    D.   Rambunctiousness

    E.   Prayerful

The answer is A.
Another synonym choice - A is correct.

Description of the Examination

The CLEP College Composition examinations assess writing skills taught in most first-year college composition courses. Those skills include analysis, argumentation, synthesis, usage, ability to recognize logical development and research. The exams cannot cover every skill (such as keeping a journal or peer editing) required in many first-year college writing courses. Candidates will, however, be expected to apply the principles and conventions used in longer writing projects to two timed writing assignments and to apply the rules of standard written English.

College Composition contains approximately 50 multiple-choice items to be answered in approximately 50 minutes and two essays to be written in 70 minutes (with 30 minutes to write the first essay and 40 minutes to read the two sources and write the second essay), for a total of approximately 120 minutes testing time. Essays must be typed on the computer.

The actual examination contains multiple-choice items and two mandatory, centrally scored essays. The essays are scored twice a month by college English faculty from throughout the country via an online scoring system. Each of the two essays is scored independently by two different readers, and the scores are then combined. This combined score is weighted approximately equally with the score from the multiple-choice section. These scores are then combined to yield the candidate's score. The resulting combined score is reported as a single scared score between 20 and 80. Separate scores are not reported for the multiple-choice and essay sections.

The College Composition Modular exam allows institutions to administer and/or score test-takers' essays after approximately 90 multiple choice questions are completed in 90 minutes (with the two essay questions to be completed in 70 minutes to complete both essay answers), for a total of approximately 160 minutes. The knowledge and skills assessed are the same as those measured by College Composition, but the format and timing allow a more extended indirect assessment of test-takers' knowledge and skills. The percentages of exam questions on each topic are the same in the College Composition exam as well as this sample College Composition Modular sample test.

Knowledge and Skills Required

The subject matter of the College Composition examination is drawn from the following topics. The percentages next to the main topics indicate the approximate percentage of exam questions on that topic for the multiple-choice items.

10% Conventions of Standard English
- measures the awareness of logical, structural and grammatical relationships within sentences. Questions relate to syntax, punctuation, concord/agreement, modifiers, active versus passive voice and additional areas

40% Revision Skills
- measures revision skills in the context of early essays, such as organization, level of detail, awareness of audience or tone, sentence variety and structure, main ideas, transitions, point of views
- Modular format includes questions that require sentence restructuring/word replacement to improve comprehension

25% Ability to Use Source Material
- measures familiarity with basic reference and research skills via the use of reference materials, evaluation of sources, integration of resources and documentation

25% Rhetorical Analysis
- measures ability to analyze writing primarily using passage based questions reviewing appeals, tone, structure, rhetorical effects

On the next page, the sample test begins. There are 90 questions that you must answer in less than 90 minutes. Then, there are essay questions that you must answer in a timed fashion: the first essay has 30 minutes and the second essay has 40 minutes to read two passages and complete and essay.

Remember, your goals for this test are those questions you answer accurately; it is not based on how many are incorrect. Take your time, and good luck.

SAMPLE TEST

CONVENTIONS OF STANDARD WRITTEN ENGLISH

DIRECTIONS: Read each item carefully, paying attention to the underlined portions. If there is an error, it will be underlined. Assume that elements of the sentence not underlined are correct. If there is an error, select the one underlined part and enter that letter on the answer sheet. If there is no error, choose E.

1. A <u>fearful</u> man, all in grey, <u>were</u> down by the river <u>standing</u> by the bunches of <u>rushes</u>. <u>No error.</u>

    A. fearful

    B. was

    C. standing

    D. rushes

    E. No error

2. When our group of <u>friends</u> goes to Italy next year, we will be <u>seeing</u> many of the <u>countries</u> famous <u>landmarks</u>. <u>No error.</u>

    A. friends

    B. seeing

    C. country's

    D. landmarks

    E. No error

3. <u>Their</u> are no walls high enough, no <u>valleys</u> deep enough, <u>to</u> keep the warriors <u>from</u> attacking the city. <u>No error.</u>

    A. There

    B. valleys

    C. to

    D. from

    E. No error

4. <u>Whenever</u> the phone rings, the dog <u>likes</u> to run to the front door to <u>see</u> who <u>has come</u> to visit. <u>No error</u>

    A. Whenever

    B. likes

    C. see

    D. has come

    E. No error

5. <u>Every one</u> must pass <u>through</u> Vanity Fair in order to get to the <u>celestial</u> city and receive <u>their</u> three golden eggs. <u>No error</u>

A. Everyone

B. through

C. celestial

D. their

E. No error

6. Suffering <u>has been</u> stronger than all other teaching, and <u>have</u> taught me to understand what <u>your</u> heart <u>use</u> to be. <u>No error</u>

A. has been

B. has

C. your

D. use

E. No error

7. The loneliest moment in <u>someone's</u> life is when they are watching <u>their</u> <u>hole</u> world fall apart, and all they can do is <u>stare</u> blankly. <u>No error</u>

A. someone's

B. their

C. whole

D. stare

E. No error

8. I have not <u>broken</u> your heart - you have <u>broke</u> it; and in <u>breaking</u> it, you <u>have</u> broken mine. <u>No error</u>

A. broke

B. broken

C. breaking

D. have

E. No error

Mr. Smith gave instructions for the painting to be hung on the wall. And then it leaped forth before his eyes: the little cottages on the river, the white clouds floating over the valley and the green of the towering mountain ranges which were seen in the distance. The painting was so vivid that it seemed almost real. Mr. Smith was now absolutely certain that the painting had been worth money.

9.   From the last sentence, one can infer that:

   A.   the painting was expensive.

   B.   the painting was cheap.

   C.   Mr. Smith was considering purchasing the painting.

   D.   Mr. Smith thought the painting was too expensive and decided not to purchase it.

   E.   None of these things is true.

10.   What is the main idea of this passage?

   A.   The painting that Mr. Smith purchased is expensive.

   B.   Mr. Smith purchased a painting.

   C.   Mr. Smith was pleased with the quality of the painting he had purchased.

   D.   The painting depicted cottages and valleys.

   E.   Mr. Smith was looking to buy some paintings.

11.   The author's purpose is to:

   A.   Inform

   B.   Entertain

   C.   Persuade

   D.   Narrate

   E.   Analyze

One of the most difficult problems plaguing American education is the assessment of teachers. No one denies that teachers ought to be answerable for what they do, but what exactly does that mean? The Oxford American Dictionary defines accountability as: the obligation to give a reckoning or explanation for one's actions.

Does a student have to learn for teaching to have taken place? Historically, teaching has not been defined in this restrictive manner; the teacher was thought to be responsible for the quantity and quality of material covered and the way in which it was presented. However, some definitions of teaching now imply that students must learn in order for teaching to have taken place.

As a teacher who tries my best to keep current on all the latest teaching strategies, I believe that those teachers who do not bother even to pick up an educational journal every once in a while should be kept under close watch. There are many teachers out there who have been teaching for decades and refuse to change their ways even if research has proven that their methods are outdated and ineffective. There is no place in the profession of teaching for these types of individuals. It is time that the American educational system clean house, for the sake of our children.

12. What is the main idea of the passage?

A. Teachers should not be answerable for what they do.

B. Teachers who do not do their job should be fired.

C. The author is a good teacher.

D. Assessment of teachers is a serious problem in society today.

E. Defining accountability.

13. From the passage, one can infer that:

A. The author considers herself a good teacher.

B. Poor teachers will be fired.

C. Students have to learn for teaching to take place.

D. The author will be fired.

E. All of these are characteristics of fables

14. What is the author's purpose in writing the passage on the previous page?

    A. To entertain

    B. To narrate

    C. To describe

    D. To persuade

    E. To make demands

15. The author states that teacher assessment is a problem for:

    A. Elementary schools

    B. Secondary schools

    C. American education

    D. Families

    E. Teachers

Disciplinary practices have been found to affect diverse areas of child development such as the acquisition of moral values, obedience to authority, and performance at school. Even though the dictionary has a specific definition of the word "discipline," it is still open to interpretation by people of different cultures.

There are four types of disciplinary styles: assertion of power, withdrawal of love, reasoning, and permissiveness. Assertion of power involves the use of force to discourage unwanted behavior. Withdrawal of love involves making the love of a parent conditional on a child's good behavior. Reasoning involves persuading the child to behave one way rather than another. Permissiveness involves allowing the child to do as he or she pleases and face the consequences of his/her actions.

16. Name the four types of disciplinary styles.

    A. Reasoning, power assertion, morality, and permissiveness.

    B. Morality, reasoning, permissiveness, and withdrawal of love.

    C. Withdrawal of love, permissiveness, power, and reasoning.

    D. Permissiveness, morality, reasoning, and power assertion.

    E. Explore, Inform, Entertain, Persuade.

17. What is the main idea of the previous passage?

    A. Different people have different ideas of what discipline is.

    B. Permissiveness is the most widely used disciplinary style.

    C. Most people agree on their definition of discipline.

    D. There are four disciplinary styles.

    E. Child development needs to focus on obedience to authority.

18. What is the author's purpose in writing this?

    A. To describe

    B. To narrate

    C. To entertain

    D. To inform

    E. To argue

19. From reading this passage, we can conclude that:

    A. The author is a teacher.

    B. The author has many children.

    C. The author has written a book about discipline.

    D. The author has done a lot of research on discipline.

    E. The author has at least two siblings.

20. What does the technique of reasoning involve?

    A. Persuading the child to behave in a certain way.

    B. Allowing the child to do as he/she pleases.

    C. Using force to discourage unwanted behavior.

    D. Making love conditional on good behavior.

    E. Distracting the child in order to get them to behave appropriately.

Each underlined portion of sentences 21-23 contains one or more errors in grammar, usage, mechanics, or sentence structure. Circle the choice that best corrects the error without changing the meaning of the original sentence. Choice E may repeat the underlined portion. Select the identical phrase if you find no error.

21. Walt Whitman was famous for <u>his composition, *Leaves of Grass*, serving as a nurse during the Civil War, and a devoted son</u>.

A. *Leaves of Grass*, his service as a nurse during the Civil War, and a devoted son.

B. composing *Leaves of Grass*, serving as a nurse during the Civil War, and being a devoted son.

C. his composition, *Leaves of Grass*, his nursing during the Civil War, and his devotion as a son.

D. serving as a nurse during the civil war, being a devoted son and *Leaves of Grass*.

E. his composition, *Leaves of Grass*, serving as a nurse during the Civil War, and a devoted son.

22. There were <u>fewer pieces</u> of evidence presented during the second trial.

A. fewer peaces

B. less peaces

C. less pieces

D. not as many peaces

E. fewer pieces

23. Wally <u>groaned, "Why</u> do I have to do an oral interpretation <u>of "The Raven."</u>

A. groaned "Why ... of 'The Raven'?"

B. groaned "Why ... of "The Raven"?

C. groaned "Why ... of "The Raven?"

D. groaned, "Why ... of "The Raven."

E. groaned, "Why... of *The Raven*?"

97

Microbiology is the study of tiny organisms that can only be seen through a magnifying glass or microscope. Scientists have used microbiology to help prevent and cure certain diseases. It has also been important in the development of new and better foods.

24. What is the main idea of this pas-sage?

    A. Microbiology has been used to prevent and cure certain diseases.

    B. Through microbiology, scientists have made discoveries that have helped many people.

    C. Microbiology is the study of tiny organisms.

    D. It is necessary to have a magnifying glass or microscope when engaged in a microbiological study.

    E. none of the above.

Many people insist on wearing "real" fur coats even though artificial furs have been available for over 30 years. It is cruel to torture animals just to be fashionable. Save an animal by wearing artificial fur coats instead of "real" ones.

25. The author's purpose is to

    A. Describe

    B. Inform

    C. Persuade

    D. Narrate

    E. Summarize

Plants are very versatile living organisms. They are constantly adapting to survive in their environments. Some plants have grown spines to protect themselves from herbivores. Plants that grow in cold regions grow close to the ground to avoid harsh winds.

26. What type of organizational pattern is the author using?

   A. Cause and Effect

   B. Generalization

   C. Comparison and Contrast

   D. Simple Listing

   E. Analogy

Rembrandt and Van Gogh were two Dutch painters. Both were from wealthy families. Both showed incredible talent at a young age. Van Gogh did not begin to paint seriously until he was twenty-seven. Rembrandt, on the other hand, had already completed many paintings by that age.

27. Which organizational pattern does the author use?

   A. Comparison and Contrast

   B. Simple Listing

   C. Cause and Effect

   D. Definition

   E. Description

Charles Lindbergh had no intention of becoming a pilot. He was enrolled in the University of Wisconsin until a flying lesson changed the entire course of his life. He began his career as a pilot by performing daredevil stunts at fairs

28. The author wrote this paragraph primarily to:

    A. describe

    B. inform

    C. entertain

    D. narrate

    E. analyze

29. Addressing someone absent or something inhuman as though present and able to respond describes a figure of speech known as:

    A. personification

    B. synecdoche

    C. metonymy

    D. apostrophe

    E. rhetorical strategy

Read the following paragraph and answer the questions below, selecting the best choice of the options presented.

(1) It was a cold and windy night. (2) Everyone was close around the fire in order to keep warm. (3) It was lonely for the little boy, who waited for his mother to bring him a marshmallow to toast on a stick. (4) His sister died just weeks ago and he really missed her.

30. In sentence (2), a better way to phrase "was close" could be:

    A. huddled

    B. gather

    C. stood

    D. left from

    E. none of these options are better

31. In sentence (4), the author is describing what emotion?

    A. hunger

    B. happiness

    C. coldness

    D. sadness

    E. anger

As she mused the pitiful vision of her mother's life laid its spell on the very quick of her being— that life of commonplace sacrifices closing in final craziness. She trembled as she heard again her mother's voice saying constantly with foolish insistence: Derevaun Seraun! Derevaun Seraun!

* [Derevaun Seraun means "The end of pleasure is pain!" (Gaelic)]

32. The following passage is written from which point of view?

   A. First person, narrator

   B. Second person, direct address

   C. Third person, omniscient

   D. First person, omniscient

   E. First person, direct address

33. To understand the origins of a word, one must study the:

   A. synonyms

   B. inflections

   C. phonetics

   D. etymology

   E. epidemiology

34. Which is the best definition for syntax?

   A. The specific order of word choices by an author to create a particular mood or feeling in the reader

   B. Writing that explains something thoroughly

   C. The background or exposition for a short story or drama

   D. Word choices that help teach a truth or moral

   E. Proper elocution

35. Which is the least true statement concerning an author's literary tone?

A. Tone is partly revealed through the selection of details.

B. Tone is the expression of the author's attitude toward his or her subject.

C. Tone can be expressed in a variety of ways by an author.

D. Tone in literature corresponds to the tone of voice a speaker uses.

E. Tone in literature is usually satiric or angry.

36. Regarding the study of poetry, which elements are least applicable to all types of poetry?

A. Setting and audience

B. Theme and tone

C. Pattern and diction

D. Diction and rhyme scheme

E. Words and symbols

There is no frigate like a book
To take us lands away,
Nor any coursers like a page
Of prancing poetry;
This traverse may the poorest take
Without oppress of toll;
How frugal is the chariot
That bears the human soul!

37. How many types of transport types does the author incorporate?

A. two

B. three

C. four

D. five

E. none

38. If the words 'frigate, coursers, and chariot' were replaced with synonyms, what would the best choice of the following options include?

A. Train, car, carriage

B. Train, horse, carriage

C. Ship, car, carriage

D. Ship, car, train

E. Ship, horse, carriage

39. What is a good paraphrase of "To take us lands away" that Ms. Dickinson writes in this poem?

   A. War makes it unsafe to travel, so we can just read about places.

   B. Poems will drive us to save our souls.

   C. Books can engage us to see new things

   D. Authors can show us how to go on vacation.

   E. It shows poems are short and fun.

Tyger! Tyger! burning bright
In the forests of the night,
What immortal hand or eye
Could frame thy fearful symmetry?

In what distant deeps or skies
Burnt the fire of thine eyes?
On what wings dare he aspire?
What the hand dare seize the flame?

And what shoulder, & what art,
Could twist the sinews of they heart?
And when thy heart began to beat,
What dread hand? & what dread feet?

40. Sinews, in the third stanza, can be best compared to:

   A. thread.

   B. a cage.

   C. rope.

   D. heart strings or emotions.

   E. burnt fire, from the second stanza.

41. Another phrase for "deeps or skies" that would fit in this poem could be:

   A. caves or planes.

   B. trees or forests.

   C. seas or air.

   D. waves or wind.

   E. oceans or lakes.

42. In line 7 of this poem, what word below most nearly means "aspire"?

   A. Soar.

   B. Plunge.

   C. Scheme.

   D. Travel.

   E. Admire.

These are morning matters, pictures you dream as the final wave heaves you up on the sand in the bright light and drying air. You remember pressure, and a curved sleep you rested against, soft, like a scallop in its shell. But the air hardens your skin; you stand; you leave the lighted shore to explore some dim headland, and soon you're lost in the leafy interior, intent, remembering nothing.

I still think of that old tomcat, mornings, when I wake. Things are tamer now; I sleep with the window shut. The cats and our rites are gone and my life is changed, but the memory remains of something powerful playing over me. I wake expectant, hoping to see a new thing. If I'm lucky I might be jogged awake by a strange bird call. I dress in a hurry, imagining the yard flapping with auks, or flamingos. This morning it was a wood duck, down at the creek. It flew away.

43. The phrase, "like a scallop in its shell" is an example of:

A. an irony.

B. a simile.

C. a metaphor.

D. personification.

E. euphemism.

44. The phrase "the air hardens your skin" within the context of the passage most likely refers to what?

A. The morning air woke the character up from dreaming.

B. The scallop shell bed the character sleeps in has opened.

C. The air dries out the character's skin.

D. The coldness of the room turns off the brain of the character.

E. The air turns the character's skin cold when the cat leaves the bed.

One of the most difficult problems plaguing American education is the assessment of teachers. No one denies that teachers ought to be answerable for what they do, but what exactly does that mean? The Oxford American Dictionary defines accountability as: the obligation to give a reckoning or explanation for one's actions.

Does a student have to learn for teaching to have taken place? Historically, teaching has not been defined in this restrictive manner; the teacher was thought to be responsible for the quantity and quality of material covered and the way in which it was presented. However, some definitions of teaching now imply that students must learn in order for teaching to have taken place.

As a teacher who tries my best to keep current on all the latest teaching strategies, I believe that those teachers who do not bother even to pick up an educational journal every once in a while should be kept under close watch. There are many teachers out there who have been teaching for decades and refuse to change their ways even if research has proven that their methods are outdated and ineffective. There is no place in the profession of teaching for these types of individuals. It is time that the American educational system clean house, for the sake of our children

45. Where does the author get her definition of "accountability?"

A. Webster's Dictionary

B. Encyclopedia Brittanica

C. Oxford Dictionary

D. World Book Encyclopedia

E. Wikipedia

46. In the second paragraph, the second sentence can best be described as:

A. compound.

B. complex.

C. run-on.

D. a fragment.

E. compound-complex.

47. Taite, Richard. "Five Things to Know About Recovery from Alcohol." *Psychology Today.* Web. (https://www.psychologytoday.com/blog/ending-addiction-good/201510/five-things-know-about-recovery-alcohol-or-drugs) October 16, 2015.

In the citation, 16 October 2015 provides what information?

A. Date printed

B. Date accessed

C. Date placed on the Internet

D. Date the last person accessed it

E. None of these are correct

48. Nelson, MD., Lewis S et al. Addressing the Opioid Epidemic. *JAMA.* 13 October 2015; 314(14): 1453-1454.

The (14) refers to:

A. the fourteenth article in the magazine.

B. the fourteenth article published by this author.

C. there are fourteen articles on opioids in this issue.

D. there are fourteen authors.

E. This is the fourteenth issue in the series, in volume 314.

49. In the *JAMA* citation previously, 1454-1454 refers to what?

   A. The number of issues this has magazine has published.

   B. How many articles have discussed opioids in the magazine's history.

   C. Page numbers for this citation.

   D. Ongoing page numbers for the table of contents in this magazine.

   E. Tagnemics

50. The word 'print' at the end of a citation is a reference for:

   A. the article is from a newspaper.

   B. the article is from a book.

   C. the article is from a periodical.

   D. the article was not accessed online.

   E. none of these selections are accurate.

51. Ciottone, Gregory et al. Disaster Medicine, Second Edition. Elsevier, digital. September 24, 2015. ISBN-13: 978-0323286657

The "et al" refers to:

   A. no hard cover copy is available.

   B. the content is digital only.

   C. this has been published in the United States.

   D. that Ciottone is the editor.

   E. more than one author should be listed.

52. Serra, Luigi. Domencio Zampieri, detto Il Domenichino. E. Calzone, ed. 1909. Princeton University.

Who is the editor?

   A. Serra Luigi

   B. Luigi Serra

   C. E. Calzone

   D. Domenico Zampieri

   E. Domenichino

53. Cattong, Bruce. "Grant and Lee: A Study in Contrasts." *The Bedford Reader*. 9th ed. Ed. X. J. Kennedy et al. Boston: Bedford/St. Martin's, 2006. 258-61. Print. This is an ex-ample of what kind of citation for-mat?

A. MLA

B. APA

C. Chicago

D. Turabian

E. None of these

54. Aloise-Young, P. A. (1993). The development of self-presentation: Self-promotion in 6- to 10-year-old children. *Social Cognition, II,* 201-222. This is an example of what kind of citation?

A. MLA

B. APA

C. Chicago

D. Turabian

E. None of these

55. Smith, John Maynard. "The Origin of Altruism." *Nature* 393 (1998): 639-40. This is an example of which kind of citation?

A. MLA

B. APA

C. Chicago

D. Turabian

E. None of these

"(1)These good folk, who have only just begun to think and act for themselves, are slow as yet to grasp the changed conditions which should attach them to these theories. (2)They have only reached those ideas which conduce to economy and to physical welfare; in the future, if some one else carries on this work of mine, they will come to understand the principles that serve to uphold and preserve public order and justice. (3)As a matter of fact, it is not sufficient to be an honest man, you must appear to be honest in the eyes of others. (4)Society does not live by moral ideas alone; its existence depends upon actions in harmony with those ideas."

56. The first sentence can best be described as:

A. compound.

B. complex.

C. run-on.

D. a fragment.

E. compound-complex.

57. The second sentence can best be described as:

A. compound.

B. complex.

C. run-on.

D. a fragment.

E. compound-complex.

58. Warren, Robert Penn. *All The King's Men.* New York: Harcourt, Brace, 1946. Print. p415.

The p415 sentence can best be described as:

A. the number of pages in the book used.

B. the last page the reader completed.

C. the citation for a portion referenced in the/a document.

D. the last page of dialogue in the book.

E. none of the choices are accurate.

59. United States. Cong. Senate. Appropriations. Schedule of Serial Set Volumes. 112 Cong., 2 sess. S. Doc. 15383A. Washington DC: U.S. Senate, 2012. Web.

15383A can best be described as:

A. amendment number.

B. edit number.

C. page number.

D. volume number

E. document number.

60. Bell, A. G. (1876). *U.S. Patent No.174,465.* Washington, DC: U.S. Patent and Trademark Office.

This is the patent citation for:

A. a lightbulb.

B. train brakes.

C. relativity.

D. telephone.

E. telegraph.

61. Mozart, W. A. (1970). *Die Zauberflöte* [The magic flute], K. 620 [Vo-cal score]. Munich, Germany: Becksche Verlagsbuchhandlung. (Original work published 1791).

The "K. 620" is the citation for:

A. the 620th note in the musical score.

B. opus, or work number.

C. the number of instruments required.

D. the number of performers required, including voices.

E. none of these are correct.

62. Harris, Ann Sutherland (PhD). Seventeenth Century Art and Architecture. Lawrence King Publishing, 2005. pxv.

The "pxv" is:

A. the version label.

B. the author's work number.

C. the date in Roman numeral.

D. the preface page number.

E. none of these are correct.

63. "Higher education has become a central part of the process by which high-income families can seek to assure that their children are more likely to have high incomes." Taylor, Timothy. How Higher Education Perpetuates Intergenerational Inequality. March 4, 2015. http://conversableeconomist.blogspot.com/2015/03/how-higher-education-perpetuates.html Accessed August 8, 2015.

When prefaced with "61" in superscript before this phrase and listed on the same page, it would be referred to as a(an):

A. footnote.

B. endnote.

C. footer.

D. header.

E. none of these are correct.

This writer has often been asked to tutor hospitalized children with cystic fibrosis. While undergoing all the precautionary measures to see these children (i.e. scrubbing thoroughly and donning sterilized protective gear- for the child's protection), she has often wondered why their parents subject these children to the pressures of schooling and trying to catch up on what they have missed because of hospitalization, which is a normal part of cystic fibrosis patients' lives. These children undergo so many tortuous treatments a day that it seems cruel to expect them to learn as normal children do, especially with their life expectancies being as short as they are.

64. What is the author's main purpose?

   A. To inform

   B. To entertain

   C. To describe

   D. To narrate

   E. To record

65. What is the main idea of this passage?

   A. There is a lot of preparation involved in visiting a patient of cystic fibrosis.

   B. Children with cystic fibrosis are incapable of living normal lives.

   C. Certain concessions should be made for children with cystic fibrosis.

   D. Children with cystic fibrosis die young.

   E. The specific ways you must decontaminate yourself to visit children.

66. What is meant by the word "precautionary" in the second sentence?

   A. Careful

   B. Protective

   C. Medical

   D. Sterilizing

   E. Reckless

67. What is the author's tone in the previous passage?

   A. Sympathetic

   B. Cruel

   C. Disbelieving

   D. Cheerful

   E. Cautious

68. What type of organizational pat-tern is the author using in the selection about cystic fibrosis?

   A. Classification

   B. Explanation

   C. Comparison and Contrast

   D. Cause and Effect

   E. Entertaining

69. How is the author so familiar with the procedures used when visiting a child with cystic fibrosis?

   A. She has read about it.

   B. She works in a hospital.

   C. She is the parent of one.

   D. She often tutors them.

   E. She had it as a child.

Disciplinary practices have been found to affect diverse areas of child development such as the acquisition of moral values, obedience to authority, and performance at school. Even though the dictionary has a specific definition of the word "discipline," it is still open to interpretation by people of different cultures.

There are four types of disciplinary styles: assertion of power, withdrawal of love, reasoning, and permissiveness. Assertion of power involves the use of force to discourage unwanted behavior. Withdrawal of love involves making the love of a parent conditional on a child's good behavior. Reasoning involves persuading the child to behave one way rather than another.

Permissiveness involves allowing the child to do as he or she pleases and face the consequences of his/her actions

70. **What is the meaning of the word "diverse" in the first sentence?**

   A. Many

   B. Related to children

   C. Disciplinary

   D. Moral

   E. Racially disparate

71. **What organizational structure is used in the first sentence of the second paragraph?**

   A. Addition

   B. Explanation

   C. Definition

   D. Simple Listing

   E. Argumentative

72. **What is the author's tone?**

   A. Disbelieving

   B. Angry

   C. Informative

   D. Optimistic

   E. None of these are correct.

73. **What is the overall organizational pattern of this passage?**

   A. Generalization

   B. Cause and Effect

   C. Addition

   D. Summary

   E. Informational

   One of the most difficult problems plaguing American education is the assessment of teachers. No one denies that teachers ought to be answerable for what they do, but what exactly does that mean? The Oxford American Dictionary defines accountability as: the obligation to give a reckoning or explanation for one's actions.
   Does a student have to learn for teaching to have taken place? Historically, teaching has not been defined in this restrictive manner; the teacher

was thought to be responsible for the quantity and quality of material covered and the way in which it was presented. However, some definitions of teaching now imply that students must learn in order for teaching to have taken place.

As a teacher who tries my best to keep current on all the latest teaching strategies, I believe that those teachers who do not bother even to pick up an educational journal every once in a while should be kept under close watch. There are many teachers out there who have been teaching for decades and refuse to change their ways even if research has proven that their methods are outdated and ineffective. There is no place in the profession of teaching for these types of individuals. It is time that the American educational system clean house, for the sake of our children

74. What is the meaning of the word "reckoning" in the third sentence?

A. Thought

B. Answer

C. Obligation

D. Explanation

E. Prayerful

75. What is the organizational pattern of the second paragraph?

A. Cause and Effect

B. Classification

C. Addition

D. Explanation

E. None of these things

76. What is the author's overall organizational pattern?

A. Classification

B. Cause and Effect

C. Definition

D. Comparison and Contrast

E. None of these things

77. The author's tone in the passage on the previous page is one of:

A. Disbelief

B. Excitement

C. Support

D. Concern

E. Empathy

78. What is meant by the word "plaguing" in the first sentence of the previous passage?

A. Causing problems

B. Causing illness

C. Causing anger

D. Causing failure

E. Causing unrest

(1)London was our present point of rest; we determined to remain several months in this wonderful and celebrated city. (2)Clerval desired the intercourse of the men of genius and talent who flourished at this time; but this was with me a secondary object; I was principally occupied with the means of obtaining the information necessary for the completion of my promise, and quickly availed myself of the letters of

introduction that I had brought with me, addressed to the most distinguished natural philosophers.

79. The fourth word in the second sentence, "intercourse", refers to:

A. intimate relations between two people

B. interactive conversation

C. an in-depth artist's class

D. a secondary outcome after a gift is given in Victorian times

E. none of these options are correct

80. In the previous passage (referenced in question 79 also), what is the main theme of the selection?

   A. Travel discussions that compare where the characters have been

   B. Discussions about information gathering and solving an issue

   C. Meeting gentlemen for coffee

   D. Identifying the thought-leaders of the time

   E. How the travelers were going to spend their time in the city.

   "Oh, Madam Mina," he said, "how can I say what I owe to you? This paper is as sunshine. It opens the gate to me. I am dazed, I am dazzled, with so much light, and yet clouds roll in behind the light every time. But that you do not, cannot comprehend. Oh, but I am grateful to you, you so clever woman. Madame," he said this very solemnly, "if ever Abraham Van Helsing can do anything for your or yours, I trust you will let me know. It will be pleasure and delight if I may serve you as a friend, as a friend, but all I have ever learned, all I can ever do, shall be for you and those you love. There are darknesses in life, and there are lights. You are one of the lights. You are one of the lights. You will have a happy life and a good life, and your husband will be blessed in you."

81. The phase "This paper is as sunshine. It opens the gate to me." means

   A. Madam Mina was holding a light in the next sentence that made it seem as bright as day.

   B. the character speaking has been given new glasses with which to see the sunshine.

   C. the character speaking simply has new information that is helpful to him.

   D. that he is making a joke to Madam Mina.

   E. none of these things.

82. Using the information only presented in the selection, he tone used by the author suggests:

   A. Madam Mina gave Van Helsing information unwillingly.

   B. one of the characters has been drinking a love potion.

   C. Madam Mina wants nothing to do with Van Helsing.

   D. that Van Helsing is making fun to Madam Mina.

   E. Van Helsing is enamored with Madam Mina because of her helpfulness.

"Mornings, he likes to sit in his new leather chair by his new living room window, looking out across the rooftops and chimney pots, the clotheslines and telegraph lines and office towers. It's the first time Manhattan, from high above, hasn't crushed him with desire. On the contrary the view makes him feel smug. All those people down there, striving, hustling, pushing, shoving, busting to get what Willie's already got. In spades. He lights a cigarette, blows a jet of smoke against the window. Suckers."

83. The subject in this passage is

   A. a character, and seems to be the lead in the story.

   B. a supporting character.

   C. has the attitude of a criminal.

   D. female.

   E. has been poor his whole life.

84. **What kind of description is the author providing of this scene?**

   A. Backstory of the character.

   B. A characterization of what the character is like.

   C. A narrative, with the end of the selection giving thoughts in the first person.

   D. The unreliable narrative about a character.

   E. The author is using a persuasive argument.

85. **What types of words are "striving, hustling, pushing, shoving, bustling"?**

   A. Adjectives

   B. Adverbs

   C. Nouns

   D. Gerunds

   E. Verbs

86. **If you had to explain the phrase "crushed him" in the paragraph above and context of the paragraph, what would be the best appropriate explanation?**

   A. The city sustained him with all the opportunity available.

   B. The city called to him to be part of its life.

   C. The city complimented him for everything he has achieved.

   D. The city had energized him to get what he felt he deserved.

   E. The city smothered him with all of its offerings.

87. **The author portrays the attitude of the character toward the people on the street below as:**

   A. Condescending.

   B. Sarcastic.

   C. Affectionate.

   D. Tolerant.

   E. Encouraged.

Solemnly he came forward and mounted the round gunrest. He faced about and blessed gravely thrice the tower, the surrounding country and the awaking mountains. Then, catching sight of Stephen Dedalus, he bent towards him and made rapid crosses in the air, gurgling in his throat and shaking his head. Stephen Dedalus, displeased and sleepy, leaned his arms on the top of the staircase and looked coldly at the shaking gurgling face that blessed him, equine in its length, and at the light untenured hair, grained and hued like pale oak.

88.   The likely setting for this paragraph is:

A.   a hospital.

B.   the battlefield.

C.   Stephen's bedroom.

D.   beside the river.

E.   unable to be determined.

89.   The description of the main character's hair leads to the conclusion that he is:

A.   a blonde.

B.   a brunette.

C.   has black hair.

D.   has grained black and white hair.

E.   is bald.

90.   The phrase "equine in its length" to describe the main character:

A.   is complementary as horses were very valuable to soldiers.

B.   could be considered sarcastic.

C.   reveals the way Stephen feels about the main character, which is not fond or complementary.

D.   was a common description of the time period.

E.   is used repeatedly in this book.

120

SAMPLE TEST ESSAY 1

As a reminder, you have 30 minutes to compose your essay and type it on the computer.

Directions: Write an essay in which you discuss the extent to which you agree or disagree with the statement below. Support your discussion with specific reasons and examples from your reading, experience or observations.

Topic: *Communication is the key for success.*

Readers will assign scores based on a matrix, or scoring guide. Here is an example outline of how both student essays will be graded on a six point scale.

SCORE OF 6 - The 6 essay presents a thesis that is coherent and well-developed. The writer's ideas are detailed, intelligent, and thoroughly elaborated. The writer's use of language and structure is correct and meaningful.

SCORE OF 5 - The 5 essay presents a thesis and offers persuasive support. The writer's ideas are usually new, mature, and thoroughly developed. A command of language and a variety of structures are evident.

SCORE OF 4 - The 4 essay presents a thesis and frequently offers a plan of development, which is usually demonstrated. The writer offers sufficient details to achieve the purpose of the essay. There is capable use of language and varied sentence structure. Errors in sentence structure and usage don't interfere with the writer's main purpose.

SCORE OF 3 - The 3 essay gives a thesis and offers a plan of development, which is usually demonstrated. The writer gives support that leans toward generalized statements or a listing. Overall, the support in a 3 essay is neither adequate or coherent enough to be convincing. There are errors in sentence structure and usage that frequently interfere with the writer's ability to state the purpose.

SCORE OF 2 - The 2 essay usually states a thesis. The writer offers support that may be incomplete. Simple and disconnected sentence structure is present. Mistakes in grammar and usage often thwart the writer's ability to state the purpose.

SCORE OF 1 - The 1 essay has a thesis that is pointless or poorly articulated. Support is shallow. The language is muddled and confusing. Many mistakes in grammar and usage.

SAMPLE ESSAY 2

As a reminder, you have 40 minutes to read these two passages and type your essay on the computer.

Directions: Write an essay in which you incorporate the two sources of information provided below. You must use both sources and you must use appropriate citation for both sources using the author's last name, the title or by any other means that adequately identifies it. Support your discussion with specific reasons and examples from your reading, experience or observations.

Assignment: Read the following sources carefully. Then write an essay in which you develop a position on whether communities have contracts to keep peace and fellow members free from harm.

Introduction: A contract is a legal agreement between people, companies, et cetera. Miriam-Webster Dictionary.

Source 1: Hobbes, Thomas. "Leviathan." England: 1651.

Except - The final cause, end or design of men (who naturally love liberty, and dominion over others) in the introduction of that restraint upon themselves in which we see them live in Commonwealths, is the foresight of their own preservation, and of a more contented live thereby; that is to say, of getting themselves out of that miserable condition of war which is necessarily consequent, as hath been shown, to the natural passions of men when there is no visible power to keep them in awe, and tie them by fear of punishment to the performance of their covenants..."

Source 2: Golding, William. "Lord of the Flies." England: 1954.

This toy of voting was almost as pleasing as the conch. Jack started to protest but the clamor changed from the general wish for a chief to an election by acclaim of Ralph himself. None of the boys could have found good reason for this; what intelligence had been shown was traceable to Piggy while the most obvious leaders was Jack. But there was a stillness about Ralph as he sat that marked him out: there was his size, and attractive appearance; and most obscurely, yet most powerfully, there was the conch. The being that had blown that, had sat waiting for them on the platform with the delicate thing balanced on his knees, was set apart.

ANSWER KEY

Question Number	Correct Answer	Your Answer	Question Number	Correct Answer	Your Answer	Question Number	Correct Answer	Your Answer
1	B		31	D		61	B	
2	C		32	C		62	D	
3	A		33	D		63	A	
4	E		34	A		64	C	
5	A		35	E		65	C	
6	B		36	A		66	B	
7	C		37	B		67	C	
8	B		38	E		68	D	
9	A		39	C		69	D	
10	C		40	D		70	A	
11	D		41	C		71	D	
12	D		42	A		72	C	
13	A		43	C		73	E	
14	D		44	A		74	D	
15	C		45	C		75	D	
16	C		46	E		76	E	
17	A		47	B		77	D	
18	D		48	E		78	A	
19	D		49	C		79	B	
20	A		50	E		80	E	
21	B		51	E		81	C	
22	E		52	C		82	E	
23	A		53	A		83	A	
24	B		54	B		84	C	
25	C		55	C		85	E	
26	A		56	B		86	E	
27	A		57	E		87	A	
28	B		58	C		88	E	
29	A		59	E		89	A	
30	A		60	D		90	C	

RATIONALES

1.   A <u>fearful</u> man, all in grey, <u>were</u> down by the river <u>standing</u> by the bunches of <u>rushes</u>. <u>No error.</u>

    A. fearful

    B. was

    C. standing

    D. rushes

    E. No error

The answer is B.
Were is plural and the subject is singular; therefore, it should be was.

2.   When our group of <u>friends</u> goes to Italy next year, we will be <u>seeing</u> many of the <u>countries</u> famous <u>landmarks</u>. <u>No error.</u>

    A. friends

    B. seeing

    C. country's

    D. landmarks

    E. No error

The answer is C.
Countries is plural, but in this sentence, the word should be possessive, or country's.

3.   Their are no walls high enough, no valleys deep enough, to keep the warriors from attacking the city. No error.

A.   There

B.   valleys

C.   to

D.   from

E.   No error

The answer is A.
Again, the word listed - their - is possessive and here, the correct word should be the location (there).

4.   Whenever the phone rings, the dog likes to run to the front door to see who has come to visit. No error

A.   Whenever

B.   likes

C.   see

D.   has come

E.   No error

The answer is E.
as everything is right.

5.   <u>Every one</u> must pass <u>through</u> Vanity Fair in order to get to the <u>celestial</u> city and receive <u>their</u> three golden eggs. <u>No error</u>

A. Everyone

B. through

C. celestial

D. their

E. No error

The answer is A.
Everyone is one word, not two (as listed).

6.   Suffering <u>has been</u> stronger than all other teaching, and <u>have</u> taught me to understand what <u>your</u> heart <u>use</u> to be. <u>No error</u>

A. has been

B. has

C. your

D. use

E. No error

The answer is B.
The incorrect verb tense is used - it lists "have" but should be "has".

7.   The loneliest moment in <u>someone's</u> life is when they are watching
      <u>their</u> <u>hole</u> world fall apart, and all they can do is <u>stare</u> blankly. <u>No</u>
      <u>error</u>

   A. someone's

   B. their

   C. whole

   D. stare

   E. No error

The answer is C.
The appropriate spelling of "hole" in this instance is "whole".

8.   I have not <u>broken</u> your heart - you have <u>broke</u> it; and in <u>breaking</u> it,
      you <u>have</u> broken mine. <u>No error</u>

   A. broke

   B. broken

   C. breaking

   D. have

   E. No error

The answer is B.
"Broke" is incorrect for the conjugation in the tense of this portion of the
phrase; it should be broken, as it is two other times in the sentence.

Mr. Smith gave instructions for the painting to be hung on the wall. And then it leaped forth before his eyes: the little cottages on the river, the white clouds floating over the valley and the green of the towering mountain ranges which were seen in the distance. The painting was so vivid that it seemed almost real. Mr. Smith was now absolutely certain that the painting had been worth money.

9.   From the last sentence, one can infer that:

A.   the painting was expensive.

B.   the painting was cheap.

C.   Mr. Smith was considering purchasing the painting.

D.   Mr. Smith thought the painting was too expensive and decided not to purchase it.

E.   None of these things is true.

The answer is A.
Choice B is incorrect because, had the painting been cheap, chances are that Mr. Smith would no have considered his purchase. Choices C and D are ruled out by the fact that the painting had already been purchased. The author makes this clear when she says, "...the painting had been worth the money."

10.   What is the main idea of this passage?

A.   The painting that Mr. Smith purchased is expensive.

B.   Mr. Smith purchased a painting.

C.   Mr. Smith was pleased with the quality of the painting he had purchased.

D.   The painting depicted cottages and valleys.

E.   Mr. Smith was looking to buy some paintings.

The answer is C.
Every sentence in the paragraph alludes to this fact.

11.   The author's purpose is to:

    A.   Inform

    B.   Entertain

    C.   Persuade

    D.   Narrate

    E.   Analyze

The answer is D.
The author is simply narrating or telling the story of Mr. Smith and his painting.

One of the most difficult problems plaguing American education is the assessment of teachers. No one denies that teachers ought to be answerable for what they do, but what exactly does that mean? The Oxford American Dictionary defines accountability as: the obligation to give a reckoning or explanation for one's actions.

Does a student have to learn for teaching to have taken place? Historically, teaching has not been defined in this restrictive manner; the teacher was thought to be responsible for the quantity and quality of material covered and the way in which it was presented. However, some definitions of teaching now imply that students must learn in order for teaching to have taken place.

As a teacher who tries my best to keep current on all the latest teaching strategies, I believe that those teachers who do not bother even to pick up an educational journal every once in a while should be kept under close watch. There are many teachers out there who have been teaching for decades and refuse to change their ways even if research has proven that their methods are outdated and ineffective. There is no place in the profession of teaching for these types of individuals. It is time that the American educational system clean house, for the sake of our children.

12.   **What is the main idea of the passage?**

   A.   Teachers should not be answerable for what they do.

   B.   Teachers who do not do their job should be fired.

   C.   The author is a good teacher.

   D.   Assessment of teachers is a serious problem in society today.

   E.   Defining accountability.

The answer is D.
Most of the passage is dedicated to elaborating on why teacher assessment is such a problem.

13.   **From the passage, one can infer that:**

   A.   The author considers herself a good teacher.

   B.   Poor teachers will be fired.

   C.   Students have to learn for teaching to take place.

   D.   The author will be fired.

   E.   All of these are characteristics of fables

The answer is A.
The first sentence of the third paragraph alludes to this.

14. What is the author's purpose in writing the passage on the previous page?

   A. To entertain

   B. To narrate

   C. To describe

   D. To persuade

   E. To make demands

The answer is D.
The author does some describing, but the majority of her statements seemed geared towards convincing the reader that teachers who are lazy or who do not keep current should be fired.

15. The author states that teacher assessment is a problem for:

   A. Elementary schools

   B. Secondary schools

   C. American education

   D. Families

   E. Teachers

The answer is C.
This fact is directly stated in the first paragraph.

   Disciplinary practices have been found to affect diverse areas of child development such as the acquisition of moral values, obedience to authority, and performance at school. Even though the dictionary has a specific definition of the word "discipline," it is still open to interpretation by people of different cultures.

   There are four types of disciplinary styles: assertion of power, withdrawal of love, reasoning, and permissiveness. Assertion of power involves the use of force to discourage unwanted behavior. Withdrawal of love involves making the love of a parent conditional on a child's good behavior. Reasoning involves persuading the child to behave one way rather than another. Permissiveness involves allowing the child to do as he or she pleases and face the consequences of his/her actions.

16.   Name the four types of disciplinary styles.

   A.   Reasoning, power assertion, morality, and permissiveness.

   B.   Morality, reasoning, permissiveness, and withdrawal of love.

   C.   Withdrawal of love, permissiveness, power, and reasoning.

   D.   Permissiveness, morality, reasoning, and power assertion.

   E.   Explore, Inform, Entertain, Persuade.

The answer is C.
This is directly stated in the second paragraph.

17.   **What is the main idea of the previous passage?**

   A.   Different people have different ideas of what discipline is.

   B.   Permissiveness is the most widely used disciplinary style.

   C.   Most people agree on their definition of discipline.

   D.   There are four disciplinary styles.

   E.   Child development needs to focus on obedience to authority.

The answer is A.
Choice C is not true, the opposite is stated in the passage. Choice B could be true, but we have no evidence of this. Choice D is just one of the many facts listed in the passage.

18.   **What is the author's purpose in writing this?**

   A.   To describe

   B.   To narrate

   C.   To entertain

   D.   To inform

   E.   To argue

The answer is D.
The author is providing the reader with information about disciplinary practices.

19.   **From reading this passage, we can conclude that:**

   A.   The author is a teacher.

   B.   The author has many children.

   C.   The author has written a book about discipline.

   D.   The author has done a lot of research on discipline.

   E.   The author has at least two siblings.

The answer is D.
Given all the facts mentioned in the passage, this is the only inference one can make.

20.   What does the technique of reasoning involve?

   A.   Persuading the child to behave in a certain way.

   B.   Allowing the child to do as he/she pleases.

   C.   Using force to discourage unwanted behavior.

   D.   Making love conditional on good behavior.

   E.   Distracting the child in order to get them to behave appropriately.

The answer is A.
This fact is directly stated in the second paragraph.

Each underlined portion of sentences 21-23 contains one or more errors in grammar, usage, mechanics, or sentence structure. Circle the choice that best corrects the error without changing the meaning of the original sentence. Choice E may repeat the underlined portion. Select the identical phrase if you find no error.

21.   Walt Whitman was famous for **his composition, *Leaves of Grass*, serving as a nurse during the Civil War, and a devoted son.**

   A.   *Leaves of Grass*, his service as a nurse during the Civil War, and a devoted son.

   B.   composing *Leaves of Grass*, serving as a nurse during the Civil War, and being a devoted son.

   C.   his composition, *Leaves of Grass*, his nursing during the Civil War, and his devotion as a son.

   D.   serving as a nurse during the civil war, being a devoted son and *Leaves of Grass*.

   E.   his composition, *Leaves of Grass*, serving as a nurse during the Civil War, and a devoted son.

The answer is B.
To be parallel, the sentence needs three gerunds. The other sentences use both gerunds and nouns, which is a lack of parallelism.

22. There were <u>fewer pieces</u> of evidence presented during the second trial.

    A. fewer peaces

    B. less peaces

    C. less pieces

    D. not as many peaces

    E. fewer pieces

The answer is E.
"Less" is impossible in the plural, and "peace" is the opposite of war, not a "piece" of evidence.

23. Wally <u>groaned, "Why</u> do I have to do an oral interpretation <u>of "The Raven."</u>

    A. groaned "Why ... of 'The Raven'?"

    B. groaned "Why ... of "The Raven"?

    C. groaned "Why ... of "The Raven?"

    D. groaned, "Why ... of "The Raven."

    E. groaned, "Why... of *The Raven*?"

The answer is A.
The question mark in a quotation that is an interrogation should be within the quotation marks. Also, when quoting a title that is styled in quotation marks (like the title of a poem or short story) within another quotation, one should use single quotation marks ('...') for the title of this work, and they should close before the final quotation mark.

Microbiology is the study of tiny organisms that can only be seen through a magnifying glass or microscope. Scientists have used microbiology to help prevent and cure certain diseases. It has also been important in the development of new and better foods.

24.   What is the main idea of this passage?

    A.   Microbiology has been used to prevent and cure certain diseases.

    B.   Through microbiology, scientists have made discoveries that have helped many people.

    C.   Microbiology is the study of tiny organisms.

    D.   It is necessary to have a magnifying glass or microscope when engaged in a microbiological study.

    E.   none of the above.

The answer is B.
Two of the sentences in the paragraph support that this is the main idea.

Many people insist on wearing "real" fur coats even though artificial furs have been available for over 30 years. It is cruel to torture animals just to be fashionable. Save an animal by wearing artificial fur coats instead of "real" ones.

25.   The author's purpose is to

    A.   Describe

    B.   Inform

    C.   Persuade

    D.   Narrate

    E.   Summarize

The answer is C.
By mentioning that artificial furs are available and that it is cruel to torture animals, the author is attempting to convince the readers to abandon "real" furs and wear artificial ones instead.

Plants are very versatile living organisms. They are constantly adapting to survive in their environments. Some plants have grown spines to protect themselves from herbivores. Plants that grow in cold regions grow close to the ground to avoid harsh winds.

26.   What type of organizational pattern is the author using?

    A.   Cause and Effect

    B.   Generalization

    C.   Comparison and Contrast

    D.   Simple Listing

    E.   Analogy

The answer is A.
The author lists some ways in which plants have changed and the reasons why.

Rembrandt and Van Gogh were two Dutch painters. Both were from wealthy families. Both showed incredible talent at a young age. Van Gogh did not begin to paint seriously until he was twenty-seven. Rembrandt, on the other hand, had already completed many paintings by that age.

27.   Which organizational pattern does the author use?

    A.   Comparison and Contrast

    B.   Simple Listing

    C.   Cause and Effect

    D.   Definition

    E.   Description

The answer is A.
Since the author is demonstrating how Rembrandt and Van Gogh were alike and how they were different, the correct answer is (A).

Charles Lindbergh had no intention of becoming a pilot. He was enrolled in the University of Wisconsin until a flying lesson changed the entire course of his life. He began his career as a pilot by performing daredevil stunts at fairs

28. The author wrote this paragraph primarily to:

A. describe

B. inform

C. entertain

D. narrate

E. analyze

The answer is B.
Since the author is simply telling us or informing us about the life of Charles Lindbergh, the correct answer here is (B).

29. Addressing someone absent or something inhuman as though present and able to respond describes a figure of speech known as:

A. personification

B. synecdoche

C. metonymy

D. apostrophe

E. rhetorical strategy

The answer is A.
as it is the definition of personification.

(1) It was a cold and windy night. (2) Everyone was close around the fire in order to keep warm. (3) It was lonely for the little boy, who waited for his mother to bring him a marshmallow to toast on a stick. (4) His sister died just weeks ago and he really missed her.

30.   In sentence (2), a better way to phrase "was close" could be:

    A. huddled

    B. gather

    C. stood

    D. left from

    E. none of these options are better

The answer is A.
Huddle means to get close, and at the end of that sentence, it describes that they were around the fire to keep warm. Thus, huddle is a better choice than B or C; D is the opposite of the activity being described.

31.   In sentence (4), the author is describing what emotion?

    A. hunger

    B. happiness

    C. coldness

    D. sadness

    E. anger

The answer is D.
The end of the sentence talks about the subject really missing his sister, and there is no words that would describe anger at her being gone. If you did not read the sentence, you may try to go off of the prior question and guess coldness, but that would be wrong. Also, happiness is the opposite of what the author is conveying and is not a correct option.

As she mused the pitiful vision of her mother's life laid its spell on the very quick of her being—that life of commonplace sacrifices closing in final craziness. She trembled as she heard again her mother's voice saying constantly with foolish insistence: Derevaun Seraun! Derevaun Seraun!

* [Derevaun Seraun means "The end of pleasure is pain!" (Gaelic)]

32.   The following passage is written from which point of view?

   A.   First person, narrator

   B.   Second person, direct address

   C.   Third person, omniscient

   D.   First person, omniscient

   E.   First person, direct address

The answer is C.
All of the options can be eliminated by seeing that the author uses the pronoun "she" which is third person. There is only one third person selection.

33.   To understand the origins of a word, one must study the:

   A.   synonyms

   B.   inflections

   C.   phonetics

   D.   etymology

   E. epidemiology

The answer is D.
As the definition of etymology is the study of the origins of words.

34. **Which is the best definition for syntax?**

A. The specific order of word choices by an author to create a particular mood or feeling in the reader

B. Writing that explains something thoroughly

C. The background or exposition for a short story or drama

D. Word choices that help teach a truth or moral

E. Proper elocution

The answer is A.
The definition of syntax is the specific order and particular word choices of an author to convey a mood or feeling to a reader.

35. **Which is the least true statement concerning an author's literary tone?**

A. Tone is partly revealed through the selection of details.

B. Tone is the expression of the author's attitude toward his or her subject.

C. Tone can be expressed in a variety of ways by an author.

D. Tone in literature corresponds to the tone of voice a speaker uses.

E. Tone in literature is usually satiric or angry.

The answer is E.
As all of the options A through D are relevant to the definition of an author's tone, E - a very lopsided and opinionated option - is the correct answer.

36. Regarding the study of poetry, which elements are least applicable to all types of poetry?

    A. Setting and audience

    B. Theme and tone

    C. Pattern and diction

    D. Diction and rhyme scheme

    E. Words and symbols

The answer is A.
Certain poems are very specific in their symbols, rhyme scheme, diction, pattern and theme. The best answer for which option is not as important to poetry is A.

There is no frigate like a book
To take us lands away,
Nor any coursers like a page
Of prancing poetry;
This traverse may the poorest take
Without oppress of toll;
How frugal is the chariot
That bears the human soul!

37. How many types of transport types does the author incorporate?

    A. two

    B. three

    C. four

    D. five

    E. none

The answer is B
There are three modes of transport in the poem. This is further confirmed in the next question.

38.　If the words 'frigate, coursers, and chariot' were replaced with synonyms, what would the best choice of the following options include?

　　A.　Train, car, carriage

　　B.　Train, horse, carriage

　　C.　Ship, car, carriage

　　D.　Ship, car, train

　　E.　Ship, horse, carriage

The answer is E.
This is an analysis question to see if you understand synonyms and is important in the composition exam. Alternative words for frigate, coursers and chariot are ship, horse and carriage.

39.　What is a good paraphrase of "To take us lands away" that Ms. Dickinson writes in this poem?

　　A.　War makes it unsafe to travel, so we can just read about places.

　　B.　Poems will drive us to save our souls.

　　C.　Books can engage us to see new things

　　D.　Authors can show us how to go on vacation.

　　E.　It shows poems are short and fun.

The answer is C.
Books, and poems, can virtually take us anywhere that we can imagine.

Tyger! Tyger! burning bright
In the forests of the night,
What immortal hand or eye
Could frame thy fearful symmetry? (line 4)

In what distant deeps or skies
Burnt the fire of thine eyes?
On what wings dare he aspire?
What the hand dare seize the flame? (line 8)

And what shoulder, & what art,
Could twist the sinews of they heart?
And when thy heart began to beat,
What dread hand? & what dread feet? (line 12)

40.   Sinews, in the third stanza, can be best compared to:

    A.   thread.

    B.   a cage.

    C.   rope.

    D.   heart strings or emotions.

    E.   burnt fire, from the second stanza.

The answer is D.
Sinews, while it is possible that anything from A through D could be correct, the only appropriate option is heart strings. Option E is simply misleading.

41.   Another phrase for "deeps or skies" that would fit in this poem
        could be:

    A.   caves or planes.

    B.   trees or forests.

    C.   seas or air.

    D.   waves or wind.

    E.   oceans or lakes.

The answer is C.
Again, this is about comprehension of the composition and your ability to
identify appropriate synonyms in context of the selection. In the other pairs,
one word may be accurate but the other option is not appropriate.

42.   In line 7 of this poem, what word below most nearly means
        "aspire"?

    A.   Soar.

    B.   Plunge.

    C.   Scheme.

    D.   Travel.

    E.   Admire.

The answer is A.
This is the best choice and the other options are not appropriate synonyms.

These are morning matters, pictures you dream as the final wave heaves you up on the sand in the bright light and drying air. You remember pressure, and a curved sleep you rested against, soft, like a scallop in its shell. But the air hardens your skin; you stand; you leave the lighted shore to explore some dim headland, and soon you're lost in the leafy interior, intent, remembering nothing.

I still think of that old tomcat, mornings, when I wake. Things are tamer now; I sleep with the window shut. The cats and our rites are gone and my life is changed, but the memory remains of something powerful playing over me. I wake expectant, hoping to see a new thing. If I'm lucky I might be jogged awake by a strange bird call. I dress in a hurry, imagining the yard flapping with auks, or flamingos. This morning it was a wood duck, down at the creek. It flew away.

43.   The phrase, "like a scallop in its shell" is an example of:

   A.   an irony.

   B.   a simile.

   C.   a metaphor.

   D.   personification.

   E.   euphemism.

The answer is C.
This is a definition type of question, and it is the only possible answer.

44.   The phrase "the air hardens your skin" within the context of the
       passage most likely refers to what?

A.   The morning air woke the character up from dreaming.

B.   The scallop shell bed the character sleeps in has opened.

C.   The air dries out the character's skin.

D.   The coldness of the room turns off the brain of the character.

E.   The air turns the character's skin cold when the cat leaves the bed.

The answer is A.
The character describes waking up in the morning, and it is the closest
rephrasing of the author's words.

One of the most difficult problems plaguing American education is the assessment of teachers. No one denies that teachers ought to be answerable for what they do, but what exactly does that mean? The Oxford American Dictionary defines accountability as: the obligation to give a reckoning or explanation for one's actions.

Does a student have to learn for teaching to have taken place? Historically, teaching has not been defined in this restrictive manner; the teacher was thought to be responsible for the quantity and quality of material covered and the way in which it was presented. However, some definitions of teaching now imply that students must learn in order for teaching to have taken place.

As a teacher who tries my best to keep current on all the latest teaching strategies, I believe that those teachers who do not bother even to pick up an educational journal every once in a while should be kept under close watch. There are many teachers out there who have been teaching for decades and refuse to change their ways even if research has proven that their methods are outdated and ineffective. There is no place in the profession of teaching for these types of individuals. It is time that the American educational system clean house, for the sake of our children

45.   Where does the author get her definition of "accountability?"

    A.   Webster's Dictionary

    B.   Encyclopedia Brittanica

    C.   Oxford Dictionary

    D.   World Book Encyclopedia

    E.   Wikipedia

The answer is C.
It is stated in the first paragraph.

46. In the second paragraph, the second sentence can best be described as:

A. compound.

B. complex.

C. run-on.

D. a fragment.

E. compound-complex

The answer is E.
A compound-complex sentence has two independent sentences are conjoined with the semi-colon.

47. Taite, Richard. "Five Things to Know About Recovery from Alcohol." *Psychology Today.* Web. (https://www.psychologytoday.com/blog/ending-addiction-good/201510/five-things-know-about-recovery-alcohol-or-drugs) October 16, 2015.

In the citation, 16 October 2015 provides what information?

A. Date printed

B. Date accessed

C. Date placed on the Internet

D. Date the last person accessed it

E. None of these are correct

The answer is B.
The date it was accessed on the Internet.

48.   Nelson, MD., Lewis S et al. Addressing the Opioid Epidemic. *JAMA*. 13 October 2015; 314(14): 1453-1454.

The (14) refers to:

A.   the fourteenth article in the magazine.

B.   the fourteenth article published by this author.

C.   there are fourteen articles on opioids in this issue.

D.   there are fourteen authors.

E.   This is the fourteenth issue in the series, in volume 314.

The answer is E.
The citation for the correct volume.

49.   In the *JAMA* citation previously, 1454-1454 refers to what?

A.   The number of issues this has magazine has published.

B.   How many articles have discussed opioids in the magazine's history

C.   Page numbers for this citation.

D.   Ongoing page numbers for the table of contents in this magazine.

E.   Tagnemics

The answer is C.
As it lists the correct page numbers for this article in the JAMA periodical.

50. The word 'print' at the end of a citation is a reference for:

A. the article is from a newspaper.

B. the article is from a book.

C. the article is from a periodical.

D. the article was not accessed online.

E. none of these selections are accurate.

The answer is E.
As A through D are all possibly accurate, option E is correct because you need more information to choose which print item is correct.

51. Ciottone, Gregory et al. Disaster Medicine, Second Edition. Elsevier, digital. September 24, 2015. ISBN-13: 978-0323286657

The "et al" refers to:

A. no hard cover copy is available.

B. the content is digital only.

C. this has been published in the United States.

D. that Ciottone is the editor.

E. more than one author should be listed.

The answer is E.
That more than one author should be listed.

52. Serra, Luigi. Domencio Zampieri, detto Il Domenichino. E. Calzone, ed. 1909. Princeton University.

Who is the editor?

A. Serra Luigi

B. Luigi Serra

C. E. Calzone

D. Domenico Zampieri

E. Domenichino

The answer is C.
As Calzone is the editor. Luigi Serra is the author, and D and E are the names and alias of the artist about whom Serra writes. Regardless of language, the citation formats are the same.

53. Cattong, Bruce. "Grant and Lee: A Study in Contrasts." *The Bedford Reader.* 9th ed. Ed. X. J. Kennedy et al. Boston: Bedford/St. Martin's, 2006. 258-61. Print. This is an ex-ample of what kind of citation for-mat?

A. MLA

B. APA

C. Chicago

D. Turabian

E. None of these

The answer is A.
As this is MLA citation format.

54. Aloise-Young, P. A. (1993). The development of self-presentation: Self-promotion in 6- to 10- year-old children. *Social Cognition, II,* 201-222. This is an example of what kind of citation?

A. MLA

B. APA

C. Chicago

D. Turabian

E. None of these

The answer is B.
As this is APA citation format.

55. Smith, John Maynard. "The Origin   of Altruism." *Nature* 393 (1998): 639-40. This is an example of which kind of citation?

A. MLA

B. APA

C. Chicago

D. Turabian

E. None of these

The answer is C
as this is Chicago citation format.

"(1)These good folk, who have only just begun to think and act for themselves, are slow as yet to grasp the changed conditions which should attach them to these theories. (2)They have only reached those ideas which conduce to economy and to physical welfare; in the future, if someone else carries on this work of mine, they will come to understand the principles that serve to uphold and preserve public order and justice. (3)As a matter of fact, it is not sufficient to be an honest man, you must appear to be honest in the eyes of others. (4)Society does not live by moral ideas alone; its existence depends upon actions in harmony with those ideas."

56.   The first sentence can best be described as:

A.   compound.

B.   complex.

C.   run-on.

D.   a fragment.

E.   compound-complex

The answer is B.
The writer uses expressions such as "protective gear" and "child's protection" to emphasize this.

57.   The second sentence can best be described as:

A.   compound.

B.   complex.

C.   run-on.

D.   a fragment.

E.   compound-complex

The answer is E.
There is a semi-colon and two independent phrases with dependent clauses - this describes compound-complex.

58.   Warren, Robert Penn. *All The King's Men.* New York: Harcourt, Brace, 1946. Print. p415.

The p415 sentence can best be described as:

A.   the number of pages in the book used.

B.   the last page the reader completed.

C.   the citation for a portion referenced in the document.

D.   the last page of dialogue in the book.

E.   none of the choices are accurate.

The answer is C.
The page number reference shows where the citation is located in the book.

59.   United States. Cong. Senate. Appropriations. Schedule of Serial Set Volumes. 112 Cong., 2 sess. S. Doc. 15383A. Washington DC: U.S. Senate, 2012. Web.

15383A can best be described as:

A.   amendment number.

B.   edit number.

C.   page number.

D.   volume number

E.   document number.

The answer is E.
Congressional documents are numbered and in this citation, the abbreviation prior to the number explains this is a document number.

60.   Bell, A. G. (1876). *U.S. Patent No. 174,465.* Washington, DC: U.S. Patent and Trademark Office.

This is the patent citation for:

A.   a lightbulb.

B.   train brakes.

C.   relativity.

D.   telephone.

E.   telegraph.

The answer is D.
As this is a patent, the name listed is the patent holder, so outside information again needs be used. Alexander Graham Bell invented the telephone.

61.   Mozart, W. A. (1970). *Die Zauberflöte* [The magic flute], K. 620 [Vocal score]. Munich, Germany: Becksche Verlagsbuchhandlung. (Original work published 1791).

The "K. 620" is the citation for:

A.   the 620th note in the musical score.

B.   opus, or work number.

C.   the number of instruments required.

D.   the number of performers required, including voices.

E.   none of these are correct.

The answer is B.
When citing music, "K." is the abbreviation during the Classical era for the German word, Kochel-Verzeichnis, and is the "opus" (latin for "work" and followed by a number).

62. Harris, Ann Sutherland (PhD). Seventeenth Century Art and Architecture. Lawrence King Publishing, 2005. pxv.   The "pxv" is:

   A.   the version label.

   B.   the author's work number.

   C.   the date in Roman numeral.

   D.   the preface page number.

   E.   none of these are correct.

The answer is D.
in reference to preface pages, which are denoted with small Roman numerals.

63. "Higher education has become a central part of the process by which high-income families can seek to assure that their children are more likely to have high incomes." Taylor, Timothy. How Higher Education Perpetuates Intergenerational Inequality. March 4, 2015. http://conversableeconomist.blogspot.com/2015/03/how-higher-education-perpetuates.html Accessed August 8, 2015.

   When prefaced with "61" in superscript before this phrase and listed on the same page, it would be referred to as a(an):

   A.   footnote.

   B.   endnote.

   C.   footer.

   D.   header.

   E.   none of these are correct.

The answer is A.

This writer has often been asked to tutor hospitalized children with cystic fibrosis. While undergoing all the precautionary measures to see these children (i.e. scrubbing thoroughly and donning sterilized protective gear-for the child's protection), she has often wondered why their parents subject these children to the pressures of schooling and trying to catch up on what they have missed because of hospitalization, which is a normal part of cystic fibrosis patients' lives. These children undergo so many tortuous treatments a day that it seems cruel to expect them to learn as normal children do, especially with their life expectancies being as short as they are.

64.   What is the author's main purpose?

    A.   To inform

    B.   To entertain

    C.   To describe

    D.   To narrate

    E.   To record

The answer is C.
The author states that she wonders "why parents subject these children to the pressures of schooling" and that "it seems cruel to expect them to learn as normal children do." In making these statements she appears to be expressing the belief that these children should not have to do what "normal" children do. They have enough to deal with – their illness itself.

65. **What is the main idea of this passage?**

   A.   There is a lot of preparation involved in visiting a patient of cystic fibrosis.

   B.   Children with cystic fibrosis are incapable of living normal lives.

   C.   Certain concessions should be made for children with cystic fibrosis.

   D.   Children with cystic fibrosis die young.

   E.   The specific ways you must decontaminate yourself to visit children.

The answer is C.
The author is simply describing her experience in working with children with cystic fibrosis.

66. **What is meant by the word "precautionary" in the second sentence?**

   A.   Careful

   B.   Protective

   C.   Medical

   D.   Sterilizing

   E.   Reckless

The answer is B.

67. **What is the author's tone in the previous passage?**

    A. Sympathetic

    B. Cruel

    C. Disbelieving

    D. Cheerful

    E. Cautious

The answer is C.
The author appears to simply be stating the facts.

68. **What type of organizational pattern is the author using in the selection about cystic fibrosis?**

    A. Classification

    B. Explanation

    C. Comparison and Contrast

    D. Cause and Effect

    E. Entertaining

The answer is D.
The author has taken a subject and shown how one disease affects the childrens' lives in a variety of ways.

69.   How is the author so familiar with the procedures used when
       visiting a child with cystic fibrosis?

A.   She has read about it.

B.   She works in a hospital.

C.   She is the parent of one.

D.   She often tutors them.

E.   She had it as a child.

The answer is D.
The author states in the selection that she tutors children with cystic fibrosis.

Disciplinary practices have been found to affect diverse areas of child development such as the acquisition of moral values, obedience to authority, and performance at school. Even though the dictionary has a specific definition of the word "discipline," it is still open to interpretation by people of different cultures.

There are four types of disciplinary styles: assertion of power, withdrawal of love, reasoning, and permissiveness. Assertion of power involves the use of force to discourage unwanted behavior. Withdrawal of love involves making the love of a parent conditional on a child's good behavior. Reasoning involves persuading the child to behave one way rather than another. Permissiveness involves allowing the child to do as he or she pleases and face the consequences of his/her actions

70.   What is the meaning of the word "diverse" in the first sentence?

   A.   Many

   B.   Related to children

   C.   Disciplinary

   D.   Moral

   E.   Racially disparate

The answer is A.
As it affects many areas of child development, like the ones mentioned at the end of the sentence.

71. **What organizational structure is used in the first sentence of the second paragraph?**

   A. Addition

   B. Explanation

   C. Definition

   D. Simple Listing

   E. Argumentative

The answer is D.
Given the options, the correct answer is D - simple listing.

72. **What is the author's tone?**

   A. Disbelieving

   B. Angry

   C. Informative

   D. Optimistic

   E. None of these are correct.

The answer is C.
The piece is informative about the topic. The other options are emotional rather than descriptive about style.

73. What is the overall organizational pattern of this passage?

    A. Generalization

    B. Cause and Effect

    C. Addition

    D. Summary

    E. Informational

The answer is E.
As in the previous question, the correct answer is informational, answer E.

One of the most difficult problems plaguing American education is the assessment of teachers. No one denies that teachers ought to be answerable for what they do, but what exactly does that mean? The Oxford American Dictionary defines accountability as: the obligation to give a reckoning or explanation for one's actions.

Does a student have to learn for teaching to have taken place? Historically, teaching has not been defined in this restrictive manner; the teacher was thought to be responsible for the quantity and quality of material covered and the way in which it was presented. However, some definitions of teaching now imply that students must learn in order for teaching to have taken place.

As a teacher who tries my best to keep current on all the latest teaching strategies, I believe that those teachers who do not bother even to pick up an educational journal every once in a while should be kept under close watch. There are many teachers out there who have been teaching for decades and refuse to change their ways even if research has proven that their methods are outdated and ineffective. There is no place in the profession of teaching for these types of individuals. It is time that the American educational system clean house, for the sake of our children

74.   What is the meaning of the word "reckoning" in the third sentence?

A. Thought

B. Answer

C. Obligation

D. Explanation

E. Prayerful

The answer is D.
As given in the definition - right after the word "reckoning".

75. **What is the organizational pattern of the second paragraph?**

   A. Cause and Effect

   B. Classification

   C. Addition

   D. Explanation

   E. None of these things

The answer is D.
As an explanation is the organizational pattern for that paragraph.

76. **What is the author's overall organizational pattern?**

   A. Classification

   B. Cause and Effect

   C. Definition

   D. Comparison and Contrast

   E. None of these things

The answer is E.
For the overall organizational pattern is not one of the options listed.

77.   The author's tone in the passage on the previous page is one of:

   A. Disbelief

   B. Excitement

   C. Support

   D. Concern

   E. Empathy

The answer is D.
The author's tone is concern, or D.

78.   What is meant by the word "plaguing" in the first sentence of the previous passage?

   A. Causing problems

   B. Causing illness

   C. Causing anger

   D. Causing failure

   E. Causing unrest

The answer is A.
Another way of saying causing problems.

(1)London was our present point of rest; we determined to remain several months in this wonderful and celebrated city. (2)Clerval desired the intercourse of the men of genius and talent who flourished at this time; but this was with me a secondary object; I was principally occupied with the means of obtaining the information necessary for the completion of my promise, and quickly availed myself of the letters of introduction that I had brought with me, addressed to the most distinguished natural philosophers.

79. The fourth word in the second sentence, "intercourse", refers to:

   A. intimate relations between two people

   B. interactive conversation

   C. an in-depth artist's class

   D. a secondary outcome after a gift is given in Victorian times

   E. none of these options are correct

The answer is B.
An interactive conversation. While the other answers may indeed be possible definitions, context is important to select the correct answer.

80. In the previous passage (referenced in question 79 also), what is the main theme of the selection?

   A. Travel discussions that compare where the characters have been

   B. Discussions about information gathering and solving an issue

   C. Meeting gentlemen for coffee

   D. Identifying the thought-leaders of the time

   E. How the travelers were going to spend their time in the city.

The answer is E.
While B is a possible answer, the most correct and appropriate answer is E, how they are going to spend time in the city, using their time wisely.

Read the following paragraph and answer the two questions that follow.

"Oh, Madam Mina," he said, "how can I say what I owe to you? This paper is as sunshine. It opens the gate to me. I am dazed, I am dazzled, with so much light, and yet clouds roll in behind the light every time. But that you do not, cannot comprehend. Oh, but I am grateful to you, you so clever woman. Madame," he said this very solemnly, "if ever Abraham Van Helsing can do anything for your or yours, I trust you will let me know. It will be pleasure and delight if I may serve you as a friend, as a friend, but all I have ever learned, all I can ever do, shall be for you and those you love. There are darknesses in life, and there are lights. You are one of the lights. You are one of the lights. You will have a happy life and a good life, and your husband will be blessed in you."

81.   The phase "This paper is as sunshine. It opens the gate to me." means

    A.   Madam Mina was holding a light in the next sentence that made it seem as bright as day.

    B.   the character speaking has been given new glasses with which to see the sunshine.

    C.   the character speaking simply has new information that is helpful to him.

    D.   that he is making a joke to Madam Mina.

    E.   none of these things.

The answer is C.
As the new information was helpful to him.

82. Using the information only presented in the selection, he tone used by the author suggests:

   A. Madam Mina gave Van Helsing information unwillingly.

   B. one of the characters has been drinking a love potion.

   C. Madam Mina wants nothing to do with Van Helsing.

   D. that Van Helsing is making fun to Madam Mina.

   E. Van Helsing is enamored with Madam Mina because of her helpfulness.

The answer is E
as Van Helsing effuses complements after Madam is helpful to him.

"Mornings, he likes to sit in his new leather chair by his new living room window, looking out across the rooftops and chimney pots, the clotheslines and telegraph lines and office towers. It's the first time Manhattan, from high above, hasn't crushed him with desire. On the contrary the view makes him feel smug. All those people down there, striving, hustling, pushing, shoving, busting to get what Willie's already got. In spades. He lights a cigarette, blows a jet of smoke against the window. Suckers."

83. The subject in this passage is

   A. a character, and seems to be the lead in the story.

   B. a supporting character.

   C. has the attitude of a criminal.

   D. female.

   E. has been poor his whole life.

The answer is A.
The other options are not substantiated by the items in the passage, so A is the best choice

84. **What kind of description is the author providing of this scene?**

    A.   Backstory of the character.

    B.   A characterization of what the character is like.

    C.   A narrative, with the end of the selection giving thoughts in the first person.

    D.   The unreliable narrative about a character.

    E.   The author is using a persuasive argument.

The answer is C
C provides the definition of a narrative. Backstory describes the past and he is speaking in the present. There are no personal descriptions and there is no topic that the character is trying to persuade the reader to adopt. And lastly, the leap of assuming the character is unreliable is not supported by the passage.

85. **What types of words are "striving, hustling, pushing, shoving, bustling"?**

    A.   Adjectives

    B.   Adverbs

    C.   Nouns

    D.   Gerunds

    E.   Verbs

The answer is E.
This is definition and the action words are all verbs.

86.   If you had to explain the phrase "crushed him" in the paragraph above and context of the paragraph, what would be the best appropriate explanation?

A.   The city sustained him with all the opportunity available.

B.   The city called to him to be part of its life.

C.   The city complimented him for everything he has achieved.

D.   The city had energized him to get what he felt he deserved.

E.   The city smothered him with all of its offerings.

The answer is E.
As the city was so attractive to him with options and in this selection, the character describes how the city used to be oppressive to him with its options.

87.   The author portrays the attitude of the character toward the people on the street below as:

A.   Condescending.

B.   Sarcastic.

C.   Affectionate.

D.   Tolerant.

E.   Encouraged.

The answer is A.
C, D and E are too "positive" and B is not applicable.

Solemnly he came forward and mounted the round gunrest. He faced about and blessed gravely thrice the tower, the surrounding country and the awaking mountains. Then, catching sight of Stephen Dedalus, he bent towards him and made rapid crosses in the air, gurgling in his throat and shaking his head. Stephen Dedalus, displeased and sleepy, leaned his arms on the top of the staircase and looked coldly at the shaking gurgling face that blessed him, equine in its length, and at the light untenured hair, grained and hued like pale oak.

88.   The likely setting for this paragraph is:

   A.   a hospital.

   B.   the battlefield.

   C.   Stephen's bedroom.

   D.   beside the river.

   E.   unable to be determined.

The answer is E.
While it may seem like a battlefield, the characters on on a stairwell (and there would likely not be stairs on a field). There is no indication that they are in a bedroom or a hospital, so these answers are blatantly wrong

89.   The description of the main character's hair leads to the conclusion that he is:

A.   a blonde.

B.   a brunette.

C.   has black hair.

D.   has grained black and white hair.

E.   is bald.

The answer is A.
Blonde, as the last lines describe his hair as the color of pale oak. Thus, brunette as well as black or black and white are wrong. Bald could be construed from "hued", but hue means color and other indicators also point to blonde.

90.   The phrase "equine in its length" to describe the main character:

A.   is complementary as horses were very valuable to soldiers.

B.   could be considered sarcastic.

C.   reveals the way Stephen feels about the main character, which is not fond or complementary.

D.   was a common description of the time period.

E.   is used repeatedly in this book.

The answer is C.
It is an insult. While A is true that horses were valuable, the correlation to a person's looks was not meant to be flattering. Sarcasm is not applicable in this example, and we cannot determine if it was either a common description of the time period or used elsewhere in the book.

Description of the Examination

The Principles of Management examination covers material that is usually taught in an introductory course in the essentials of management and organization. The fact that such courses are offered by different types of institutions and in a number of fields other than business has been taken into account in the preparation of this examination. It requires a knowledge of human resources and operational and functional aspects of management.

The examination contains approximately 100 questions to be answered in 90 minutes. Some of these are pretest questions that will not be scored. Any time candidates spend on tutorials and providing personal information is in addition to the actual testing time.

Knowledge and Skills Required

Questions on the Principles of Management examination require candidates to demonstrate one or more of the following abilities in the approximate proportions indicated.

- Specific factual knowledge, recall, and general understanding of purposes, functions, and techniques of management (about 10 percent of the exam)
- Understanding of and ability to associate the meaning of specific terminology with important management ideas, processes, techniques, concepts, and elements (about 40 percent of the exam)
- Understanding of theory and significant underlying assumptions, concepts, and limitations of management data, including a comprehension of the rationale of procedures, methods, and analyses (about 40 percent of the exam)
- Application of knowledge, general concepts, and principles to specific problems (about 10 percent of the exam)

The subject matter of the Principles of Management examination is drawn from the following topics. The percentages next to the main topics indicate the approximate percentage of exam questions on that topic.

15-25%   Organization and Human Resources
- Personnel Administration
- Human Relations and Motivation
- Training and Development
- Performance Appraisal
- Organizational Development
- Legal Concerns
- Workforce Diversity

- Recruiting and Selecting
- Compensation and Benefits
- Collective Bargaining

10-20% **Operational Aspects of Management**
- Operations Planning and Control
- Work Scheduling
- Quality Management
- Information Processing and Management
- Strategic Planning and Analysis
- Productivity

45-55% **Functional Aspects of Management**
- Planning
- Organizing
- Leading
- Controlling
- Authority
- Decision Making
- Organization Charts
- Leadership
- Organizational Structure
- Budgeting
- Problem Solving
- Group Dynamics and Team Functions

- Conflict Resolution
- Communication
- Change
- Organizational Theory
- Historical Aspects

10-20% **International Management and Contemporary Issues**
- Value Dimensions
- Regional Economic Integration
- Trading Alliances
- Global Environment
- Social Responsibilities of Business
- Ethics
- Systems
- Environment
- Government Regulation
- Management Theories and Theorists
- E-Business
- Creativity and Innovation

SAMPLE TEST

DIRECTIONS: Read each item and select the best response.

1. **According to equity theory:**

   A. (Employee B's rewards/Employee A's input) = (Employee A's rewards/Employee B's input)

   B. (Employee A's rewards/Employee A's input) = (Employee B's rewards/Employee B's input)

   C. (Employee A's rewards/Employee B's input) = (Employee B's rewards/Employee A's input)

   D. (Employee A's rewards/Employee A's input) > (Employee B's rewards/Employee B's input)

   E. (Employee A's rewards/Employee A's input) < (Employee B's rewards/Employee B's input)

2. **Productivity is:**

   A. Input*Output

   B. Input/Output

   C. Output/Input

   D. (Output-Input)/Output

   E. (Input-Output)/Input

3. **The use of a neutral third party tasked with resolving a dispute but who doesn't have the authority to enforce the outcome is known as:**

   A. Mediation

   B. Conciliation

   C. Arbitration

   D. Bargaining

   E. Litigation

4. ___ is not one of Porter's five forces of environmental scanning:

   A. Bargaining power of suppliers

   B. Regulation of governments

   C. Bargaining power of customers

   D. Threat of new entrants

   E. Threat of substitutes

5. ___ is an example of ethnocentrism:

   A. Opening a wholly-foreign owned enterprise before attempting licensing

   B. Mistranslations of promotional materials

   C. Managing team dynamics in foreign offices as in home offices

   D. Using the same asset management analytics in each global office

   E. Structuring a business by functional division rather than geography

6. ___ is an example of the maintenance group role:

   A. Making acquisition decisions for upcoming projects

   B. Collecting feedback on an internal policy change

   C. Alleviating office friction during end of fiscal year

   D. Playing "Devil's Advocate"

   E. Scheduling project milestones in line with final deadline

7. The highest degree of group autonomy is found in ___ groups:

   A. Traditional

   B. Semi-autonomous

   C. Cross-functional

   D. Self-managed

   E. Virtual

8. A management method training employees on the operations of the company and the role of their primary function within it:

A. Job enlargement

B. Job rotation

C. Job enrichment

D. Job reengineering

E. Job intensification

9. Equity theory requires the use of objective measurements of input because:

A. So that employees know what to expect in their rewards

B. The endowment effect means each person values their own contributions more than equivalent contributions by others

C. So that inputs and outputs can be readily calculated

D. To set a prediction reference point relative to actual outcomes

E. To set a reference point for negotiations in future exchanges

10. What type of plan is this "Over the next 5 years we will expand the total market by targeting previously untouched demographics":

A. Strategic

B. Tactical

C. Operational

D. Project

E. Contingency

11. Who is in charge of establishing operational plans:

A. Middle managers

B. First-line managers

C. Executive managers

D. Financial managers

E. Shift managers

12. The best contingency plans:

A. Deviate from the optimal plan at the point of change, preserving the value of the previous steps

B. Are fully established plans wholly separate from the optimal plan

C. Set alternatives for each step which feed back into the optimal plan

D. Should be pursued simultaneously to the optimal plan

E. Should only be developed if the optimal plan fails

13. In change management, all the following are part of the unfreezing process except:

    A. Surveying employees about their jobs and how they can be improved

    B. Quantify the operational, competitive, and financial impact of elements to be changed

    C. Reinforcing the negative aspects of current methods in the minds of the staff

    D. Communicating controlled isolation of the problem with plans for improvement that doesn't extend into the rest of the organization

    E. Implementing new policies

14. At 6σ, the ideal goal of Six Sigma quality management, there are ____ DPMO with a ____ percentage yield:

    A. 0.019, 99.9999981

    B. 3.4, 99.99966

    C. 233, 99.977

    D. 6,210, 99.38

    E. 66,807, 93.3

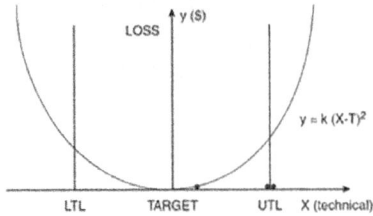

$$y = k(X-T)^2$$

LTL   TARGET   UTL   X (technical)

15. The Taguchi Loss Function states:

   A. Deviations from target specifications create a loss which increases exponentially and must not exceed upper and lower limits

   B. Quality management operations must be effective enough to be financially viable, but not to the point that its costs exceed its benefits

   C. The defective parts per million opportunities will increase the costs of fixing/reconstructing defective output more than the costs of preventing them

   D. Increasing losses create deviations from planned growth rates which become unsustainable at upper and lower limits

   E. Losses are a function of parabolic curves

16. $100,000 earned at complete project Planned 10 week deadline, linear PV $60,000 EV at 5 weeks What is the SPI:

   A. 120%

   B. 83%

   C. 10%

   D. -10%

   E. 100%

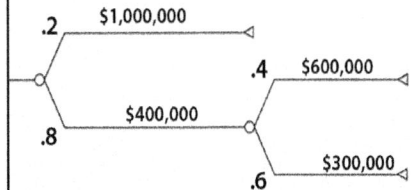

17. The adjusted values at the 2nd node of this decision tree are:

   A. -$200,000, $100,000

   B. $240,000, $180,000

   C. $300,000, -$300,000

   D. $200,000, $320,000

   E. $240,000, $300,000

Severity / Probability		Frequent	Likely	Occasional	Seldom	Unlikely
		A	B	C	D	E
Catastrophic	I	E	E	H	H	M
Critical	II	E	H	H	M	L
Moderate	III	H	M	M	L	L
Negligible	IV	M	L	L	L	L

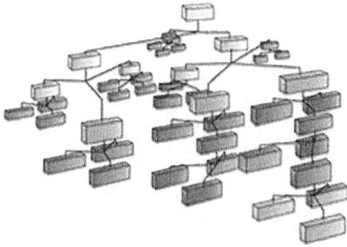

18. In the management of a fire department, the risk to individual staff members is:

A. None

B. Low (L)

C. Moderate (M)

D. High (H)

E. Extreme (E)

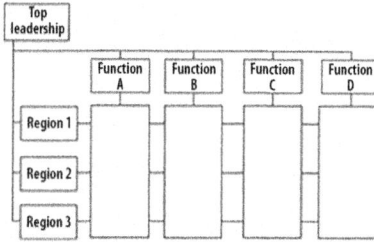

19. Models such as this are most commonly used to depict:

A. Organizational hierarchy

B. Product portfolio

C. Subsidiary structure

D. Capital assets

E. Team motivation drivers

20. This represents:

A. Divisional management

B. Matrix management

C. Micromanagement

D. Tight matrix

E. Organizational spreadsheet

184

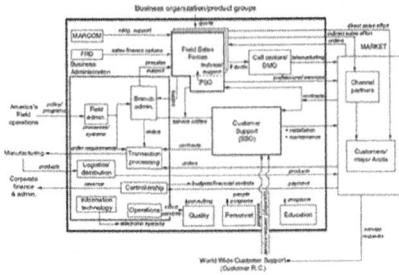

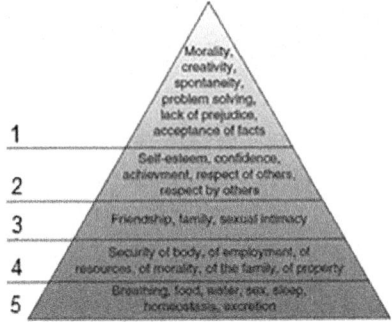

21. This is called ____ which represents ____:

A. Process flowchart, dynamic operations of an organization

B. Organizational structure, management hierarchy

C. Schematic diagram, an electrical circuit

D. Organizational structure, dynamic operations of an organization

E. Process flowchart, management hierarchy

22. In Maslow's Hierarchy of Needs, self-actualization is found at:

A. 1

B. 2

C. 3

D. 4

E. 5

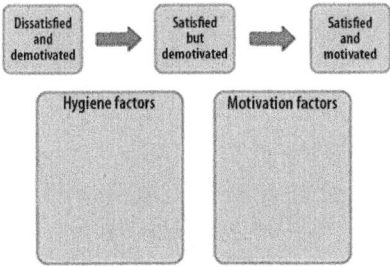

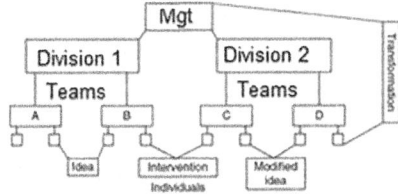

24. **This graph illustrates:**

A. Structure of authority

B. Team-based project management

C. Organizational decision making process

D. Bottom-up communication

E. The flow of information in managing continuous improvement

23. **In Herzberg's Two-Factor Theory of Motivation, ____ is a hygiene factor and ___ is a motivator:**

A. Wages, prestige

B. Responsibility, working conditions

C. Promotions, job security

D. Sense of purpose, clear expectations

E. Recognition, professional relationships

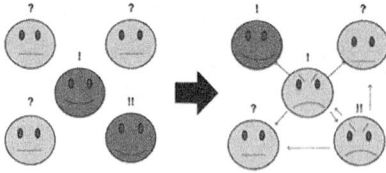

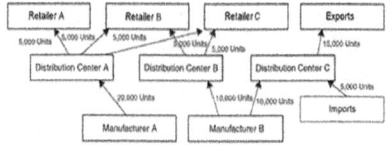

25.   This diagram on conflict creation illustrates the need for:

A.   Clear direction and dissemination of information from management

B.   The need for arbitration during the decision making process

C.   Multiple styles of negotiations

D.   Constructive forms of persuasion

E.   Team development programs

26.   Which manufacturer has the lowest-risk supply chain:

A.   Manufacturer B because 100% of their production has multiple channels to the end consumer

B.   Manufacturer A because their primary distribution center sells to 50% more retailers than 2nd highest

C.   Manufacturer A because they are not competing with foreign imports

D.   Manufacturer B because they have domestic and foreign sales

E.   Both manufacturers A and B have equal risk of disrupted supply chains

27. ___ is a form of ___ given to first-line managers, though ___ is often reserved for middle management:

A. Reward authority, legitimate power, coercive authority

B. Personal power, legitimate power, positional authority

C. Referent authority, personal power, coercive authority

D. Reward authority, personal power, coercive authority

E. Coercive authority, legitimate power, positional authority

28. ___ is acquired by being charismatic or motivational, rather than having any formal power:

A. Expert authority

B. Referent authority

C. Positional authority

D. Reward authority

E. Coercive authority

29. Compartmentalization of operations to prevent interaction and communication is typically used to:

A. This is never done in a healthy organization

B. To create an immersive environment during job rotation training

C. To prevent interaction between men and women in some highly orthodox cultures

D. To prevent conflict with competing individuals or teams

E. Prevent any person from having access to the whole of proprietary information

30. The point in the team development process in which members conflict with each other as they establish roles and culture is called:

A. Forming

B. Storming

C. Norming

D. Performing

E. Adjourning

31. The point in which a manager will most likely need to validate the credentials of a member is:

A. Adjourning

B. Forming

C. Storming

D. Norming

E. Performing

32. According to Kohlberg's Stages of Moral Development, how should a manager address an individual at Stage 4:

A. Emphasize conditioning systems of reward and punishment

B. Emphasize personal gain to be earned in negotiated terms

C. Emphasize the importance of policies and organizational authority

D. Emphasize the mutual benefits of constructed operations and dynamics

E. Emphasize conforming to organizational roles and cultures as a means of acceptance

33. According to Kohlberg's Moral Development, how should a manager address an individual at Stage 3:

    A. Emphasize conforming to organizational roles and cultures as a means of acceptance

    B. Emphasize the importance of policies and organizational authority

    C. Emphasize the mutual benefits of constructed operations and dynamics

    D. Emphasize conditioning systems of reward and punishment

    E. Emphasize personal gain to be earned in negotiated terms

34. Motivation is thematically represented as:

    A. (Expectancy*Value)/(1+ Impulsiveness*Delay)

    B. Expectancy*Value

    C. (Expectancy*Value)/(1 +Impulsiveness)

    D. Expected Value – Expected Costs

    E. Expected Value/(Impulsiveness* Delay)

35. **The negotiating style which includes offering either fake or inconsequential concessions in order to gain on those things which matter to you is called:**

    A. Accommodating

    B. Avoiding

    C. Collaborating

    D. Competing

    E. Compromising

36. The negotiating style which involves intentionally keeping negotiations on aspects which are not issues of conflict in order to draw the other person in is called:

    A. Collaborating

    B. Competing

    C. Avoiding

    D. Accommodating

    E. Compromising

37. Employees each produce 10 units per day, units sell for $100 each with a total cost of $90 per unit entirely composed of labor. If it takes 5 days to train a new employee, what is the turnover cost:

    A. $5,000

    B. $4,500

    C. $500

    D. $450

    E. $0

38. Per day, experienced staff produce 500 units and earn $100.
    Per day, new staff produce 300 units and earn $50.
    Training takes 5 days and each unit produced is worth $1
    The calculation to analyze the wage productivity differential is:

    A. $(500/100)n - ((300/50)n-250)$

    B. $((300/50)n-250)-(500/100)n$

    C. $(100/500)n-(300/50)n$

    D. $(500/100)n-(300/50)n$

    E. $(500-300)n/100-250$

39. Setup costs = $10
    Demand = 100
    Production cost = $20
    Interest rate = 100%
    EOQ is:

    A. 5

    B. 10

    C. 50

    D. 100

    E. 500

COSTS	IN-HOUSE	OUTSOURCED
Billing department costs	$118,000	$4,000
Software and hardware costs	$7,500	$500
Direct claim processing costs	$3,600	$122,500
Software and hardware costs	$5,500	$2,000
% of billings collected	60%	70%
Collections	$1,370,900	$1,623,000
Collections costs	$129,100	$127,000
Collections, net of costs		

40. **Decide whether to outsource:**

    A. Do not outsource to prevent losing $254,200

    B. Outsource to gain $254,200

    C. Do both to gain $254,200

    D. End function completely to prevent losing $254,200

    E. Panic

41. **It is best to use an authoratarian leadership style when:**

    A. During skill development programs

    B. When interpersonal conflict begins to hinder basic work functions

    C. When seeking input for revision of internal policies

    D. When managing skilled experts working in creative conditions

    E. During times of crisis when change must be rapid

42. A pacesetting leadership style intended to facilitate the staff's activities is best used when:

A. When managing skilled experts working in creative conditions

B. When seeking input for revision of internal policies

C. When interpersonal conflict begins to hinder basic work functions

D. During times of crisis when change must be rapid

E. During skill development programs

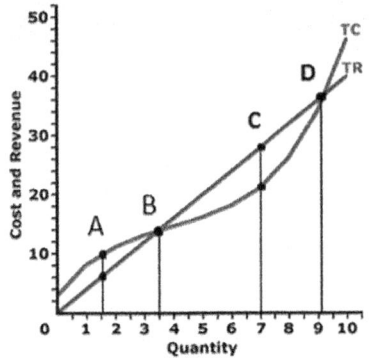

43. For profit-maximizing firms efficiency is optimized at ___ and for revenue-maximizing firms at ___:

A. B, C

B. D, C

C. C, D

D. C, B

E. B, D

44. Under generic competitive conditions, productive efficiency is achieved at:

A. MC=FC

B. FC=AC

C. VC=FC

D. MC=AC

E. MC=TC

45. **Which is not a type of team dysfunction:**

   A. Groupthink

   B. Interpersonal conflict

   C. Freeriding

   D. Comprehensive input

   E. Lack of individualization

46. **Analysis paralysis typically results from:**

   A. Lack of decisive confidence

   B. Too much information

   C. Too little information

   D. Too much or too little information

   E. Rapidly changing business environment

47. **The shareholder wealth maximization model is concerned with:**

   A. Increasing current profitability

   B. Increasing the value of company equity

   C. Maximizing the value that the company creates for those which it influences

   D. Increasing company revenue growth

   E. Increasing NPV of company investments

48. **Which of the following is not a stakeholder:**

   A. Competitors

   B. Shareholders

   C. Employees

   D. Customers

   E. Partners

49. **Agency problems result from:**

    A. Executives who manage a company in a manner contrary to that which benefits the shareholders

    B. Executives who manage a company in a manner contrary to that which benefits the stakeholders

    C. Contradictions between the benefits of the shareholders and stakeholders

    D. Managers who embezzle money from the company

    E. Inefficient functions such as bid rigging and nepotism

50. **A short organization is one which has:**

    A. Few degrees of management with a larger volume of staff per manager

    B. More degrees of management with a lower volume of staff per manager

    C. Few degrees of management with a lower volume of staff per manager

    D. More degrees of management with a with a larger volume of staff per manager

    E. Few degrees of management with higher staff empowerment

51. **SIPOC analysis includes each except:**

    A. Competitors

    B. Supplier

    C. Inputs

    D. Processes

    E. Outputs

52. According to Lean-Six Sigma, the 8 sources of waste include everything except:

   A. Defects

   B. Overproduction

   C. Non-utilized talent

   D. Overtime

   E. Inventory-in-process

53. The most integrated way to create a direct presence within a foreign market is through:

   A. WFOE

   B. Licensing

   C. Joint venture

   D. Exporting

   E. Outsourcing

54. In SWOT, ___ is an example of "W" and ____ is an example of "O":

   A. Small HR pool in area, small population leading to insufficient revenues

   B. Efficient inventory management, cost-leader strategy from low costs

   C. Low brand recognition, cult following with potential for niche market strategy

   D. High materials costs, price competition

   E. Unique product, lack of sustainable advantage due to no IP registration

55. Something must be ___ and ___ to maintain a sustainable competitive advantage:

   A. Valuable, exchangeable

   B. Unsubstitutable, irreplaceable

   C. Rare, inimitable

   D. Rare, exchangeable

   E. Valuable, irreplaceable

56. ___ is the person who influences decisions by using indirect information to guide other to come to the desired conclusion:

   A. Idea planters

   B. Predictors

   C. Trend setters

   D. Persuaders

   E. Negotiators

57. According to JIT ___:

   A. Reserve inventory should always be held to account for variations from predicted sales volume

   B. The only reserve inventory to be held is that which will be used in the next month

   C. The only reserve inventory to be held is that which will be used biweekly

   D. The only reserve inventory to be held is that which will be used in the next week

   E. No reserve inventory should be held

58. How is PESTEL different in a global environment than a domestic one:

A. Economical factors must include a corrective index to account for different economic structures

B. Sociocultural factors become impossible to predict in foreign nations

C. The interaction between nations creates dynamics more complex than both nations by themselves

D. You must include political factors

E. There is no difference

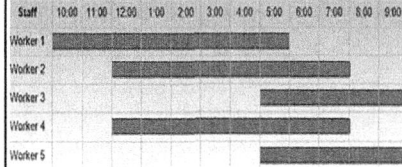

59. What does this say about operations:

A. Open from 10am-9pm with a shift change at 7pm and mornings are busier than evening

B. Open from 10am-9pm with a shift change at 5pm and mornings are busier than evenings

C. A one-day project starting at 10am with a deadline of 9pm has up to 5 workers on it at any time

D. One person opens at 10am, 2 people close at 9pm, and there are 4 employees to the manager

E. The period of 5pm-7pm is the busiest, requiring the most people

60. Decentralization requires
    ____ in order to _____:

    A. Decreased authority in
       first-line management,
       empower employees

    B. Increased authority in
       middle management,
       maintain control

    C. Increased authority in
       first-line management,
       be responsive to
       customers

    D. Empowerment of
       middle management,
       make decisions

    E. Centralization,
       maintain order

61. The Foreign Corrupt
    Practices Act:

    A. Bans the bribing of
       domestic officials by
       US or foreign citizens

    B. Bans the bribing of
       domestic officials by
       foreigners, and holds
       foreign corporations
       listed domestically to
       SEC laws

    C. Bans US citizens from
       banning foreign
       officials or domestic
       officials

    D. Bans the bribing of
       foreign officials, bans
       the bribing of
       domestic officials by
       foreigners

    E. Bans the bribing of
       foreign officials, and
       holds foreign
       corporations listed
       domestically to SEC
       laws

62. According to _____, management involves using the scientific method to break-down each function into rigid specializations in a mass-production environment:

A. Henri Fayol

B. David Aaker

C. FW Taylor

D. Charon Drotter

E. Max Weber

63. Henry Ford, founder of the Ford Motor Company, paid twice the standard salary because:

A. It allowed employees to purchase the products they were making

B. Paying standard wages gave people little incentive to stay, creating huge turnover costs

C. To attract highly-skilled workers

D. To increase aggregate demand using the income effect

E. To motivate employees to be more productive

64. According to _____, management must include participative setting of objectives:

A. Frederick Herzberg

B. Geert Hoftsede

C. Abraham Maslow

D. FW Taylor

E. Peter Drucker

65. Lower wages do not lead to higher employment because:

A. Fewer people are willing to work at a given price level despite their need to survive

B. Companies will never hire more people than they need to meet . production demand, regardless of wage level

C. Lower wages cause greater per-person output

D. Higher employment requires higher price levels to increase supply

E. Unions prevent labor negotiations

66. According to Blanchard and Hersey, the ___ management style is used when employees are most developed, and ___ when they are least developed:

A. Coaching, directing

B. Delegating, supporting

C. Coaching, supporting

D. Delegating, directing

E. Directing, delegating

67. **The 20-70-10 rule states:**

   A. Employees in the bottom 70% of productivity must be replaced, those in the top 10% supported, and the remaining 20% coached

   B. Employees get 10% of their skills from training, 70% from working, and the remaining 20% from work socialization

   C. Employees in the bottom 20% of productivity must be replaced, those in the top 10% supported, and the remaining 70% coached

   D. Employees in the bottom 10% of productivity must be replaced, those in the top 20% supported, and the remaining 70% coached

   E. Employees get 70% of their skills from training, 10% from working, and the remaining 20% from work socialization

68. **According to Hofstede, the degree to which a culture values gain and achievement over social cohesion is called:**

   A. Indulgence

   B. Masculinity

   C. Individualism

   D. Time orientation

   E. Power distance

69. **Hofstede and GLOBE share which cultural dimension:**

   A. Uncertainty avoidance

   B. Gender egalitarianism

   C. Performance orientation

   D. In-group collectivism

   E. Humane orientation

70. According to the original Civil Rights Act of 1964, it was legal to discriminate employment based on:

A. Disability

B. Gender

C. Race

D. Religion

E. Color

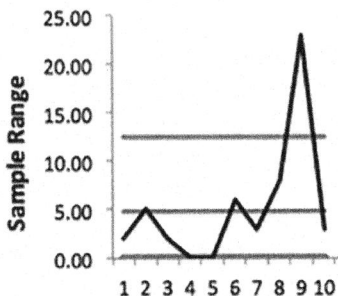

71. In statistical process control, this is typical of:

A. A systematic flaw causing consistent variability

B. An anomalous or temporary flaw in the production cycle

C. Volatile production growth

D. Seasonal production variations

E. Normal production quality

72. A behavior is considered unlawful harassment when:

A. The behavior is not appropriate in the workplace

B. An individual perceives the behavior as offensive

C. It is persistent or severe enough to make the workplace intimidating

D. The behavior breaks other laws

E. The behavior is socially inappropriate

73. **A company is held liable for harassment within the workplace when:**

   A. Companies are never held liable, only people

   B. It fails to act on any harassment brought to its attention

   C. It fails to provide workplace equality training during orientation

   D. It fails to act on harassment brought to its attention, or immediately when supervisors harass

   E. Companies are always immediately liable for what happens

74. **___ is not a type of compensation:**

   A. Wages

   B. Insurance benefits

   C. Flex time

   D. 401(k) matching

   E. Pensions

75. **Each limits the bargaining power of individual employees except:**

   A. The high cost of developing new skills relative to low income

   B. Government regulation

   C. The majority of labor does not have the savings to survive for extended negotiations or job search

   D. Low skill requirements for those jobs most vulnerable

   E. Lack of equivalent access to legal and PR resources

76. **Performance appraisals must be all except:**

   A. Performed regularly

   B. Clear and specific

   C. Objectively measured

   D. Strict

   E. Individualized

77. Which is not a tool used to create a cohesive virtual environment:

A. Instant messaging

B. Cloud computing

C. Database management systems

D. Collaborative workspace

E. Video conferencing

78. _____ is not one of the reasons workplace diversity is important:

A. Different perspectives increases innovation and improves idea pool

B. Larger labor pools increase total labor potential

C. Affirmative action requires special consideration for underrepresented groups

D. Demographic equivalence improves responsiveness to changing markets

E. Workplace diversity expands market size and/or market share

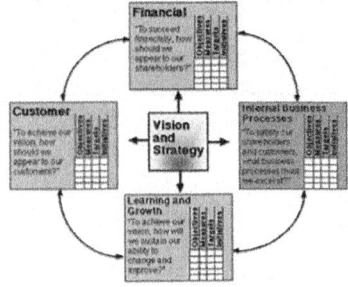

79. This is _____, which _____:

A. Balanced scorecard, evaluates the degree to which different functions are prepared to pursue a strategy initiative before execution

B. Balanced scorecard, assesses the degree to which operations support the overall strategy

C. Balanced scorecard, calculates the resource utilization of different functions dedicated to a strategic initiative

D. Strategic operations chart, defines the way in which organizational operations must function to achieve strategic goals

E. Strategy control graph, assesses the degree to which operations support the overall strategy

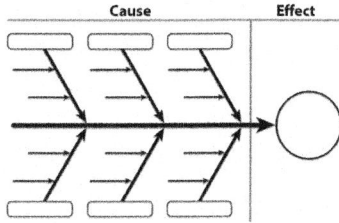

80. This is ____ :

A. Causal loop diagram

B. Cause-effect graph

C. Why-because analysis

D. Ishikawa diagram

E. Causal diagram

81. In a corporation, top management is hired by:

A. Board of directors

B. Shareholders

C. Stakeholders

D. Executives

E. Front-line management

82. In a corporation, board of directors is hired by:

A. Board of directors

B. Shareholders

C. Stakeholders

D. Executives

E. Front-line management

83. The four functions of management does not include:

A. Planning

B. Organizing

C. Marketing

D. Leading

E. Controlling

84. According to Mintzberg, the role of the manager which involves communicating information to people outside the organization is:

    A. Disseminator

    B. Spokesperson

    C. Monitor

    D. Figurehead

    E. Liaison

85. According to Mintzberg, the role of the manager which includes networking within and outside the organization is:

    A. Liaison

    B. Spokesperson

    C. Figurehead

    D. Disseminator

    E. Monitor

86. According to Mintzberg, the role of the manager which involves defending the interests of the business is:

    A. Disturbance handler

    B. Entrepreneur

    C. Negotiator

    D. Resource allocator

    E. Leader

87. Which are traditionally listed as part of the managerial skill set:

    A. Technical skills, human skills

    B. Human skills, marketing skills

    C. Conceptual skills, accounting skills

    D. Technical skills, marketing skills

    E. Human skills, accounting skills

88.   ___ refers to those actions and behaviors which people believe to be important:

  A.   Morals

  B.   Principles

  C.   Beliefs

  D.   Values

  E.   Ethics

89.   Setting goals does not:

  A.   Function has a comprehensive plan

  B.   Provide guidance and direction

  C.   Create a foundation for organized planning

  D.   Establish challenging milestones to motivate staff

  E.   Provide a method for evaluating performance

90.   The official parameters set by an organization outlining an activity or response is called:

  A.   Regulations

  B.   Rules

  C.   Procedures

  D.   Laws

  E.   Norms

91.   Which type of grand strategy can involve selling current business units:

  A.   Retrenchment

  B.   Global

  C.   Growth

  D.   Stability

  E.   Business

92. According to the rational model, the decision-making process includes everything except:

    A. Assess options

    B. Determine the point of acceptable satisficing

    C. Make decision

    D. Define the problem

    E. Evaluate results

93. Which is a potential disadvantage of group decision-making:

    A. Greater error recognition

    B. Improved morale through participation

    C. Greater acceptance of decision by staff

    D. Diffusion of responsibility

    E. Expanded knowledge pool

94. Techniques teams can use to stimulate creative problem solving include everything except ___, which is typically used by individuals:

    A. Brainstorming

    B. Delphi technique

    C. Cross-fertilization

    D. Nominal group technique

    E. Devil's advocacy

95. Fast, repetitive production environments are facilitated by a ___, and creative environments of dynamic challenges by a ___:

    A. Industrial system, organic system

    B. Mechanistic system, organic system

    C. Natural system, Mechanistic system

    D. Industrial system, natural system

    E. Mechanistic system, mechanistic system

96. Horizontal organizations are unique because:

A. They formed as a result of horizontal integration with other organizations

B. They have a small number of employees per manager

C. They emphasize functional integration and personal empowerment over hierarchy

D. They give greater authority to employees than management

E. They are the inverse of vertical organizations

97. Perceptual errors in leadership do not include:

A. Halo effect

B. Strictness or leniency

C. Expectancy effect

D. Projection effect

E. Selective perception

98. Which type of team is best when highly specialized operations are involved:

A. Dysfunctional team

B. Cross-functional team

C. Functional team

D. Vertical team

E. Project

99. What type of team is best for executive operations:

A. Dysfunctional team

B. Cross-functional team

C. Functional team

D. Vertical team

E. Project team

100. **Groupthink is:**

A. A form of group brainstorming

B. The collective culture of an organization

C. The aggregate knowledge set of a team

D. The innovation created in large groups of highly specialized people

E. A state in which conformity takes priority over critical thought

ANSWER KEY

Question Number	Correct Answer	Your Answer	Question Number	Correct Answer	Your Answer	Question Number	Correct Answer	Your Answer
1	B		36	C		71	B	
2	C		37	A		72	C	
3	C		38	A		73	D	
4	B		39	B		74	C	
5	C		40	B		75	B	
6	C		41	E		76	D	
7	D		42	A		77	C	
8	B		43	C		78	C	
9	B		44	D		79	B	
10	A		45	D		80	D	
11	B		46	A		81	A	
12	C		47	B		82	B	
13	E		48	A		83	C	
14	B		49	A		84	B	
15	A		50	A		85	A	
16	A		51	A		86	C	
17	B		52	D		87	A	
18	E		53	A		88	D	
19	A		54	C		89	A	
20	B		55	C		90	C	
21	A		56	A		91	A	
22	A		57	E		92	B	
23	A		58	C		93	D	
24	E		59	B		94	C	
25	A		60	C		95	B	
26	A		61	E		96	C	
27	A		62	C		97	B	
28	B		63	B		98	C	
29	E		64	E		99	B	
30	B		65	B		100	E	
31	B		66	D				
32	C		67	C				
33	A		68	B				
34	A		69	A				
35	E		70	A				

RATIONALES

1. According to equity theory:

    A. (Employee B's rewards/Employee A's input) = (Employee A's rewards/Employee B's input)

    B. (Employee A's rewards/Employee A's input) = (Employee B's rewards/Employee B's input)

    C. (Employee A's rewards/Employee B's input) = (Employee B's rewards/Employee A's input)

    D. (Employee A's rewards/Employee A's input) > (Employee B's rewards/Employee B's input)

    E. (Employee A's rewards/Employee A's input) < (Employee B's rewards/Employee B's input)

The answer is B
Equity theory states that an employee compares the amount of work they do and the amount of reward they get to that of others.

2. Productivity is:

    A. Input*Output

    B. Input/Output

    C. Output/Input

    D. (Output-Input)/Output

    E. (Input-Output)/Input

The answer is C
The amount of output produced per unit of input is simple measure of productivity

3.   The use of a neutral third party tasked with resolving a dispute but who doesn't have the authority to enforce the outcome is known as:

   A.   Mediation

   B.   Conciliation

   C.   Arbitration

   D.   Bargaining

   E.   Litigation

The answer is C
Arbitration involves the use of an impartial "judge" who attempts to help people find a solution, and makes a determination, but it is not legally binding.

4.   ___ is not one of Porter's five forces of environmental scanning:

   A.   Bargaining power of suppliers

   B.   Regulation of governments

   C.   Bargaining power of customers

   D.   Threat of new entrants

   E.   Threat of substitutes

The answer is B
Suppliers, Customers, Competitors, new entrants, substitutes

5.   ___ is an example of ethnocentrism:

   A.   Opening a wholly-foreign owned enterprise before attempting licensing

   B.   Mistranslations of promotional materials

   C.   Managing team dynamics in foreign offices as in home offices

   D.   Using the same asset management analytics in each global office

   E.   Structuring a business by functional division rather than geography

The answer is C
Ethnocentrism occurs when you apply domestic standards of behavior to foreign workers.

6.   ___ is an example of the maintenance group role:

   A.   Making acquisition decisions for upcoming projects

   B.   Collecting feedback on an internal policy change

   C.   Alleviating office friction during end of fiscal year

   D.   Playing "Devil's Advocate"

   E.   Scheduling project milestones in line with final deadline

The answer is C
Maintenance means doing what's necessary to maximize cohesion within a group.

7.   The highest degree of group autonomy is found in _____ groups:

A.   Traditional

B.   Semi-autonomous

C.   Cross-functional

D.   Self-managed

E.   Virtual

The answer is D
Self-managed groups make most or all operational decisions themselves.

8.   A management method training employees on the operations of the company and the role of their primary function within it:

A.   Job enlargement

B.   Job rotation

C.   Job enrichment

D.   Job reengineering

E.   Job intensification

The answer is B
By briefly performing other jobs within the organization, you can learn the details of the inputs, outputs, and processes of others, improving coordination between job roles.

9.   Equity theory requires the use of objective measurements of input because:

A.   So that employees know what to expect in their rewards

B.   The endowment effect means each person values their own contributions more than equivalent contributions by others

C.   So that inputs and outputs can be readily calculated

D.   To set a prediction reference point relative to actual outcomes

E.   To set a reference point for negotiations in future exchanges

The answer is B
Each person places more value of their own contributions than on the contributions of others, making relative reward seem persistently inequitable, but this can be alleviated by tying rewards to clear and constant performance metrics.

10.   What type of plan is this
"Over the next 5 years we will expand the total market by targeting previously untouched demographics":

A.   Strategic

B.   Tactical

C.   Operational

D.   Project

E.   Contingency

The answer is A
Strategic plans deal with the broad direction a company takes, rather than the detailed functions which allow it to pursue its strategy. That's also the difference between a CEO and a COO – CEO makes a plan, COO makes it happen.

11.   Who is in charge of establishing operational plans:

   A.   Middle managers

   B.   First-line managers

   C.   Executive managers

   D.   Financial managers

   E.   Shift managers

The answer is B
First-line managers are the people who direct the day-to-day activities of production staff.

12.   The best contingency plans:

   A.   Deviate from the optimal plan at the point of change, preserving the value of the previous steps

   B.   Are fully established plans wholly separate from the optimal plan

   C.   Set alternatives for each step which feed back into the optimal plan

   D.   Should be pursued simultaneously to the optimal plan

   E.   Should only be developed if the optimal plan fails

The answer is C
To avoid sunk costs from aimless floundering, each step in a plan has its own contingency plan to get back on track.

13.　In change management, all the following are part of the unfreezing process except:

A.　Surveying employees about their jobs and how they can be improved

B.　Quantify the operational, competitive, and financial impact of elements to be changed

C.　Reinforcing the negative aspects of current methods in the minds of the staff

D.　Communicating controlled isolation of the problem with plans for improvement that doesn't extend into the rest of the organization

E.　Implementing new policies

The answer is E
Unfreezing involves preparing the organization to change by sowing discontent with those things which are going to be changed.

14.　At 6σ, the ideal goal of Six Sigma quality management, there are ____ DPMO with a ____ percentage yield:

A.　0.019, 99.9999981

B.　3.4, 99.99966

C.　233, 99.977

D.　6,210, 99.38

E.　66,807, 93.3

The answer is B
3.4 defective parts per million opportunities lies at 6 standard deviations from the mean, according to 6σ.

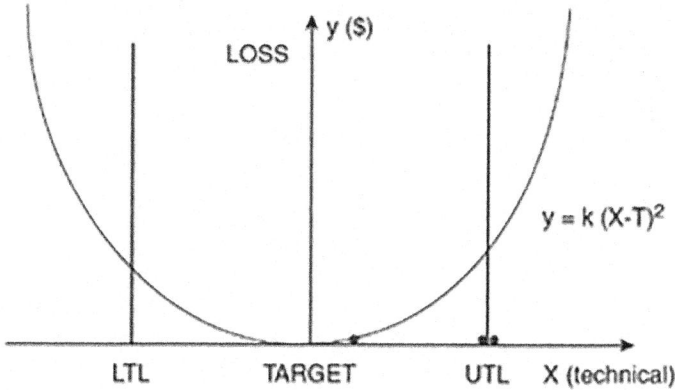

LOSS y ($)

$y = k (X-T)^2$

LTL   TARGET   UTL   X (technical)

15.   **The Taguchi Loss Function states:**

A. Deviations from target specifications create a loss which increases exponentially and must not exceed upper and lower limits

B. Quality management operations must be effective enough to be financially viable, but not to the point that its costs exceed its benefits

C. The defective parts per million opportunities will increase the costs of fixing/reconstructing defective output more than the costs of preventing them

D. Increasing losses create deviations from planned growth rates which become unsustainable at upper and lower limits

E. Losses are a function of parabolic curves

The answer is A

As a quality management tool, the TLF is used to estimate the amount of loss associated with missed specification targets.

16. $100,000 earned at complete project
Planned 10 week deadline, linear PV
$60,000 EV at 5 weeks
What is the SPI:

    A. 120%

    B. 83%

    C. 10%

    D. -10%

    E. 100%

The answer is A
If a project is exactly on budget and deadline then the schedule performance index will be 100%. If it's ahead of schedule and/or under budget, it'll be over 100%.

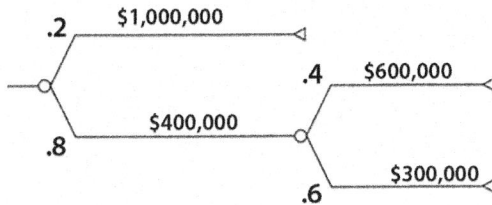

17. The adjusted values at the 2nd node of this decision tree are:

    A. -$200,000, $100,000

    B. $240,000, $180,000

    C. $300,000, -$300,000

    D. $200,000, $320,000

    E. $240,000, $300,000

The answer is B
Each potential choice is valued using a combination of the earned value of success, adjusted for the probability of success.

Severity	Probability	Frequent	Likely	Occasional	Seldom	Unlikely
		A	B	C	D	E
Catastrophic	I	E	E	H	H	M
Critical	II	E	H	H	M	L
Moderate	III	H	M	M	L	L
Negligible	IV	M	L	L	L	L

18. In the management of a fire department, the risk to individual staff members is:

A. None

B. Low (L)

C. Moderate (M)

D. High (H)

E. Extreme (E)

The answer is E

Fire fighters are at least likely to encounter a fire as it is the nature of their jobs, and the threat fire poses is quite high. Such an extreme risk warrants a large degree of mitigation.

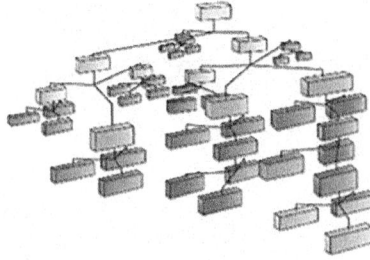

19. Models such as this are most commonly used to depict:

A. Organizational hierarchy

B. Product portfolio

C. Subsidiary structure

D. Capital assets

E. Team motivation drivers

The answer is A
Positional authority structure determines the shape, and each box is a different job, with its own functions, required skills, etc.

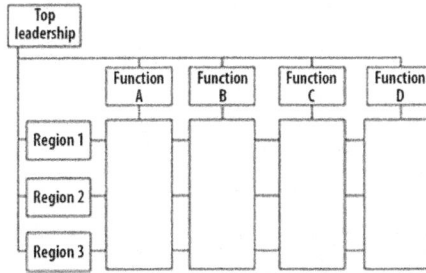

20. **This represents:**

    A. Divisional management

    B. Matrix management

    C. Micromanagement

    D. Tight matrix

    E. Organizational spreadsheet

The answer is B
Matrix structures are difficult to execute due to the high potential for conflicting requests, orders, and loyalties.

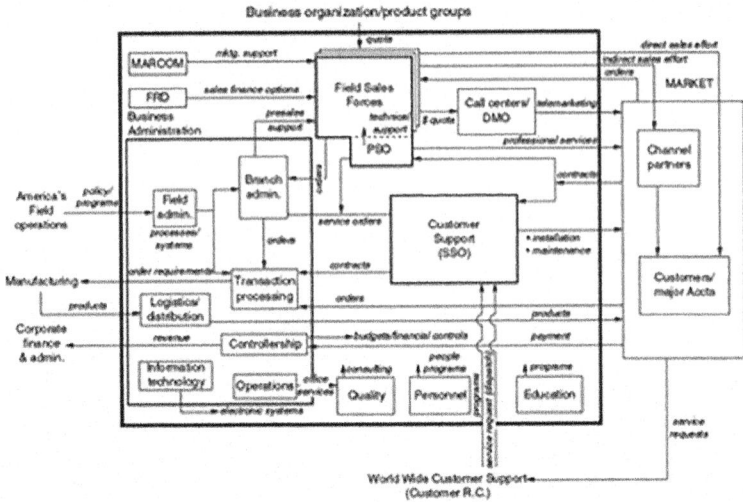

Business organization/product groups

World Wide Customer Support
(Customer R.C.)

21.   This is called ____ which represents ____:

A.   Process flowchart, dynamic operations of an organization

B.   Organizational structure, management hierarchy

C.   Schematic diagram, an electrical circuit

D.   Organizational structure, dynamic operations of an organization

E.   Process flowchart, management hierarchy

The answer is A
Every function of an organization can be modeled using a process flowchart.

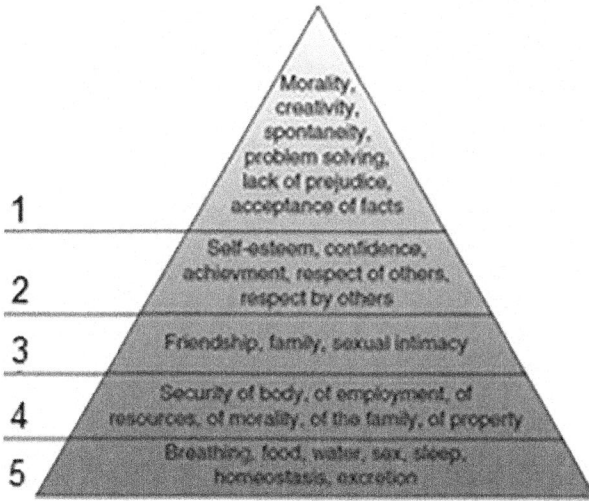

22.   In Maslow's Hierarchy of Needs, self-actualization is found at:

A.   1

B.   2

C.   3

D.   4

E.   5

The answer is A

Typically, before a person can pursue self-actualization, they must first meet their baser needs, such as getting paid enough for shelter, and having confidence in their abilities. This is what makes pursuing the life of an artist or writer often so challenging – the pursuit starts with self-actualization.

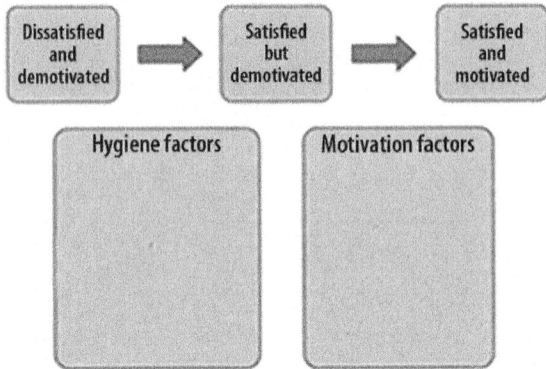

23. In Herzberg's Two-Factor Theory of Motivation, ____ is a hygiene factor and ___ is a motivator:

A. Wages, prestige

B. Responsibility, working conditions

C. Promotions, job security

D. Sense of purpose, clear expectations

E. Recognition, professional relationships

The answer is A
Hygiene factors will keep their jobs over hygiene factors, reducing the costs of employment turnover, but for them to strive for excellence they must be motivated.

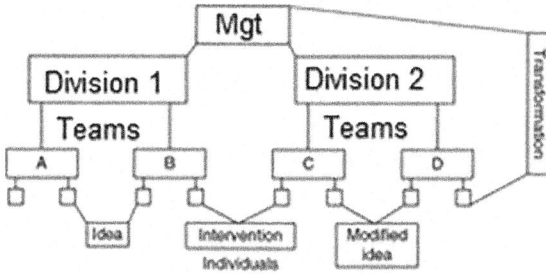

24.   **This graph illustrates:**

A.   Structure of authority

B.   Team-based project management

C.   Organizational decision making process

D.   Bottom-up communication

E.   The flow of information in managing continuous improvement

The answer is E
A productive company culture starts with management, but is customized by individuals, shaping the way management makes future decisions about the people and structures of which culture is composed.

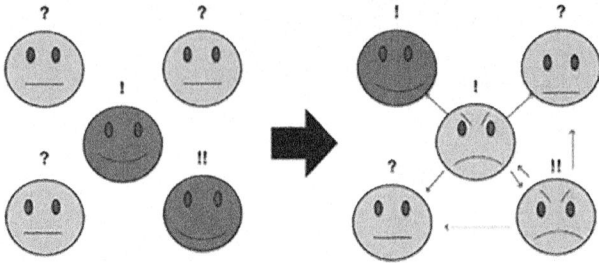

25. This diagram on conflict creation illustrates the need for:

A. Clear direction and dissemination of information from management

B. The need for arbitration during the decision making process

C. Multiple styles of negotiations

D. Constructive forms of persuasion

E. Team development programs

The answer is A
Conflict comes from differences in ideas about the way things should be. Confusion or lack of clear direction breeds a lot of conflict.

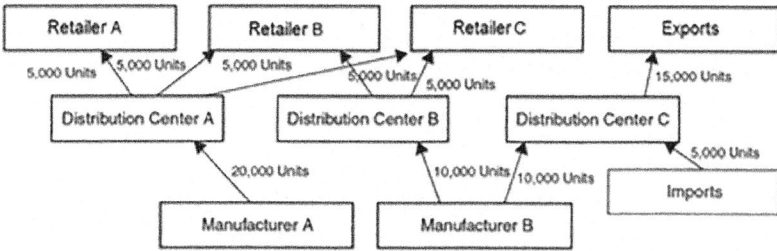

26.   Which manufacturer has the lowest-risk supply chain:

A.   Manufacturer B because 100% of their production has multiple channels to the end consumer

B.   Manufacturer A because their primary distribution center sells to 50% more retailers than 2nd highest

C.   Manufacturer A because they are not competing with foreign imports

D.   Manufacturer B because they have domestic and foreign sales

E.   Both manufacturers A and B have equal risk of disrupted supply chains

The answer is A
Ensuring you have multiple options – plans and contingency plans – is the key to mitigating risk.

27. ___ is a form of ___ given to first-line managers, though ___ is often reserved for middle management:

A. Reward authority, legitimate power, coercive authority

B. Personal power, legitimate power, positional authority

C. Referent authority, personal power, coercive authority

D. Reward authority, personal power, coercive authority

E. Coercive authority, legitimate power, positional authority

The answer is A
The authority to give bonuses, hold contests, and so forth improves the dynamic between managers and employees, but those things which can harm morale is frequently reserved for managers which the employees don't usually interact with regularly.

28. ___ is acquired by being charismatic or motivational, rather than having any formal power:

A. Expert authority

B. Referent authority

C. Positional authority

D. Reward authority

E. Coercive authority

The answer is B
Much of the power people hold over us is freely given just by nature of the social dynamic; expert authority is given because someone knows more about a topic than you, and referent authority is given just because that person can talk us into acting.

29.   Compartmentalization of operations to prevent interaction and communication is typically used to:

A.   This is never done in a healthy organization

B.   To create an immersive environment during job rotation training

C.   To prevent interaction between men and women in some highly orthodox cultures

D.   To prevent conflict with competing individuals or teams

E.   Prevent any person from having access to the whole of proprietary information

The answer is E
For secret, proprietary information related to your strategic advantage or core operations, it can be useful to split the function into multiple parts and separate those parts so that "the right hand doesn't know what the left is doing", so to speak.

30.   The point in the team development process in which members conflict with each other as they establish roles and culture is called:

A.   Forming

B.   Storming

C.   Norming

D.   Performing

E.   Adjourning

The answer is B
Until the members of a team all hold the same ideas of how operations and interpersonal interactions should be, minor conflicts will persist.

31. The point in which a manager will most likely need to validate the credentials of a member is:

    A. Adjourning

    B. Forming

    C. Storming

    D. Norming

    E. Performing

The answer is B
If someone is introduced to a team and the rest of the team isn't familiar with them, it's up to management to validate competence in order to expedite the building of trust and incorporation into a group.

32. According to Kohlberg's Stages of Moral Development, how should a manager address an individual at Stage 4:

    A. Emphasize conditioning systems of reward and punishment

    B. Emphasize personal gain to be earned in negotiated terms

    C. Emphasize the importance of policies and organizational authority

    D. Emphasize the mutual benefits of constructed operations and dynamics

    E. Emphasize conforming to organizational roles and cultures as a means of acceptance

The answer is C
People at Stage 4 look to authority and structure to make decisions of morality

33. According to Kohlberg's Moral Development, how should a manager address an individual at Stage 3:

   A. Emphasize conforming to organizational roles and cultures as a means of acceptance

   B. Emphasize the importance of policies and organizational authority

   C. Emphasize the mutual benefits of constructed operations and dynamics

   D. Emphasize conditioning systems of reward and punishment

   E. Emphasize personal gain to be earned in negotiated terms

The answer is A
People at Stage 3 rely on assessments of what other people want, and what will maximize social inclusion, for moral decisions.

34. **Motivation is mathematically represented as:**

   A. (Expectancy*Value)/(1+Impulsiveness*Delay)

   B. Expectancy*Value

   C. (Expectancy*Value)/(1+Impulsiveness)

   D. Expected Value – Expected Costs

   E. Expected Value/(Impulsiveness*Delay)

The answer is A
Motivation is driven by future expectations, but mitigated by a person's inability to maintain a given level of activity over longer periods of time.

35.   The negotiating style which includes offering either fake or inconsequential concessions in order to gain on those things which matter to you is called:

   A.   Accommodating

   B.   Avoiding

   C.   Collaborating

   D.   Competing

   E.   Compromising

The answer is E

False compromise that is clear to others can create distrust, actually making the true issues at hand more difficult to negotiate. Best to be as genuine as possible.

36.   The negotiating style which involves intentionally keeping negotiations on aspects which are not issues of conflict in order to draw the other person in is called:

   A.   Collaborating

   B.   Competing

   C.   Avoiding

   D.   Accommodating

   E.   Compromising

The answer is C

Avoiding the true topics of contention can make secondary matters easier to resolve if you don't intend to use them as negotiation pieces, and it creates a unique dynamic wherein the other person is pursuing you, thus putting them at a disadvantage so long as you can maintain avoidance longer than their ability to be patient about it.

37. Employees each produce 10 units per day, units sell for $100 each with a total cost of $90 per unit entirely composed of labor. If it takes 5 days to train a new employee, what is the turnover cost:

A. $5,000

B. $4,500

C. $500

D. $450

E. $0

The answer is A

Even assuming management can instantly replace a lost employee, the training period results in $1,000 per day of lost revenues, which is the amount of differential between maintaining an employee and training a new one.

38. Per day, experienced staff produce 500 units and earn $100.
Per day, new staff produce 300 units and earn $50.
Training takes 5 days and each unit produced is worth $1
The calculation to analyze the wage productivity differential is:

A. $(500/100)n - ((300/50)n-250)$

B. $((300/50)n-250)-(500/100)n$

C. $(100/500)n-(300/50)n$

D. $(500/100)n-(300/50)n$

E. $(500-300)n/100-250$

The answer is A

In changing labor markets, new employees often don't have the same amount of bargaining power, allowing for lower relative costs, but the cost savings must be more than the amount of lost productivity and the cost of training.

236

39. Setup costs = $10
    Demand = 100
    Production cost = $20
    Interest rate = 100%
    EOQ is:

    A. 5

    B. 10

    C. 50

    D. 100

    E. 500

The answer is B
$\sqrt{(2SD)/(PI)}$

COSTS	IN-HOUSE	OUTSOURCED
Billing department costs	$118,000	$4,000
Software and hardware costs	$7,500	$500
Direct claim processing costs	$3,600	$122,500
Software and hardware costs	$5,500	$2,000
% of billings collected	60%	70%
Collections	$1,370,900	$1,623,000
Collections costs	$129,100	$127,000
Collections, net of costs		

40. Decide whether to outsource:

    A. Do not outsource to prevent losing $254,200

    B. Outsource to gain $254,200

    C. Do both to gain $254,200

    D. End function completely to prevent losing $254,200

    E. Panic

The answer is B
Using transfer pricing, the amount of cost and revenue created from each production function can be calculated, and then if an outside company can perform that function more effectively then outsourcing it the best option.

41.   It is best to use an authoratarian leadership style when:

A.   During skill development programs

B.   When interpersonal conflict begins to hinder basic work functions

C.   When seeking input for revision of internal policies

D.   When managing skilled experts working in creative conditions

E.   During times of crisis when change must be rapid

The answer is E
Authoritarian leadership is the fastest and most decisive, but is likely to be rejected by others unless it is acknowledged that such emergency actions are warranted.

42.   A pacesetting leadership style intended to facilitate the staff's activities is best used when:

A.   When managing skilled experts working in creative conditions

B.   When seeking input for revision of internal policies

C.   When interpersonal conflict begins to hinder basic work functions

D.   During times of crisis when change must be rapid

E.   During skill development programs

The answer is A
If employees already have the expertise and motivation to accomplish their goals, then it is up to management to create an environment where they can best apply their skills.

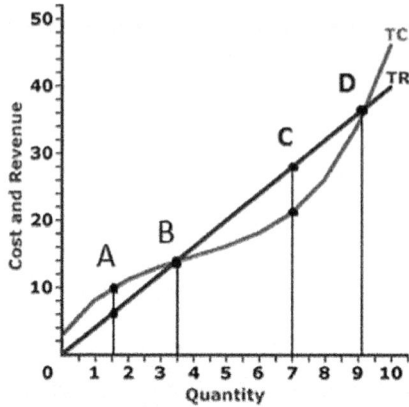

43. For profit-maximizing firms efficiency is optimized at __ and for revenue-maximizing firms at ___:

   A. B, C

   B. D, C

   C. C, D

   D. C, B

   E. B, D

The answer is C

Profit maximization is best when using a differentiation/quality strategy, while revenue maximization is best for price leadership strategies.

44.   Under generic competitive conditions, productive efficiency is achieved at:

   A.   MC=FC

   B.   FC=AC

   C.   VC=FC

   D.   MC=AC

   E.   MC=TC

The answer is D
Marginal cost will start under average cost due to the role of fixed cost, bringing average cost down, but after marginal cost surpasses average cost, then the average will increase again.

45.   **Which is not a type of team dysfunction:**

   A.   Groupthink

   B.   Interpersonal conflict

   C.   Freeriding

   D.   Comprehensive input

   E.   Lack of individualization

The answer is D
Teams have a lot of problems that need to be controlled, but having more people contribute their ideas and feedback is a good thing.

46. **Analysis paralysis typically results from:**

   A. Lack of decisive confidence

   B. Too much information

   C. Too little information

   D. Too much or too little information

   E. Rapidly changing business environment

The answer is A

All decisions are made without perfect information, and if faced with too much information it's up to management to quickly decide what information to use and how quickly the decision must be made.

47. **The shareholder wealth maximization model is concerned with:**

   A. Increasing current profitability

   B. Increasing the value of company equity

   C. Maximizing the value that the company creates for those which it influences

   D. Increasing company revenue growth

   E. Increasing NPV of company investments

The answer is B

It is up to management to do whatever is best for the owners of a company, and in a corporation the owners are the shareholders.

48.   Which of the following is not a stakeholder:

A.   Competitors

B.   Shareholders

C.   Employees

D.   Customers

E.   Partners

The answer is A
The formal definition of a stakeholder is "those groups without whose support the organization would cease to exist."

49.   **Agency problems result from:**

A.   Executives who manage a company in a manner contrary to that which benefits the shareholders

B.   Executives who manage a company in a manner contrary to that which benefits the stakeholders

C.   Contradictions between the benefits of the shareholders and stakeholders

D.   Managers who embezzle money from the company

E.   Inefficient functions such as bid rigging and nepotism

The answer is A
The separation of ownership and management creates conflicts of interest and other problems of agency.

50. **A short organization is one which has:**

    A. Few degrees of management with a larger volume of staff per manager

    B. More degrees of management with a lower volume of staff per manager

    C. Few degrees of management with a lower volume of staff per manager

    D. More degrees of management with a with a larger volume of staff per manager

    E. Few degrees of management with higher staff empowerment

The answer is A

"Tall" and "short" refer to the height of the organizational structure – the number of levels of authority in a chain of command.

51. **SIPOC analysis includes each except:**

    A. Competitors

    B. Supplier

    C. Inputs

    D. Processes

    E. Outputs

The answer is A

The "C" stands for customers – SIPOC is all about value creation.

52.   According to Lean-Six Sigma, the 8 sources of waste include everything except:

   A.   Defects

   B.   Overproduction

   C.   Non-utilized talent

   D.   Overtime

   E.   Inventory-in-process

The answer is D
The sources of waste can be remembered using "DOWNTIME", but overtime contributes to production, not waste.

53.   The most integrated way to create a direct presence within a foreign market is through:

   A.   WFOE

   B.   Licensing

   C.   Joint venture

   D.   Exporting

   E.   Outsourcing

The answer is A
Subsidiary ownership is most immersive option of foreign expansion

54. In SWOT, ___ is an example of "W" and ____ is an example of "O":

    A. Small HR pool in area, small population leading to insufficient revenues

    B. Efficient inventory management, cost-leader strategy from low costs

    C. Low brand recognition, cult following with potential for niche market strategy

    D. High materials costs, price competition

    E. Unique product, lack of sustainable advantage due to no IP registration

The answer is C
Sometimes companies with low brand recognition garner the attention of niche markets specifically because they are aren't well-known yet.

55. Something must be ___ and ___ to maintain a sustainable competitive advantage:

    A. Valuable, exchangeable

    B. Unsubstitutable, irreplaceable

    C. Rare, inimitable

    D. Rare, exchangeable

    E. Valuable, irreplaceable

The answer is C
Rare, valuable, inimitable, unsubstitutable

56.   ___ is the person who influences decisions by using indirect information to guide other to come to the desired conclusion:

A.   Idea planters

B.   Predictors

C.   Trend setters

D.   Persuaders

E.   Negotiators

The answer is A
Idea planters stimulate inception within others

57.   **According to JIT ____:**

A.   Reserve inventory should always be held to account for variations from predicted sales volume

B.   The only reserve inventory to be held is that which will be used in the next month

C.   The only reserve inventory to be held is that which will be used biweekly

D.   The only reserve inventory to be held is that which will be used in the next week

E.   No reserve inventory should be held

The answer is E
It's the goal of just-in-time inventory management to strive to make products available just as customers need them in order to limit storage costs.

58. **How is PESTEL different in a global environment than a domestic one:**

A. Economical factors must include a corrective index to account for different economic structures

B. Sociocultural factors become impossible to predict in foreign nations

C. The interaction between nations creates dynamics more complex than both nations by themselves

D. You must include political factors

E. There is no difference

The answer is C
Each nation has its own environment, but the way these environments influence each other adds a complexity that must also be considered.

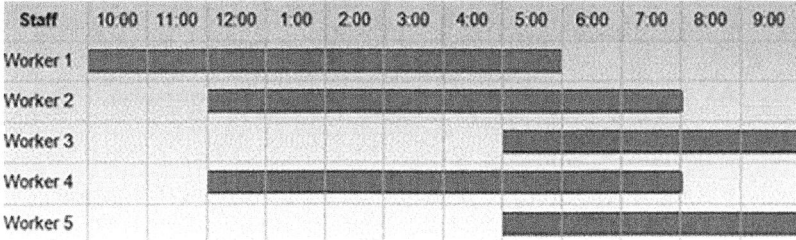

Staff	10:00	11:00	12:00	1:00	2:00	3:00	4:00	5:00	6:00	7:00	8:00	9:00
Worker 1												
Worker 2												
Worker 3												
Worker 4												
Worker 5												

59.   What does this say about operations:

A.   Open from 10am-9pm with a shift change at 7pm and mornings are busier than evening

B.   Open from 10am-9pm with a shift change at 5pm and mornings are busier than evenings

C.   A one-day project starting at 10am with a deadline of 9pm has up to 5 workers on it at any time

D.   One person opens at 10am, 2 people close at 9pm, and there are 4 employees to the manager

E.   The period of 5pm-7pm is the busiest, requiring the most people

The answer is B
Gantt charts are a great way to visualize staff scheduling.

60.   Decentralization requires ____ in order to ____:

A.   Decreased authority in first-line management, empower
     employees

B.   Increased authority in middle management, maintain control

C.   Increased authority in first-line management, be responsive to
     customers

D.   Empowerment of middle management, make decisions

E.   Centralization, maintain order

The answer is C
If lower-level staff aren't empowered to make decisions, decentralization will
bring operations to a halt.

61.   **The Foreign Corrupt Practices Act:**

A.   Bans the bribing of domestic officials by US or foreign citizens

B.   Bans the bribing of domestic officials by foreigners, and holds
     foreign corporations listed domestically to SEC laws

C.   Bans US citizens from banning foreign officials or domestic
     officials

D.   Bans the bribing of foreign officials, bans the bribing of domestic
     officials by foreigners

E.   Bans the bribing of foreign officials, and holds foreign
     corporations listed domestically to SEC laws

The answer is E
The FCPA dictates the interaction of Americans with foreign officials, and the
manner in which foreign corporations interact with domestic shareholders.

62. According to _____, management involves using the scientific method to break-down each function into rigid specializations in a mass-production environment:

 A. Henri Fayol

 B. David Aaker

 C. FW Taylor

 D. Charon Drotter

 E. Max Weber

The answer is C
This has been dubbed Taylorism.

63. **Henry Ford, founder of the Ford Motor Company, paid twice the standard salary because:**

 A. It allowed employees to purchase the products they were making

 B. Paying standard wages gave people little incentive to stay, creating huge turnover costs

 C. To attract highly-skilled workers

 D. To increase aggregate demand using the income effect

 E. To motivate employees to be more productive

The answer is B
The turnover costs associated

64. According to ____, management must include participative setting of objectives:

    A. Frederick Herzberg

    B. Geert Hoftsede

    C. Abraham Maslow

    D. FW Taylor

    E. Peter Drucker

The answer is E
When employees are included in setting objectives, they take greater ownership and have greater acceptance of them.

65. Lower wages do not lead to higher employment because:

    A. Fewer people are willing to work at a given price level despite their need to survive

    B. Companies will never hire more people than they need to meet production demand, regardless of wage level

    C. Lower wages cause greater per-person output

    D. Higher employment requires higher price levels to increase supply

    E. Unions prevent labor negotiations

The answer is B
At the same time, companies will continue to hire as many people as they need to meet production demands regardless of gradual increases in minimum wages.

66.   According to Blanchard and Hersey, the ___ management style is used when employees are most developed, and ___ when they are least developed:

A.   Coaching, directing

B.   Delegating, supporting

C.   Coaching, supporting

D.   Delegating, directing

E.   Directing, delegating

The answer is D
Managers can continuously give autonomy to individual employees, changing the management style from directing, to coaching, to supporting, to delegating.

67.   **The 20-70-10 rule states:**

A.   Employees in the bottom 70% of productivity must be replaced, those in the top 10% supported, and the remaining 20% coached

B.   Employees get 10% of their skills from training, 70% from working, and the remaining 20% from work socialization

C.   Employees in the bottom 20% of productivity must be replaced, those in the top 10% supported, and the remaining 70% coached

D.   Employees in the bottom 10% of productivity must be replaced, those in the top 20% supported, and the remaining 70% coached

E.   Employees get 70% of their skills from training, 10% from working, and the remaining 20% from work socialization

The answer is C
The 20-70-10 rule has been largely rejected for its tendency to create frictional, low-morale working environment in which 1/5 of the company is constantly at risk.

68.   According to Hofstede, the degree to which a culture values gain and achievement over social cohesion is called:

A.   Indulgence

B.   Masculinity

C.   Individualism

D.   Time orientation

E.   Power distance

The answer is B
The dimension of masculinity/femininity has been criticized for its application of gender stereotypes to the label.

69.   Hofstede and GLOBE share which cultural dimension:

A.   Uncertainty avoidance

B.   Gender egalitarianism

C.   Performance orientation

D.   In-group collectivism

E.   Humane orientation

The answer is A
Power distance is also found in both.

70.   According to the original Civil Rights Act of 1964, it was legal to discriminate employment based on:

A.   Disability

B.   Gender

C.   Race

D.   Religion

E.   Color

The answer is A
The Age Discrimination Act of 1967 makes it illegal to discriminate against those aged 40 and over, but not under the age of 40.

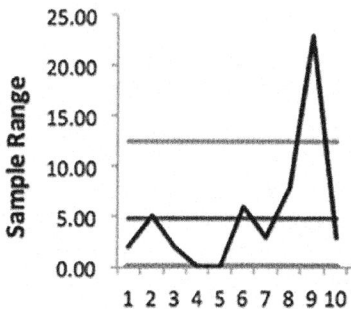

71.   In statistical process control, this is typical of:

A.   A systematic flaw causing consistent variability

B.   An anomalous or temporary flaw in the production cycle

C.   Volatile production growth

D.   Seasonal production variations

E.   Normal production quality

The answer is B
Short, periodic deviations of quality outside production parameters result from problems which are not systematic, making them more difficult to identify.

72.   **A behavior is considered unlawful harassment when:**

A.   The behavior is not appropriate in the workplace

B.   An individual perceives the behavior as offensive

C.   It is persistent or severe enough to make the workplace intimidating

D.   The behavior breaks other laws

E.   The behavior is socially inappropriate

The answer is C
Even if a behavior is not considered acceptable, to be considered unlawful there must either be a consistent pattern of that behavior, or the behavior must be relatively severe.

73.   **A company is held liable for harassment within the workplace when:**

A.   Companies are never held liable, only people

B.   It fails to act on any harassment brought to its attention

C.   It fails to provide workplace equality training during orientation

D.   It fails to act on harassment brought to its attention, or immediately when supervisors harass

E.   Companies are always immediately liable for what happens

The answer is D
If a behavior is not brought to the attention of management then they can't necessarily be expected to know it's happening, but if the behavior comes from a manager then they inherently know about it

74.   __ is not a type of compensation:

A.   Wages

B.   Insurance benefits

C.   Flex time

D.   401(k) matching

E.   Pensions

The answer is C
Flex time is a benefit, but it is not a form of remuneration.

75.   **Each limits the bargaining power of individual employees except:**

A.   The high cost of developing new skills relative to low income

B.   Government regulation

C.   The majority of labor does not have the savings to survive for extended negotiations or job search

D.   Low skill requirements for those jobs most vulnerable

E.   Lack of equivalent access to legal and PR resources

The answer is B
With the rise of unions in the early-20th century, government regulation actually facilitated the right to collective bargaining.

76. **Performance appraisals must be all except:**

A. Performed regularly

B. Clear and specific

C. Objectively measured

D. Strict

E. Individualized

The answer is D
Rather than strict or lenient, it's important to be fair.

77. **Which is not a tool used to create a cohesive virtual environment:**

A. Instant messaging

B. Cloud computing

C. Database management systems

D. Collaborative workspace

E. Video conferencing

The answer is C
Databases do not increase connectivity between individuals in a virtual organization, but they can be shared using methods which do.

78.   _____ is not one of the reasons workplace diversity is important:

   A.   Different perspectives increases innovation and improves idea
        pool

   B.   Larger labor pools increase total labor potential

   C.   Affirmative action requires special consideration for
        underrepresented groups

   D.   Demographic equivalence improves responsiveness to changing
        markets

   E.   Workplace diversity expands market size and/or market share

The answer is C
Data has shown that increased diversity improves the growth of both the
organization, and the economy as a whole.

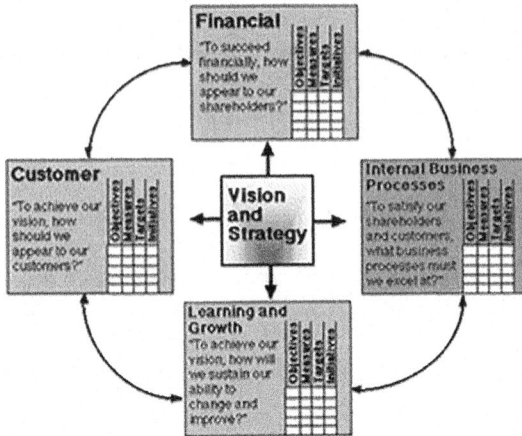

79. This is ____, which ____:

A. Balanced scorecard, evaluates the degree to which different functions are prepared to pursue a strategy initiative before execution

B. Balanced scorecard, assesses the degree to which operations support the overall strategy

C. Balanced scorecard, calculates the resource utilization of different functions dedicated to a strategic initiative

D. Strategic operations chart, defines the way in which organizational operations must function to achieve strategic goals

E. Strategy control graph, assesses the degree to which operations support the overall strategy

The answer is B:
It's used to visualize the degree to which the functions of an organization are all working toward a single goal.

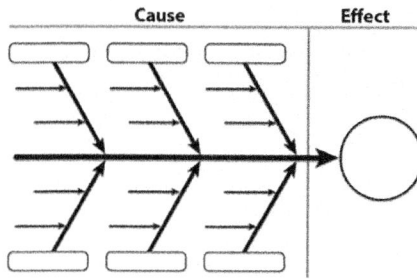

80. This is ____ :

    A. Causal loop diagram

    B. Cause-effect graph

    C. Why-because analysis

    D. Ishikawa diagram

    E. Causal diagram

The answer is D
Developed by Kaoru Ishikawa, this is colloquially known as a fishbone diagram.

81. In a corporation, top management is hired by:

    A. Board of directors

    B. Shareholders

    C. Stakeholders

    D. Executives

    E. Front-line management

The answer is A
The board of directors is in charge of hiring executive management, among other things. This often leads to conflicts of interest and agency problems as the boards of directors often place themselves into those management roles.

82.   In a corporation, board of directors is hired by:

A.   Board of directors

B.   Shareholders

C.   Stakeholders

D.   Executives

E.   Front-line management

The answer is B
Though it's difficult to coordinate the shareholders of a large corporation with broadly distributed shares, this is what's required to fire someone from the board of directors should decisions be made which are clearly contrary to the best interests of the shareholders.

83.   The four functions of management does not include:

A.   Planning

B.   Organizing

C.   Marketing

D.   Leading

E.   Controlling

The answer is C
Planning, organizing, leading, controlling

84. According to Mintzberg, the role of the manager which involves communicating information to people outside the organization is:

   A. Disseminator

   B. Spokesperson

   C. Monitor

   D. Figurehead

   E. Liaison

The answer is B
This is one of the informational roles, and contrasts the role of Disseminator, which involves communicating to people inside the organization.

85. According to Mintzberg, the role of the manager which includes networking within and outside the organization is:

   A. Liaison

   B. Spokesperson

   C. Figurehead

   D. Disseminator

   E. Monitor

The answer is A
This is one of the interpersonal roles, requiring a manager to function as a representative of the company.

86.　According to Mintzberg, the role of the manager which involves defending the interests of the business is:

A.　Disturbance handler

B.　Entrepreneur

C.　Negotiator

D.　Resource allocator

E.　Leader

The answer is C
This is one of the decisional categories, which is the only category with 4 roles rather than 3.

87.　Which are traditionally listed as part of the managerial skill set:

A.　Technical skills, human skills

B.　Human skills, marketing skills

C.　Conceptual skills, accounting skills

D.　Technical skills, marketing skills

E.　Human skills, accounting skills

The answer is A
Technical, human, conceptual

88. ___ refers to those actions and behaviors which people believe to be important:

A. Morals

B. Principles

C. Beliefs

D. Values

E. Ethics

The answer is D
Both individuals and companies have values

89. **Setting goals does not:**
     (Functional Aspects of Management)

A. Function has a comprehensive plan

B. Provide guidance and direction

C. Create a foundation for organized planning

D. Establish challenging milestones to motivate staff

E. Provide a method for evaluating performance

The answer is A
Goals are only one small part of a plan, intended to guide the actions which lead to the successful fulfillment of the plan.

90. **The official parameters set by an organization outlining an activity or response is called:**

   A. Regulations

   B. Rules

   C. Procedures

   D. Laws

   E. Norms

The answer is C
Procedures vary in how strictly they must be followed, sometimes being more lax such as social norms, or sometimes more strict even to the degree that a violation breaks the law.

91. **Which type of grand strategy can involve selling current business units:**

   A. Retrenchment

   B. Global

   C. Growth

   D. Stability

   E. Business

The answer is A
"Retrenchment" is a fancy way of saying that the company needs to get smaller if it wants to survive at all.

92. According to the rational model, the decision-making process includes everything except:

A. Assess options

B. Determine the point of acceptable satisficing

C. Make decision

D. Define the problem

E. Evaluate results

The answer is B
Satisficing is not a part of the rational model, although an assessment of the cost of one's own time relative to the benefits of additional decision-making is a rational consideration.

93. Which is a potential disadvantage of group decision-making:

A. Greater error recognition

B. Improved morale through participation

C. Greater acceptance of decision by staff

D. Diffusion of responsibility

E. Expanded knowledge pool

The answer is D
If no one can be held fully responsible, or they don't feel they can be, then decisions will often be more risky.

94. Techniques teams can use to stimulate creative problem solving include everything except ___, which is typically used by individuals:

A. Brainstorming

B. Delphi technique

C. Cross-fertilization

D. Nominal group technique

E. Devil's advocacy

The answer is C
Cross-fertilization occurs when an individual contacts a professional from another field for information.

95. Fast, repetitive production environments are facilitated by a ___, and creative environments of dynamic challenges by a ___:

A. Industrial system, organic system

B. Mechanistic system, organic system

C. Natural system, Mechanistic system

D. Industrial system, natural system

E. Mechanistic system, mechanistic system

The answer is B
The operating environment must be conducive to the type of operations being performed.

96.   **Horizontal organizations are unique because:**

A.   They formed as a result of horizontal integration with other organizations

B.   They have a small number of employees per manager

C.   They emphasize functional integration and personal empowerment over hierarchy

D.   They give greater authority to employees than management

E.   They are the inverse of vertical organizations

The answer is C
Horizontal organizations have greater cross-functionality than traditional models.

97.   **Perceptual errors in leadership do not include:**

A.   Halo effect

B.   Strictness or leniency

C.   Expectancy effect

D.   Projection effect

E.   Selective perception

The answer is B
Strictness and leniency is erroneous, but not perceptual

98.   Which type of team is best when highly specialized operations are involved:

    A.   Dysfunctional team

    B.   Cross-functional team

    C.   Functional team

    D.   Vertical team

    E.   Project

The answer is C
A group of experts in a single field can accomplish highly specialized tasks

99.   What type of team is best for executive operations:

    A.   Dysfunctional team

    B.   Cross-functional team

    C.   Functional team

    D.   Vertical team

    E.   Project team

The answer is B
Teams of people from different organizational functions are effective in determining things like product development.

100. **Groupthink is:**

A. A form of group brainstorming

B. The collective culture of an organization

C. The aggregate knowledge set of a team

D. The innovation created in large groups of highly specialized people

E. A state in which conformity takes priority over critical thought

The answer is E
Groupthink generally involves one person becoming the authority figure who is surrounded by "yes men", although blind agreement with the first person to have an idea also occurs, as people try to trade thought and responsibility for social inclusion.

Description of the Examination

The College Mathematics exam covers material generally taught in a college course for nonmathematics majors and majors in fields not requiring knowledge of advanced mathematics.

The examination contains approximately 60 questions to be answered in 90 minutes. Some of these are pretest questions that will not be scored. Any time test takers spend on tutorials and providing personal information is in addition to the actual testing time.

An online scientific (nongraphing) calculator will be available during the examination. Although a calculator is not necessary to answer most of the questions, there may be a few problems whose solutions are difficult to obtain without using a calculator. Since no calculator is allowed during the examination except for the online calculator provided, is it recommended that prior to the examination you become familiar with the use of the online calculator.

For more information about downloading the practice version of the scientific (nongraphing) calculator, please visit the College Mathematics description on the CLEP website, **clep.collegeboard.org**

It is assumed that test takes are familiar with currently taught mathematics vocabulary, symbols, and notation.

Knowledge and Skills Required

Questions on the College Mathematics examination require test takers to demonstrate the following abilities in the approximate proportion indicated.

- Solving routine, straightforward problems (about 50% of the examination)
- Solving nonroutine problems requiring an understanding of concepts and the application of skills and concepts (about 50% of the examination)

The subject matter of the College Mathematics examination is drawn from the following topics. The percentages next to the main topics indicate the approximate percentage of exam questions on that topic.

20%   Algebra
- Solving equations, linear inequalities, and systems of linear equations by analytical and graphical methods
- Interpretation, representation, and evaluation of functions: numerical,

graphical, symbolic, and descriptive methods
- Graphs of functions: translations, horizontal and vertical reflections, and symmetry about the x-axis, the y-axis, and the origin
- Linear and exponential growth
- Applications

10% Counting and Probability
- Counting problems: the multiplication rule, combinations and permutations
- Probability: union, intersection, independent events, mutually exclusive events, complementary events, conditional probabilities, and expected value
- Applications

15% Data Analysis and Statistics
- Data interpretation and representation: tables, bar graphs, line graphs, circle graphs, pie charts, scatterplots, and histograms
- Numerical summaries of data:

mean (average), median, mode, and range
- Standard deviation, normal distribution (conceptual questions only)
- Applications

20% Financial Mathematics
- Percents, percent change, markups, discounts, taxes, profit, and loss
- Interest: simple, compound, continuous interest, effective interest rate, effective annual yield or annual percentage rate (APR)
- Present value and future value
- Applications

10% Geometry
- Properties of triangles and quadrilaterals: perimeter, area, similarity, and the Pythagorean theorem
- Parallel and perpendicular lines
- Properties of circles: circumference, area, central angles, inscribed angles, and sectors
- Applications

15% **Logic and Sets**
- Logical operations and statements: conditional statements, conjunctions, disjunctions, negations, hypotheses, logical conclusions, converses, inverses, counterexamples, contrapositives, logical equivalence
- Set relationships, subsets, disjoint sets, equality of sets, and Venn diagrams
- Operations on sets: union, intersection, complement, and Cartesian product
- Applications

10% **Numbers**
- Properties of numbers and their operations: integers and rational, irrational, and real numbers (including recognizing rational and irrational numbers)
- Elementary number theory: factors and divisibility, primes and composites, odd and even integers, and the fundamental theorem of arithmetic

- Measurement: unit conversion, scientific notation, and numerical precision
- Absolute value
- Applications

SAMPLE TEST

DIRECTIONS: Read each item and select the best response.

1. Which of the following is closed under division?

    I. $\left\{\dfrac{1}{3}, 1, 3\right\}$

    II. $\{-1, 1\}$
    III. $\{-1, 0, 1\}$

    A. I only

    B. II only

    C. III only

    D. I and II

    E. II and III

2. Which of the following is always composite if x is an odd positive integer and y is an even positive integer greater than 1?

    A. $x + y$

    B. $|x + y|$

    C. $x + 2y$

    D. $3x + y$

    E. $3xy$

3. Find the LCM of 25, 18, and 24.

    A. 1200

    B. 1800

    C. 2400

    D. 3600

    E. 10,800

4. Solve for x:
    $|3x| + 6 = 21$

    A. $[9, -5]$

    B. $[-9, 5]$

    C. $[-5, 0, 5]$

    D. $[-5, 5]$

    E. $[-9, 9]$

5. Which graph represents the solution set for

$x^2 - 5x > -6$?

A.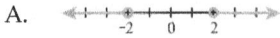

B.

C.

D.

E.

6. What is the equation of the graph shown below?

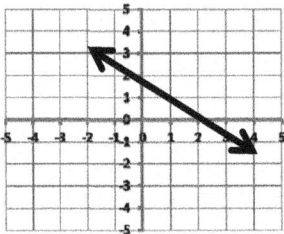

A. $x + 2y = 4$

B. $x - 2y = 4$

C. $2x + y = 4$

D. $x + 2y = -4$

E. $x - 2y = -4$

7. Solve the following inequality: $-2x > 4$

A. $x > -2$

B. $x < -2$

C. $x > 2$

D. $x > -8$

E. $x < 2$

8. Which equation represents a circle centered on the origin with radius 3?

A. $x^2 + y^2 = 3$

B. $x^2 + y^2 = 6$

C. $x^2 + y^2 = 9$

D. $x^2 + y^2 = 36$

E. $x^2 - y^2 = 9$

9. Given that D is a distance, M is a mass, T is a time, and V is a velocity, which of the following units could be used to measure $\dfrac{MTV}{D}$?

   A. feet

   B. meters

   C. grams

   D. seconds

   E. miles per hour

10. Cubic meters are used to measure which of the following?

    A. Distance

    B. Length

    C. Area

    D. Volume

    E. Mass

11. What figure best describes a data set in which many items are clustered near the median value with a smaller number of values less than or greater than the median at greater distances on each side?

    A. A parabola

    B. A normal curve

    C. A line of best fit

    D. A Cartesian curve

    E. A Newtonian curve

12. If you prove a theorem by showing that an attempt to prove the opposite of the theorem leads to a contradiction, you are using the logical strategy called:

    A. Inductive reasoning

    B. Exhaustive proof

    C. Proof by attraction

    D. Direct proof

    E. Indirect proof

13. Compute the area of the shaded region, given a radius of 7 meters. Point O is the center.

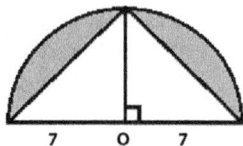

7 O 7

A. 14.0

B. 28.0

C. 55.9

D. 104.9

E. 153.9

14. A garden measures 25 m by 40 m, including a circular fishpond with radius 3 m. What is the area of the garden not including the fishpond?

A. 101.7 m²

B. 111.2 m²

C. 971.7 m²

D. 981.2 m²

E. 990.6 m²

15. The base of cone A has 3 times as great an area as the base of cone B, but the height of cone A is only $\frac{1}{3}$ the height of cone B. Which statement is true?

A. Cone A has 9 times the volume of cone B.

B. Cone A has 3 times the volume of cone B.

C. Cone A and cone B have the same volume.

D. Cone B has 3 times the volume of cone A.

E. Cone B has 9 times the volume of cone A.

16. Find the area of the figure depicted below.

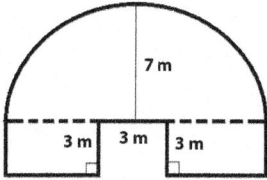

A. 109.9 m^2

B. 118.9 m^2

C. 142.9 m^2

D. 144.9 m^2

E. 186.9 m^2

17. State the domain of the function
$$f(x) = \frac{2x - 14}{x^2 - 9}.$$

A. $x \neq 3$

B. $x \neq 3, 7$

C. $x \neq 3, -3$

D. $x \neq 7$

E. $x = 3, -3, 7$

18. Which of the following is a factor of the expression $6x^2 - 5x - 14$?

A. $3x + 7$

B. $6x + 7$

C. $6x - 7$

D. $6x - 5$

E. $x + 2$

19. Solve for x by factoring:
$$x^2 + x - 6 = 0$$

A. $x = (-3, 2)$

B. $x = (3, -2)$

C. $x = (-6, 1)$

D. $x = (6, -1)$

E. no real solutions

20. Which of the following is equivalent to $\sqrt[b]{x^a}$?

    A. $x^{\frac{a}{b}}$

    B. $x^{\frac{b}{a}}$

    C. $a^{\frac{x}{b}}$

    D. $b^{\frac{x}{a}}$

    E. $a^{\frac{b}{x}}$

21. Given $f(x) = 2x + 1$ and $g(x) = x^2 - 1$, determine $g(f(x))$.

    A. $4x^2 + 4x - 1$

    B. $4x^2 + 4x + 1$

    C. $4x^2$

    D. $4x^2 - 1$

    E. $4x^2 + 4x$

22. Compute the median for the following data set: $\{9, 11, 18, 13, 12, 21\}$

    A. 12

    B. 12.5

    C. 13

    D. 14

    E. 15.5

23. Which graph represents the equation?

$$y = x^2 + 3x?$$

A.

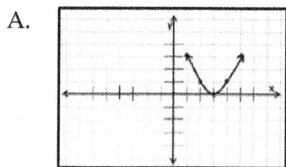

B.

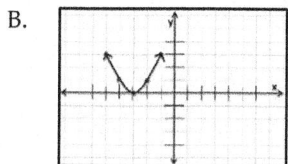

C.

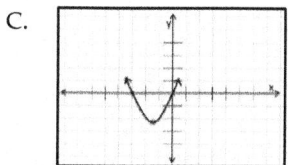

D.

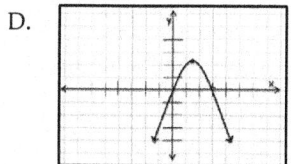

E.

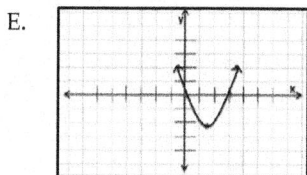

24. What would be the best measure of central tendency for the following collection of high temperatures on 10 successive days?

{27, 24, 33, 24, 36, 65, 34, 30, 28, 29}

A. Mean

B. Either mean or median

C. Median

D. Mode

E. Either median or mode

25. If the correlation between two variables is zero, the association between the two variables is

A. Negative linear

B. Positive linear

C. Quadratic

D. Direct variation

E. Random

26. Which of the following is not a valid method of collecting statistical data?

   A. Random sampling

   B. Systematic sampling

   C. Volunteer response

   D. Weighted sampling

   E. Cylindrical sampling

27. A jar contains 3 red marbles and 7 green ones. What is the probability that a marble picked at random from the jar will be red?

   A. $\dfrac{1}{3}$

   B. $\dfrac{1}{7}$

   C. $\dfrac{3}{7}$

   D. $\dfrac{3}{10}$

   E. $\dfrac{7}{10}$

28. A die is rolled several times. What is the probability that a 6 will not appear before the fourth roll of the die?

   A. $\dfrac{125}{216}$

   B. $\dfrac{625}{1296}$

   C. $\dfrac{1}{2}$

   D. $\dfrac{5}{6}$

   E. $\dfrac{1}{216}$

29. There is a 30% chance of rain this Saturday and a 30% chance of rain on Sunday as well. What is the chance of rain on both days?

   A. 9%

   B. 30%

   C. 49%

   D. 60%

   E. 70%

30. Which equation matches the data in the table?

x	3	4	5	6
y	7	8	9	10

A. $y = 2x - 1$

B. $y = 2x + 1$

C. $y = -x + 10$

D. $y = x + 4$

E. $y = x - 4$

31. Which table could be generated by the equation?

$$y = x^2 + 2x - 1?$$

A.

x	1	2	3	4
y	2	5	8	11

B.

x	1	2	3	4
y	4	9	16	25

C.

x	1	2	3	4
y	1	5	11	19

D.

x	1	2	3	4
y	2	7	13	21

E.

x	1	2	3	4
y	2	7	14	23

32. The fees charged by a parking garage are as follows:

Hours	1	2	3	4	5
Fee	$12	$19	$26	$33	$40

How would you summarize the fees charged?

A. $12 an hour

B. $5 plus $7 per hour

C. $15 an hour with a $3 discount

D. $4 plus $8 per hour

E. $3 plus $9 per hour

33. Which of the following is a solution to
$x^2 + 4x + 4 = 25$?

A. 2

B. −2

C. −7

D. −3

E. 5

34. Solve the following system of equations:

$$2x + y = 8$$
$$4x + 2y = 20$$

A. $x = 2, y = 4$

B. $x = 3, y = 1$

C. $x = 4, y = 0$

D. no solutions

E. an infinite number of solutions

35. If an initial deposit of $10,000 is made to a savings account with interest compounded continuously at an annual rate of 6%, how much money is in the account after 5 years?

A. $13,498.59

B. $3498.59

C. $13,382.26

D. $3,382.26

E. $13,000.00

36. A dance team comes prepared with a tango, a waltz, a disco number, a salsa routine, and a ballet selection. In how many different orders can they present their routines?

   A. 5

   B. 25

   C. 120

   D. 625

   E. 3125

37. You can choose 3 selections from a buffet table with 8 dishes. How many different plates can you choose?

   A. 6

   B. 24

   C. 56

   D. 336

   E. 6561

38. Leah has 4 blouses, 3 skirts, and 6 pairs of shoes. How many different outfits can she dress herself in?

   A. 12

   B. 13

   C. 24

   D. 72

   E. 720

39. Hiroshi surveys his classmates to find what percent of them come to school on the bus, by car, by subway, by bicycle, or on foot. What is the best way to display his results?

   A. A line graph

   B. A box plot

   C. A stem-and-leaf plot

   D. A scatterplot

   E. A circle graph

40. Which equation could be used as a line of best fit for the scatterplot below?

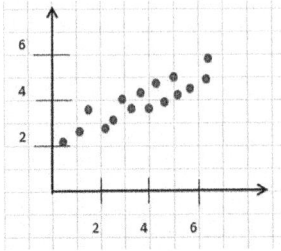

A. $y = \frac{1}{2}x + 2$

B. $y = 2x + 2$

C. $y = -2x + 2$

D. $y = \frac{1}{2}x - 2$

E. $y = \frac{1}{2}x + 2$

41. To find the standard variation of a data set, you first compute the square of the distance of each data item from the mean of all the data items. Then what do you do?

A. Add all the squared distances and take the square root of the result.

B. Find the mean of the squared distances and take the square root of the result.

C. Multiply the squared distances and take the nth root of the result.

D. Multiply the square root of the sum of the squared distances by the mean of the squared distances.

E. Multiply the sum of the squared distances by the square root of the mean of the squared distances.

42. In which data set is the mode greater than the median?

   A. {9,11,11,12,14}

   B. {13,15,17,19,21}

   C. {8,11,12,12,19}

   D. {9,9,9,14,20}

   E. {7,11,13,14,14}

43. Of the 200 students in the junior class, 8% are in the Spanish Club. How many juniors are in the Spanish Club?

   A. 4

   B. 8

   C. 16

   D. 20

   E. 25

44. When Olga bought a boat for $1750, she paid an excise tax of $78.75. What was the percent of the tax?

   A. 4.5%

   B. 5.5%

   C. 6.3%

   D. 7%

   E. 7.5%

45. A bank account pays 5% interest yearly. How large an amount would have to be deposited to earn $75 interest in a year?

   A. $375

   B. $875

   C. $1200

   D. $1500

   E. $3750

46. A stock previously trading at $96 a share is now trading at $88 a share. What is the percent of change in the value of the stock?

   A. −8%

   B. −8.3%

   C. −12%

   D. −12.5%

   E. −16%

47. The admission price to tour the Haunted House has been changed from $25 to $30. What is the percent of change in the admission price?

   A. 5%

   B. 16.7%

   C. 20%

   D. 25%

   E. 30%

48. Eileen's Bakery had expenses of $62,500 last year and sales of $68,750. What was the profit as a percent of the expenses?

   A. 6.25%

   B. 10%

   C. 12%

   D. 15%

   E. 16.7%

49. Tim's Typewriters had expenses of $26,200 last year and sales of $19,912. What was the loss as a percent of the expenses?

   A. 7%

   B. 8%

   C. 16.7%

   D. 20%

   E. 24%

50. A stock that had been selling at $30 a share increased its share price by 20%. Later in the day the same stock suffered a 20% decrease in its share price. What was the price at the end of the day?

    A. $24

    B. $28.80

    C. $30

    D. $33

    E. $36

51. A sweater is marked " 25% off." The sale price is $36. What was the price before the discount?

    A. $27

    B. $32

    C. $40

    D. $45

    E. $48

52. The sum of $1440 is deposited in a bank which pays 6% simple interest per year. After how many years will there be $1872 in the account?

    A. 2.5 years

    B. 3 years

    C. 4 years

    D. 5 years

    E. 8 years

53. A bank pays 5% interest on deposits, compounded yearly. If $14,000 is deposited, how much will be in the account 3 years later?

    A. $14,350

    B. $15,435

    C. $16,100

    D. $16,206.75

    E. $17,500

54. Which statement is logically equivalent to the following: If it's raining, my roof is leaking.

   A. If my roof isn't leaking, it isn't raining.

   B. If my roof is leaking, it's raining.

   C. If it isn't raining, my roof isn't leaking.

   D. If my roof is leaking, it's not raining

   E. If it's raining, my roof isn't leaking.

55. What is the union of set A and set B?

   Set A: {2,4,5,9,11}
   Set B: {3,5,8,11,13}

   A. {2, 3, 4, 5, 5, 8, 9, 11, 11, 13}

   B. {2, 3, 4, 5, 8, 9, 11, 13}

   C. {5, 11}

   D. {2, 3, 4, 8, 9, 13}

   E. {5, 9, 13, 20, 24}

56. What is the intersection of set A and set B?

   Set A: {1,3,7,9,10,12,14}
   Set B: {1,4,7,8,11,12,15}

   A. {1, 1, 3, 4, 7, 7, 8, 9, 10, 11, 12, 12, 14, 15}

   B. {1, 3, 4, 7, 8, 9, 10, 11, 12, 14, 15}

   C. {1, 7, 12}

   D. {1, 1, 7, 7, 12, 12}

   E. {3, 4, 8, 9, 10, 11, 14, 15}

57. Which statement is NOT implied by the Venn diagram below?

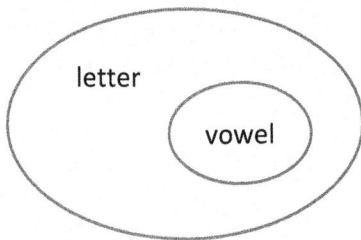

   A. No vowels are not letters.

   B. All vowels are letters.

   C. Some letters are vowels.

   D. Some letters are not vowels.

   E. Some vowels are not letters.

289

58. A total of 150 students have signed up for musical activities. There are 82 students in the choir and 80 students in the band. How many students are in both the band and the choir?

   A. 12

   B. 24

   C. 42

   D. 70

   E. 162

59. Chris's older brother Mike is 2 years younger than Florence. When Tom's younger sister Rhoda was 8, Chris was 3 Florence is not older than Rhoda. Name the five people in ascending order of age.

   A. Tom, Rhoda, Florence, Mike, Chris

   B. Tom, Florence, Rhoda, Mike, Chris

   C. Chris, Mike, Florence, Rhoda, Tom

   D. Chris, Mike, Rhoda, Florence, Tom

   E. Chris, Rhoda, Mike, Florence, Tom

60. Disprove the following statement by offering a counterexample: "Multiplying two numbers together produces a larger number than either of the two original numbers."

   A. $\sqrt{2} \times \sqrt{2}$

   B. 1.25×1.78

   C. -3×-3

   D. 0.5×0.6

   E. -0.8×-0.3

ANSWER KEY

Question Number	Correct Answer	Your Answer	Question Number	Correct Answer	Your Answer
1	B		31	E	
2	E		32	B	
3	B		33	C	
4	D		34	D	
5	E		35	A	
6	A		36	C	
7	B		37	C	
8	C		38	D	
9	C		39	E	
10	D		40	A	
11	B		41	B	
12	E		42	E	
13	B		43	C	
14	C		44	A	
15	C		45	D	
16	A		46	B	
17	C		47	C	
18	B		48	B	
19	A		49	E	
20	A		50	B	
21	E		51	E	
22	B		52	D	
23	C		53	D	
24	C		54	A	
25	E		55	B	
26	E		56	C	
27	D		57	E	
28	A		58	A	
29	A		59	C	
30	D		60	D	

RATIONALES

1. Which of the following is closed under division?

$$\text{I. } \left\{\frac{1}{3}, 1, 3\right\}$$
$$\text{II. } \{-1, 1\}$$
$$\text{III. } \{-1, 0, 1\}$$

A. I only

B. II only

C. III only

D. I and II

E. II and III

The answer is B

Set I is not closed under division, because $\dfrac{1}{3}$ divided by 3 is $\dfrac{1}{9}$, a number outside the set. Set III is not closed under division, because it is not possible to divide either –1 or 1 by 0.

2. Which of the following is always composite if x is an odd positive integer and y is an even positive integer greater than 1 ?

A. $x + y$

B. $|x + y|$

C. $x + 2y$

D. $3x + y$

E. $3xy$

The answer is E

$3xy$ must be composite, since 3, x, and y are all factors.

292

3.   Find the LCM of 25, 18, and 24.

    A. 1200

    B. 1800

    C. 2400

    D. 3600

    E. 10,800

The answer is B
The LCM must contain 2 factors of 5 to be a multiple of 25. It must contain 2 factors of 3 and a factor of 2 to be a multiple of 18. And it must contain 3 factors of 2 and a factor of 3 to be a multiple of 24. Therefore, the LCM must contain the following factors: $5 \times 5 \times 3 \times 3 \times 2 \times 2 \times 2 = 1800$

4.   Solve for x: $|3x| + 6 = 21$

    A. $[9, -5]$

    B. $[-9, 5]$

    C. $[-5, 0, 5]$

    D. $[-5, 5]$

    E. $[-9, 9]$

The answer is D
Write two equations to express the two possibilities:

$$3x + 6 = 21$$
$$-3x + 6 = 21$$

Solving the two equations gives 5 and –5.

5.   **Which graph represents the solution set for** $x^2 - 5x > -6$?

A.

B.

C.

D.

E.

The answer is E

Gathering all terms on the left gives $x^2 - 5x + 6 > 0$. Replace the inequality symbol with an equals sign and solve for x: $x = 2$, and $x = 3$. A graph of the parabola makes clear that it is greater than 0 for x-values less than 2 or greater than 3 or greater, but less than 0 when $2 \leq x \leq 3$.

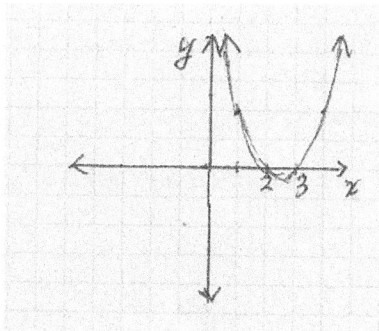

6.   What is the equation of the graph shown below?

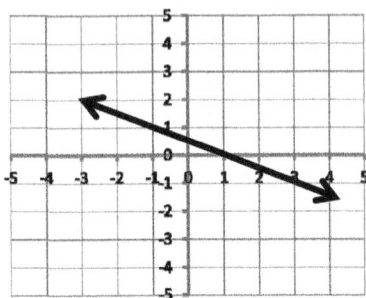

A. $x + 2y = 4$

B. $x - 2y = 4$

C. $2x + y = 4$

D. $x + 2y = -4$

E. $x - 2y = -4$

The answer is A
Replacing x with 0 gives a y-intercept of 2. Replacing y with 0 gives an x-intercept of 4. The equation is linear, so a line can be drawn between the two points to complete the graph.

7.   Solve the following inequality: $-2x > 4$

A. $x > -2$

B. $x < -2$

C. $x > 2$

D. $x > -8$

E. $x < 2$

The answer is B
To solve for x, you must divide by –2, but dividing by a negative number reverses the inequality, so the result is $x < -2$.

8.   Which equation represents a circle centered on the origin with radius 3 ?

    A. $x^2 + y^2 = 3$

    B. $x^2 + y^2 = 6$

    C. $x^2 + y^2 = 9$

    D. $x^2 + y^2 = 36$

    E. $x^2 - y^2 = 9$

The answer is C

The equation for a circle centered on the origin is $x^2 + y^2 = r^2$. Since $r = 3$, the equation in this case is $x^2 + y^2 = 9$.

9.   Given that D is a distance, M is a mass, T is a time, and V is a velocity, which of the following units could be used to measure $\dfrac{MTV}{D}$?

    A.   feet

    B.   meters

    C.   grams

    D.   seconds

    E.   miles per hour

The answer is C

Try some sample units and see how they interact:
Let the distance be in miles, the mass be in grams, the time be in hours, and the velocity in miles per hour. Then the units to express $\dfrac{MTV}{D}$ would be

$$g \times h \times \frac{mi}{h} \times \frac{1}{mi}$$ Hours and miles cancel out, leaving only grams.

10. Cubic meters are used to measure which of the following?

    A. Distance

    B. Length

    C. Area

    D. Volume

    E. Mass

The answer is D
Distance and length are measured in linear meters. Area is measured in square meters. Mass is not measured in meters of any kind. Of the choices, only volume is measured in cubic meters.

11. What figure best describes a data set in which many items are clustered near the median value with a smaller number of values less than or greater than the median at greater distances on each side?

    A. A parabola

    B. A normal curve

    C. A line of best fit

    D. A Cartesian curve

    E. A Newtonian curve

The answer is B
The figure described is a normal curve, called normal because data from the natural world tend to present a shape in which median values are commoner than extreme ones.

12.   If you prove a theorem by showing that an attempt to prove the opposite of the theorem leads to a contradiction, you are using the logical strategy called:

A.   Inductive reasoning

B.   Exhaustive proof

C.   Proof by attraction

D.   Direct proof

E.   Indirect proof

The answer is E
Such a proof is called "indirect" because it uses the opposite of the theorem instead of the theorem itself.

13.   Compute the area of the shaded region, given a radius of 7 meters. Point O is the center.

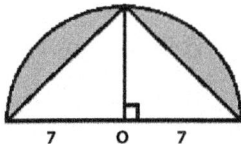

A.   14.0

B.   28.0

C.   55.9

D.   104.9

E.   153.9

The answer is B

The area of the half circle is $\dfrac{49\pi}{2}$ The two triangles are equivalent to a

square 7 meters on a side. So the shaded area $= \dfrac{49\pi}{2} - 49 \approx 28.0.$

14. A garden measures 25 m by 40 m, including a circular fishpond with radius 3 m. What is the area of the garden not including the fishpond?

    A. 101.7 m^2

    B. 111.2 m^2

    C. 971.7 m^2

    D. 981.2 m^2

    E. 990.6 m^2

The answer is C

The area of the garden is $25 \times 40 = 1000 \text{ m}^2$. The area of the fishpond is $3^2 \pi \approx 28.3 \text{ m}^2$. The difference is about 971.7 m².

15. The base of cone A has 3 times as great an area as the base of cone B, but the height of cone A is only $\frac{1}{3}$ the height of cone B.

Which statement is true?

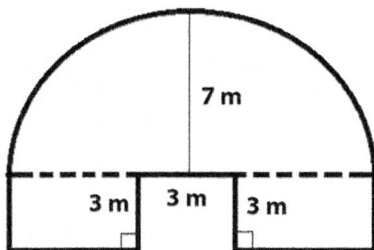

A. Cone A has 9 times the volume of cone B.

B. Cone A has 3 times the volume of cone B

C. Cone A and cone B have the same volume.

D. Cone B has 3 times the volume of cone A.

E. Cone B has 9 times the volume of cone A.

The answer is C

Let h be the height of cone B and let b be the area of the base of cone B. Using the formula for the volume of a cone, the volume of cone B is $\frac{1}{3}bh.$. The base of cone $A = 3b$, while the height of cone $A = \frac{h}{3}$. Therefore, the volume of cone A is $\frac{1}{3}(3b)\left(\frac{h}{3}\right) = \frac{1}{3}bh$, the same as cone B.

16. Find the area of the figure depicted below.

    A. 109.9 m^2

    B. 118.9 m^2

    C. 142.9 m^2

    D. 144.9 m^2

    E. 186.9 m^2

The answer is A

The area of the circle is $\dfrac{49\pi}{2}$. The dotted line equals a diameter, twice the length of the radius, or 14. Subtracting the gap of 3 m, the two rectangles add up to a length of 11 m times a width of 3 m So the total area is

$$\dfrac{49\pi}{2}+33 \approx 109.9 \text{ m}^2.$$

17. State the domain of the function $f(x)=\dfrac{2x-14}{x^2-9}$.

    A. $x \neq 3$

    B. $x \neq 3,7$

    C. $x \neq 3,-3$

    D. $x \neq 7$

    E. $x = 3,-3,7$

The answer is C

The domain must exclude values of x that would cause the denominator of the function to equal 0. Therefore, both –3 and 3 are excluded from the domain.

18.   Which of the following is a factor of the expression
$6x^2 - 5x - 14$?

A. $3x + 7$

B. $6x + 7$

C. $6x - 7$

D. $6x - 5$

E. $x + 2$

The answer is B
To factor the expression, multiply 6 times 14 to get 84. Then look for two factors of 84 that differ by 5: 7 and 12. Use these factors to rewrite the middle term as $7x - 12x$. You can then factor the expression as $(6x + 7)(x - 2)$.

19.   Solve for x by factoring: $x^2 + x - 6 = 0$

A. $x = (-3, 2)$

B. $x = (3, -2)$

C. $x = (-6, 1)$

D. $x = (6, -1)$

E.   no real solutions

The answer is A
Factoring the left side of the equation gives us $(x + 3)(x - 2) = 0$. Setting each factor equal to 0 gives us solutions of –3 and 2.

20.   Which of the following is equivalent to $\sqrt[b]{x^a}$?

A. $x^{\frac{a}{b}}$

B. $x^{\frac{b}{a}}$

C. $a^{\frac{x}{b}}$

D. $b^{\frac{x}{a}}$

E. $a^{\frac{b}{x}}$

The answer is A
Taking the bth root of x^a is equivalent to dividing the exponent of x^a by b.

21.   Given $f(x) = 2x + 1$ and $g(x) = x^2 - 1$, determine $g(f(x))$.

A. $4x^2 + 4x - 1$

B. $4x^2 + 4x + 1$

C. $4x^2$

D. $4x^2 - 1$

E. $4x^2 + 4x$

The answer is E
If $f(x) = 2x + 1,\ g(f(x)) = (2x + 1)^2 - 1 = 4x^2 - 4x.$

22. **Compute the median for the following data set:**
{9, 11, 18, 13, 12, 21}

A. 12

B. 12.5

C. 13

D. 14

E. 15.5

The answer is B

In ascending order, the set is {9, 11, 12, 13, 18, 21}

Since there are an even number of data items, the median is halfway between the two most central items when the items are put in ascending order, in this case the third and fourth.

23. **Which graph represents the equation?**

$$y = x^2 + 3x?$$

A.

B.

C.

D.

E.

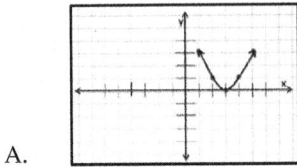

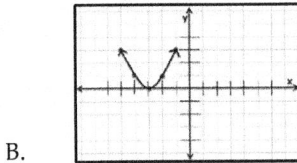

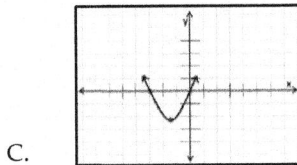

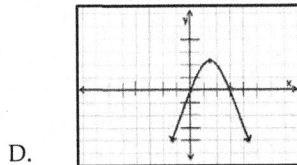

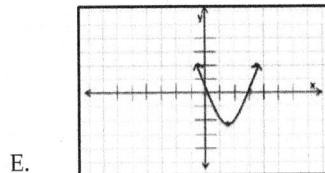

The answer is C

Since $x^2 + 3x$ can be factored as $x(x+3)$, the function has zeroes at 0 and
–3. Since the first term is positive, the parabola opens up. Choice C fits these
specifications.

24. What would be the best measure of central tendency for the following collection of high temperatures on 10 successive days?

$$\{27, 24, 33, 24, 36, 65, 34, 30, 28, 29\}$$

A. Mean

B. Either mean or median

C. Median

D. Mode

E. Either median or mode

The answer is C
Since the data contains an outlier, the mean would be skewed too high. The mode is the smallest data item and therefore also not a good representation. The median is the best available representation of the data as a whole.

25. If the correlation between two variables is zero, the association between the two variables is

A. Negative linear

B. Positive linear

C. Quadratic

D. Direct variation

E. Random

The answer is E
Choices A, B, C, and D all describe some form of correlation between the two variables. Only a random association shows zero correlation.

26. Which of the following is not a valid method of collecting statistical data?

A. Random sampling

B. Systematic sampling

C. Volunteer response

D. Weighted sampling

E. Cylindrical sampling

The answer is E
Choices A, B, C, D describe methods of data collection with varying degrees of potential usefulness and prohibition. There is no such thing as cylindrical sampling.

27. A jar contains 3 red marbles and 7 green ones. What is the probability that a marble picked at random from the jar will be red?

A. $\dfrac{1}{3}$

B. $\dfrac{1}{7}$

C. $\dfrac{3}{7}$

D. $\dfrac{3}{10}$

E. $\dfrac{7}{10}$

The answer is D
Three marbles are red out of a total of 10 marbles, yielding a probability of 3/10.

307

28.   A die is rolled several times. What is the probability that a 6 will not appear before the fourth roll of the die?

A. $\dfrac{125}{216}$

B. $\dfrac{625}{1296}$

C. $\dfrac{1}{2}$

D. $\dfrac{5}{6}$

E. $\dfrac{1}{216}$

The answer is A

Each time the die is rolled, the chance of rolling a number other than 6 is $\dfrac{5}{6}$.

The probability that this will happen three times is $\dfrac{5}{6} \times \dfrac{5}{6} \times \dfrac{5}{6} = \dfrac{125}{216}$.

29.   There is a 30% chance of rain this Saturday and a 30% chance of rain on Sunday as well. What is the chance of rain on both days?

   A.   9%

   B.   30%

   C.   49%

   D.   60%

   E.   70%

The answer is A
The probability of two things both happening is the product of the two probabilities: 0.3(0.3) = 0.09 = 9%.

30.   Which equation matches the data in the table?

x	3	4	5	6
y	7	8	9	10

   A. $y = 2x - 1$

   B. $y = 2x + 1$

   C. $y = -x + 10$

   D. $y = x + 4$

   E. $y = x - 4$

The answer is D
Each y-value is 4 greater than the corresponding x-value.

31. Which table could be generated by the equation?

$$y = x^2 + 2x - 1?$$

A.

x	1	2	3	4
y	2	5	8	11

B.

x	1	2	3	4
y	4	9	16	25

C.

x	1	2	3	4
y	1	5	11	19

D.

x	1	2	3	4
y	2	7	14	23

E.

x	1	2	3	4
y	2	7	13	21

The answer is E

Substitute <u>each</u> x-value into the equation and see if the result matches the y-value. Only in table E do all the y-values correspond to the values found by substituting the x-values into the equation.

32.   The fees charged by a parking garage are as follows:

Hours	1	2	3	4	5
Fee	$12	$19	$26	$33	$40

How would you summarize the fees charged?

A. $12 an hour

B. $5 plus $7 per hour

C. $15 an hour with a $3 discount

D. $4 plus $8 per hour

E. $3 plus $9 per hour

The answer is B
Each additional hour costs $7 more, so the rate must be $7 an hour, which leaves $5 as the initial fee.

33.   Which of the following is a solution to $x^2 + 4x + 4 = 25$?

A. 2

B. −2

C. −7

D. −3

E. 5

The answer is C
Taking the square root of both sides yields $x + 2 = \pm 5$. Therefore, $x = 3$ or −7.

34.   Solve the following system of equations:

$$2x + y = 8$$
$$4x + 2y = 20$$

A. $x = 2, y = 4$

B. $x = 3, y = 1$

C. $x = 4, y = 0$

D.   no solutions

E.   an infinite number of solutions

The answer is D
Multiply the first equation by 2 and subtract from the second equation. The result is $0 = 4$. A system of equations that resolves to an untrue statement has no solutions.

35.   **If an initial deposit of $10,000 is made to a savings account with interest compounded continuously at an annual rate of 6%, how much money is in the account after 5 years?**

A, $13,498.59

B. $3498.59

C. $13,382.26

D. $3,382.26

E. $13,000.00

The answer is A
Continuously compounded interest is calculated using the formula Pe^{rt}, where P is the amount of the principal, r is the annual rate, and t is the time in years.

$$10,000 \times e^{0.06 \times 5} = 10,000 e^{0.3} \approx 13,498.59.$$

36.   A dance team comes prepared with a tango, a waltz, a disco number, a salsa routine, and a ballet selection. In how many different orders can they present their routines?

A. 5

B. 25

C. 120

D. 625

E. 3125

The answer is C
Any of the 5 routines could be the first number. The second number could be any of the remaining 4, the third could be any of the remaining 3, and so on. The total number of choices is $5 \times 4 \times 3 \times 2 \times 1 = 120$.

37.   You can choose 3 selections from a buffet table with 8 dishes. How many different plates can you choose?

A. 6

B. 24

C. 56

D. 336

E. 6561

The answer is C
Since the order of items on your plate does not matter, it is combinations rather than permutations we need to find. The number of combinations of k items out of n possible selections is given by the formula $\dfrac{n!}{(n-k)!k!}$.

$$\frac{8!}{5!3!} = 56$$

38. Leah has 4 blouses, 3 skirts, and 6 pairs of shoes. How many different outfits can she dress herself in?

   A. 12

   B. 13

   C. 24

   D. 72

   E. 720

The answer is D
By the Fundamental Counting Principle, the number of different outfits is $4 \times 3 \times 6 = 72.$

39. Hiroshi surveys his classmates to find what percent of them come to school on the bus, by car, by subway, by bicycle, or on foot. What is the best way to display his results?

   A. A line graph

   B. A box plot

   C. A stem-and-leaf plot

   D. A scatterplot

   E. A circle graph

The answer is E
A circle graph is the best way to display what portion of the whole data set is occupied by each item.

40. Which equation could be used as a line of best fit for the scatterplot below?

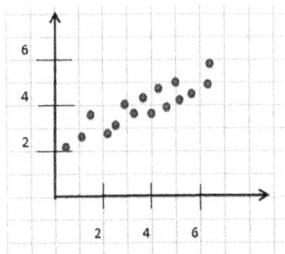

A. $y = \dfrac{1}{2}x + 2$

B. $y = 2x + 2$

C. $y = -2x + 2$

D. $y = \dfrac{1}{2}x - 2$

E. $y = 2x - 2$

The answer is A

The data appear to start around 2, and the y-values are generally rising less fast than the x-values, so the slope appears to be less than 1. $\dfrac{1}{2}x + 2$ is the best fit among the choices.

41. To find the standard variation of a data set, you first compute the square of the distance of each data item from the mean of all the data items. Then what do you do?

    A. Add all the squared distances and take the square root of the result.

    B. Find the mean of the squared distances and take the square root of the result.

    C. Multiply the squared distances and take the nth root of the result.

    D. Multiply the square root of the sum of the squared distances by the mean of the squared distances.

    E. Multiply the sum of the squared distances by the square root of the mean of the squared distances.

The answer is B
Choice B correctly completes the process of finding a standard variation.

42. In which data set is the mode greater than the median?

    A. $\{9,11,11,12,14\}$

    B. $\{13,15,17,19,21\}$

    C. $\{8,11,12,12,19\}$

    D. $\{9,9,9,14,20\}$

    E. $\{7,11,13,14,14\}$

The answer is E
In choice E, the median is 13 and the mode 14.

43.   Of the 200 students in the junior class, 8% are in the Spanish Club. How many juniors are in the Spanish Club?

A. 4

B. 8

C. 16

D. 20

E. 25

The answer is C
The number of juniors in the Spanish club is 8 % of 200 or 16.

44.   When Olga bought a boat for $1750, she paid an excise tax of $78.75. What was the percent of the tax?

A. 4.5%

B. 5.5%

C. 6.3%

D. 7%

E. 7.5%

The answer is A
To find the percent of tax, divide the tax by the sales price and multiply by 100.

$$\frac{78.75}{1750} \times 100 = 4.5,$$ so the tax rate is 4.5%.

45. A bank account pays 5% interest yearly. How large an amount would have to be deposited to earn $75 interest in a year?

    A. $375

    B. $875

    C. $1200

    D. $1500

    E. $3750

The answer is D
If a principal of x dollars earns $75 at 5% interest, then $0.5x = 75$. Multiplying both sides by 20 yields $x = 1500$, so the amount of the principal must be $1500.

46. A stock previously trading at $96 a share is now trading at $88 a share. What is the percent of change in the value of the stock?

    A. −8%

    B. −8.3%

    C. −12%

    D. −12.5%

    E. −16%

The answer is B
The percent of change is found by dividing the amount of the change by the original value, then multiplying by 100. The change is −$8, and the original amount is $96. $\dfrac{-8}{96} \times 100 \approx -8.3,$ So the stock price has changed about −8.3%.

318

47. The admission price to tour the Haunted House has been changed from $25 to $30. What is the percent of change in the admission price?

   A.   5%

   B.   16.7%

   C.   20%

   D.   25%

   E.   30%

The answer is C

The amount of change is +$5, and the original value is $25. $\dfrac{5}{25} = \dfrac{1}{5} = 20\%$.

48. Eileen's Bakery had expenses of $62,500 last year and sales of $68,750. What was the profit as a percent of the expenses?

   A.   6.25%

   B.   10%

   C.   12%

   D.   15%

   E.   16.7%

The answer is B

The amount of change is $6,250. $\dfrac{6250}{62500} = \dfrac{1}{10} = 10\%$.

49.   Tim's Typewriters had expenses of $26,200 last year and sales of $19,912. What was the loss as a percent of the expenses?

A. 7%

B. 8%

C. 16.7%

D. 20%

E. 24%

The answer is E
The amount of loss was $6288, and 6288./26200 = 24%.

50.   A stock that had been selling at $30 a share increased its share price by 20%. Later in the day the same stock suffered a 20% decrease in its share price. What was the price at the end of the day?

A. $24

B. $28.80

C. $30

D. $33

E. $36

The answer is B
After the $30 price increased by 20%, it was $36.

51. A sweater is marked "25% off." The sale price is $36. What was the price before the discount?

   A. $27

   B. $32

   C. $40

   D. $45

   E. $48

The answer is E
If the original price has been decreased by 25%, the sale price is 75% of the original. Solving $36 = 0.75x$ yields $x = 48$.

52. The sum of $1440 is deposited in a bank which pays 6% simple interest per year. After how many years will there be $1872 in the account?

   A. 2.5 years

   B. 3 years

   C. 4 years

   D. 5 years

   E. 8 years

The answer is D
After each year is completed, the amount in the account is increased by $0.06(1440) = $86.40 dollars. The number of years required to bring the account to $1872 is $\dfrac{1872-1440}{86.40} = \dfrac{432}{86.40} = 5$

321

53.   A bank pays 5% interest on deposits, compounded yearly. If
       $14,000 is deposited, how much will be in the account 3 years
       later?

    A. $14,350

    B. $15,435

    C. $16,100

    D. $16,206.75

    E. $17,500

The answer is D
The amount in the account after 3 years will be
$$14,000 \times 1.05^3 = \$16.206.75.$$

54.   Which statement is logically equivalent to the following: If it's
       raining, my roof is leaking.

    A. If my roof isn't leaking, it isn't raining.

    B. If my roof is leaking, it's raining.

    C. If it isn't raining, my roof isn't leaking.

    D. If my roof is leaking, it's not raining

    E. If it's raining, my roof isn't leaking.

The answer is A
The contrapositive of a true statement is also true. In this case, rain always
makes my roof leak, so the absence of a leak could only be explained by the
absence of rain.

55.   What is the union of set A and set B?

Set A: {2,4,5,9,11}
Set B: {3,5,8,11,13}

A.   {2,3,4,5,5,8,9,11,11,13}

B.   {2,3,4,5,8,9,11,13}

C.   {5,11}

D.   {2,3,4,8,9,13}

E.   {5,9,13,20,24}

The answer is B
The union of the two sets contains every number that is in either set.
Numbers that are in both sets are included only once in the union set.

56.   What is the intersection of set A and set B?

Set A: {1,3,7,9,10,12,14}
Set B: {1,4,7,8,11,12,15}

A.   {1,1,3,4,7,7,8,9,10,11,12,12,14,15}

B.   {1,3,4,7,8,9,10,11,12,14,15}

C.   {1,7,12}

D.   {1,1,7,7,12,12}

E.   {3,4,8,9,10,11,14,15}

The answer is C
The intersection of the two sets contains only those numbers that are in both
sets.

57.   Which statement is NOT implied by the Venn diagram below?

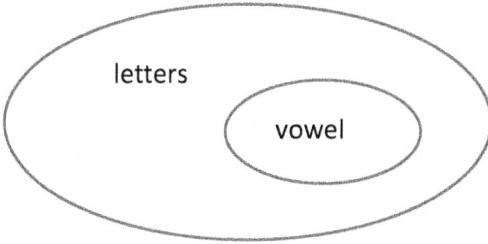

A.   No vowels are not letters.

B.   All vowels are letters.

C.   Some letters are vowels.

D.   Some letters are not vowels.

E.   Some vowels are not letters.

The answer is E

The diagram shows that the class of vowels is totally included in the class of letters, so there are no vowels that are not letters.

58.   A total of 150 students have signed up for musical activities. There are 82 students in the choir and 80 students in the band. How many students are in both the band and the choir?

A. 12

B. 24

C. 42

D. 70

E. 162

The answer is A
The sum of 82 choir members and 80 band members is 162, but only 150 students are involved. The explanation is that 12 students are in both the band and choir, and are therefore counted twice when the two memberships are added.

59.   Chris's older brother Mike is 2 years younger than Florence. When Tom's younger sister Rhoda was 8 , Chris was 3. Florence is younger than Rhoda. Name the five people in ascending order of age.

A.   Tom, Rhoda, Florence, Mike, Chris

B.   Tom, Florence, Rhoda, Mike, Chris

C.   Chris, Mike, Florence, Rhoda, Tom

D.   Chris, Mike, Rhoda, Florence, Tom

E.   Chris, Rhoda, Mike, Florence, Tom

The answer is C
Statement 1 allows as to put Chris, Mike, and Florence in ascending order. The second statement allows us to put Rhoda and Tom in ascending order. Since Florence is younger than Rhoda, both Rhoda and Tom are older than Chris, Mike, and Florence, allowing us to put all five in ascending order.

60.   Disprove the following statement by offering a counterexample:
        "Multiplying two numbers together produces a larger number than
        either of the two original numbers."

   A. $\sqrt{2} \times \sqrt{2}$

   B. 1.25×1.78

   C. -3×-3

   D. 0.5×0.6

   E. -0.8×-0.3

The answer is D

The product of 0.5 and 0.6 is 0.3, which is smaller than either of the two
original numbers. The other multiplications produce a product larger than
either of the numbers multiplied.

Description of the Examination

The Introductory Psychology examination covers material that is usually taught in a one-semester undergraduate course in introductory psychology. It stresses basic facts, concepts and generally accepted principles in thirteen areas listed in the following section.

The examination contains approximately 95 questions to be answered in 90 minutes. Some of these are pretest questions that will not be scored. Any time candidates spend on tutorials and providing personal information is in addition to the actual testing time.

Please note that the questions on the CLEP Introductory Psychology exam will continue to adhere to the terminology, criteria and classifications referred to in the fourth edition of the *Diagnostic and Statistical Manual of Mental Disorders* (DSM-IV-TR) until further notice.

Knowledge and Skills Required

Questions on the Introductory Psychology examination require candidates to demonstrate one or more of the following abilities.
- Knowledge of terminology, principles and theory
- Ability to comprehend, evaluate and analyze problem situations
- Ability to apply knowledge to new situations

The subject matter of the Introductory Psychology examination is drawn from the following topics. The percentages next to the main topics indicate the approximate percentage of exam questions on that topic.

8%-9% **History, Approaches, Methods**
- History of psychology
- Approaches: biological, behavioral, cognitive, humanistic, psychodynamic
- Research methods: experimental, clinical, correlations
- Ethics in research

8%-9% **Biological Bases of Behavior**
- Endocrine system
- Etiology
- Functional organization of the nervous system
- Genetics
- Neuroanatomy
- Physiological techniques

7%-8% **Sensation and Perception**
- Attention
- Other senses: somesthesis,

olfaction, gustation, vestibular system
- Perceptual development
- Perceptual process
- Receptor processes: vision, audition
- Sensory mechanisms: thresholds, adaptation

5%-6% States of Consciousness
- Hypnosis and meditation
- Psychoactive drug effects
- Sleep and dreaming

10%-11% Learning
- Biological bases
- Classical conditioning
- Cognitive process in learning
- Observational learning
- Operant conditioning

8%-9% Cognition
- Intelligence and creativity
- Language
- Memory
- Thinking and problem solving

7%-8% Motivation and Emotion
- Biological bases
- Hunger, thirst, sex, pain
- Social motivation
- Theories of emotion
- Theories of motivation

8%-9% Developmental Psychology
- Dimensions of development: physical, cognitive, social, moral
- Gender identity and sex roles
- Heredity-environment issues
- Research methods: longitudinal, cross-sectional
- Theories of development

7%-8% Personality
- Assessment techniques
- Growth and adjustment
- Personality theories and approaches
- Research methods: idiographic, nomothetic

- Self-concept, self-esteem

8%-9% Psychological Disorders and Health
- Affective disorders
- Anxiety disorders
- Dissociative disorders
- Health, stress and coping
- Personality disorders
- Psychoses
- Somatoform disorders
- Theories of psychopathology

7%-8% Treatment of Psychological Disorders
- Behavioral therapies
- Biological and drug therapies
- Cognitive therapies
- Community and preventive approaches
- Insight therapies: psychodynamic

and humanistic approaches

7%-8% Social Psychology
- Aggression/antisocial behavior
- Attitudes and attitude change
- Attribution processes
- Conformity, compliance, obedience
- Group dynamics
- Interpersonal perception

3%-4% Statistics, Tests and Measurement
- Descriptive statistics
- Inferential statistics
- Measurement of intelligence
- Mental handicapping conditions
- Reliability and validity
- Samples, populations, norms
- Types of tests

SAMPLE TEST

DIRECTIONS: Read each item and select the best response.

1. Which of the following describes an expression of favor or disfavor for a person, place, thing, or event?

    A. Attitude

    B. Belief

    C. Cognition

    D. Drive

    E. Behavior

2. Which of the following is a theory by Ajzen and Fishbein that outlines a model for the prediction of behavioral intention?

    A. Cognitive Dissonance Theory

    B. Social Judgment Theory

    C. Theory of Reasoned Action

    D. Information Integration Theory

    E. Congruity Theory

3. According to Petty and Cacioppo's Elaboration Likelihood Model, when a person is persuaded by the likeability of a speaker, he or she is using which processing route?

    A. Central

    B. Heuristic

    C. Peripheral

    D. Systemic

    E. None of the above

4. Which of the following psychologists coined the term *group dynamics* to describe the positive and negative forces within groups of people?

    A. Maslow

    B. Lewin

    C. Freud

    D. Pavlov

    E. Skinner

5. Which of the following "deals with how the social perceiver uses information to arrive at causal explanations for events?"

   A. Cognitive Dissonance Theory
   B. Classical conditioning
   C. Psychoanalysis
   D. Attribution Theory
   E. Frequency Theory

6. Which of the following describes obedience?

   A. The act of changing one's beliefs and attitudes to match those of other members of a social group

   B. The act of following orders without question because they come from a legitimate authority

   C. The act of adapting one's actions to another's wishes or rules

   D. The act of influencing another's attitudes, beliefs, or behaviors

   E. The act of establishing credibility and authority

7. Paul is driving to work when another driver cuts him off in traffic. Paul begins shouting and pounding on the steering wheel. Paul is exhibiting _____.

A. passive aggression

B. passivity

C. instrumental aggression

D. dissociative rage

E. impulsive aggression

8. According to Maslow's Hierarchy of Needs, humans must satisfy their physiological needs before they will desire to satisfy which other category of needs?

A. Safety

B. Belonging

C. Esteem

D. Self-actualization

E. All of the above

9. Which of the following is considered a prosocial emotion?

A. Anger

B. Sadness

C. Shame

D. Happiness

E. Awe

10. Which of the following statements is true of long-term memory?

A. Long-term memory has nearly infinite storage capacity.

B. Long-term memory is also known as working memory.

C. Long-term memory allows people to temporarily store and manipulate visual images.

D. Long-term memory has a shorter duration than working memory.

E. None of the above statements are true of long-term memory.

11. The term *chunking* refers to

    A. transferring memories from short-term to long-term

    B. combining small bits of information into larger, familiar pieces

    C. sensory memory

    D. repeating information over and over to increase the duration of time in which it stays in short-term memory

    E. an organizational process for cataloguing memories

12. The smallest units of speech are called

    A. vowels

    B. syllables

    C. phonemes

    D. semantic

    E. syntax

13. Which of the following terms describes the process by which memories fade over time?

    A. Memory loss

    B. Memory fade

    C. Memory decay

    D. Memory delay

    E. Memory recall

14. The study of psychology began in _____ and was established by _____.

    A. The United States; Freud

    B. Germany; Freud

    C. Germany; Ebbinghaus

    D. The United States; Skinner

    E. France; Piaget

15. Conduction aphasia is caused by which of the following?

   A. Disruptions in the connection between the Wernicke's and Broca's areas

   B. Disruptions in the ability to consolidate information at a neural level

   C. Short-term memory loss due to retrograde amnesia

   D. Blockage of neural circuits in working memory

   E. Damage to the cerebellum

16. An experiment that produces identical results each time is considered which of the following?

   A. Valid, but not reliable

   B. Reliable, but not valid

   C. Valid and reliable

   D. Reliable with questionable validity

   E. Valid with questionable reliability

17. The assumption that maladaptive thought patterns and behaviors are learned is associated with which of the following?

   A. Behavioral therapy

   B. Cognitive therapy

   C. Psychoanalytic therapy

   D. Rogerian therapy

   E. Group therapy

18. You have conducted two experiments in which you failed to get the same result although the conditions under which both experiments are identical. It is clear that the measurement lacks which of the following?

   A. Face validity

   B. Construct validity

   C. Inter-rater reliability

   D. Reliability

   E. Internal validity

19. When is punishment most effective is changing or suppressing behavior?

A. Punishment is most effective when it is delayed, inconsistent, and mild.

B. Punishment is most effective when it is immediate, consistent, and intense.

C. Punishment is most effective when it is explained.

D. Punishment is most effective when it is immediate, consistent, and mild.

E. Punishment is most effective when it is vague.

20. A psychologist administers the same IQ test three times to the same subject and receives identical or similar results each time. However, many scholars argue that IQ tests do not measure intelligence, but rather measure one's test-taking ability. This suggests that IQ tests are which of the following?

A. Valid but not reliable

B. Both valid and reliable

C. Neither valid nor reliable

D. Reliable but not valid

E. Lacking internal reliability

335

21. Which of the following attempts to establish an unpleasant response to the object that produces an undesired behavior?

    A. Systematic desensitization

    B. Implosion therapy

    C. Aversive classical conditioning

    D. Punishment

    E. Unconditioned stimulus

22. The ability to imitate the behavior of others and perform the same behavior under the same or similar conditions describes which of the following?

    A. Modeling

    B. Shaping

    C. Imitation

    D. Reinforcement

    E. Play

23. Which approach to psychology suggests that people are controlled by their environments?

    A. Humanism

    B. Behaviorism

    C. Psychodynamic

    D. Cognitive

    E. Biological

24. Which of the following statements best describes the evolutionary perspective of psychology?

A. The evolutionary approach explains human behavior in terms of classical and operational conditioning.

B. The evolutionary approach studies the effects of genes on human behavior.

C. The evolutionary approach seeks to understand the function of different mental processes.

D. The evolutionary approach explains human behavior in terms of the selective pressures that shape behavior.

E. The evolutionary approach seeks to study the whole person.

25. Which of the following psychologist founded the psychodynamic perspective of psychology?

A. Sigmund Freud

B. Ivan Pavlov

C. B. F. Skinner

D. Abraham Maslow

E. Carl Rogers

26. Jane's experiment did not produce significant results and she is afraid that her paper will not get published. She decides to change some of the numbers in her data to get the outcome she desired. Jane has violated which general principle of ethics, according to the APA?

A. Beneficence

B. Fidelity

C. Responsibility

D. Justice

E. Integrity

27. With which of the following research methods does the observer have direct contact with the group he or she is observing?

A. Field experiment

B. Participant observation

C. Laboratory experiment

D. Natural observation

E. Controlled observation

28. The requirement that researchers explain to potential participants the purpose and nature of a study, as well as any possible risks associated with participation, is known as

A. informed consent

B. integrity

C. researcher responsibility

D. liability

E. confidentiality

29. Which of the following topics do cognitive psychologists study?

A. Behavior

B. Emotion

C. Self-actualization

D. Memory and learning

E. Genes and DNA

30. Which of the following psychologists can be categorized as a humanist?

A. Sigmund Freud

B. Ivan Pavlov

C. B. F. Skinner

D. Abraham Maslow

E. Wilhelm Wundt

31. Which of the following prevents a person from moving while experiencing dreams?

A. REM atonia

B. NREM sleep

C. Muscle relaxers

D. Beta waves

E. Alpha waves

32. During the beginning of sleep, when a person is still relatively awake, the brain produces

   A. Rapid Eye Movement

   B. Beta Waves

   C. Alpha waves

   D. Hallucinations

   E. None of the above

33. Dreaming most often occurs during which phase of sleep?

   A. Stage 1 (theta waves)

   B. Stage 2 (sleep spindles)

   C. Stage 3 (delta waves)

   D. Stage 4 (REM)

   E. Dreaming occurs in all of the above stages

34. Which of the following is NOT considered a benefit of meditation?

   A. Greater capacity for empathy

   B. Decreased stress

   C. Increased anxiety

   D. Increased gray matter in the brain

   E. Improved sleep

35. Research on sleep provides evidence to support the ideas that

   A. sleep is not necessary in the production of brain proteins

   B. all individuals require at least 8 hours of sleep each night for optimal functioning

   C. low-quality sleep and sleep deprivation negatively impact mood

   D. sleep does not impact learning

   E. sleep is not essential to well-being

36. A dog learns that when it rings a bell, its owner will let it outside. This is an example of which kind of learning?

    A. Modeling

    B. Classical conditioning

    C. Instrumental conditioning

    D. Stimulus control

    E. Operant conditioning

37. Which of the following types of learning involves reinforcement and punishment?

    A. Operant conditioning

    B. Classical conditioning

    C. Habituation

    D. Instrumental conditioning

    E. Modeling

38. Which of the following types of learning involves a stimulus and response?

    A. Operant conditioning

    B. Classical conditioning

    C. Habituation

    D. Instrumental conditioning

    E. Modeling

39. Which of the following depicts Freud's stages of psychosexual development in the correct order?

    A. Oral, phallic, anal, latent, genital

    B. Genital, phallic, anal, latent, oral

    C. Phallic, oral, anal, genital, latent

    D. Oral, anal, phallic, latent, genital

    E. Anal, oral, latent, phallic, genital

40. According to Piaget, the sensorimotor stage occurs between which ages?

    A. 0-2 years

    B. 2-7 years

    C. 7-11 years

    D. 11-15 years

    E. 15+ years

41. Piaget's theory of cognitive development is concerned with which population?

    A. Newborn babies

    B. Children of all ages

    C. Young adults

    D. Mature adults

    E. Elderly adults

42. Which theory explains how parent-child relationships emerge and influence subsequent development?

    A. Psychoanalytic theory

    B. Social learning theory

    C. Cognitive development

    D. Attachment theory

    E. None of the above

43. Developmental psychologists often prefer which type of research design?

    A. Experimental

    B. Participant observation

    C. Case study

    D. Cross-sectional

    E. Longitudinal

44. On which level of Kohlberg's moral stages is a child whose morality is based on rules and punishments?

   A. Level I. Pre-conventional/premoral

   B. Level II: Conventional/Role conformity

   C. Level III: Post-conventional/Self-accepted moral principles

   D. Level IV: Fully moral

   E. None of the above

45. Which of the following disorders is characterized by hallucinations and delusions such as hearing voices?

   A. Depression

   B. Obsessive compulsive disorder

   C. Bipolar disorder

   D. Schizophrenia

   E. Mania

46. Which of the following drugs has stimulant and hallucinogenic effects?

   A. Molly

   B. Adderall

   C. Marijuana

   D. Cocaine

   E. Pain killers

47. Jimmy is experiencing recurring negative thoughts, a loss of interest in activities that used to excite him, trouble sleeping, and a loss of appetite. From which of the following disorders is Jimmy most likely suffering?

   A. Depression

   B. Obsessive compulsive disorder

   C. Bipolar disorder

   D. Schizophrenia

   E. Mania

48. Which of the following anxiety disorders is characterized by a fear of losing control, being trapped, or panicking in public places?

A. Acrophrobia

B. Agoraphobia

C. Generalized anxiety disorder

D. Post-traumatic stress disorder

E. General panic attack

49. Antidepressants are often associated with which of the following side effects?

A. Insomnia

B. Dry mouth

C. An increase in suicidal thoughts

D. Decreased sexual drive and function

E. All of the above

50. Which of the following types of disorders is characterized by real physical symptoms that cannot be fully explained by a medical condition, the effects of a drug, or another mental disorder?

A. Personality disorders

B. Anxiety disorders

C. Somatoform disorders

D. Affective disorders

E. Dissociative disorders

51. Which of the following personality disorders is characterized by an exaggerate sense of self-importance, a strong desire to be admired, and a lack of empathy?

A. Borderline personality disorder

B. Histrionic personality disorder

C. Avoidant personality disorder

D. Narcissistic personality disorder

E. Antisocial personality disorder

52. People with which of the following personality disorders often lack empathy and remorse, and exhibit aggressive, impulsive, reckless, or irresponsible behavior?

    A. Borderline personality disorder

    B. Histrionic personality disorder

    C. Avoidant personality disorder

    D. Narcissistic personality disorder

    E. Antisocial personality disorder

53. A person who experiences depressive and manic episodes may have which of the following disorders?

    A. Depression

    B. Obsessive compulsive disorder

    C. Bipolar disorder

    D. Schizophrenia

    E. Mania

54. Hypochondria is an example of which of the following types of disorders?

    A. Personality disorders

    B. Anxiety disorders

    C. Somatoform disorders

    D. Affective disorders

    E. Dissociative disorders

55. The _____ nervous system prepares the body for action, while the _____ nervous system keeps the body still.

    A. Sympathetic, parasympathetic

    B. Autonomic, sympathetic

    C. Parasympathetic, autonomic

    D. Sympathetic, autonomic

    E. Parasympathetic, sympathetic

56. Which of the following theories of emotion suggests that people experience emotions because they perceive physiological changes in their bodies?

   A. Cognitive appraisal

   B. Schachter and Singer's Two-Factor Theory

   C. Evolutionary Theory

   D. James-Lange Theory

   E. Cannon-Bard Theory

57. Which of the following terms describes a theoretical construct that is used to explain the reasons for people's actions, desires, and needs?

   A. Emotion

   B. Empathy

   C. Motivation

   D. Hunger

   E. Thirst

58. Which of the following is an example of intrinsic motivation?

   A. Money

   B. Receiving an award

   C. Feeling a sense of accomplishment

   D. Winning a prize

   E. A cheering crowd

59. Which of the following drugs is commonly abused by college students because its stimulant effects can aid in studying?

   A. Cocaine

   B. Marijuana

   C. Adderall

   D. Alcohol

   E. All of the above

60. Which of the following theories suggests that we are motivated to take action based on our biological needs?

A. Drive reduction theory

B. Arousal theory

C. Instinct theory

D. Maslow's Hierarchy of Needs

E. Goal-setting theory

61. Which of the following theories of emotion argues that one's experience of emotion depends on their physiological arousal and cognitive interpretation of that arousal?

A. Cognitive appraisal

B. Schachter and Singer's Two-Factor Theory

C. Evolutionary Theory

D. James-Lange Theory

E. Cannon-Bard Theory

62. Which of the following is the correct term for vision that comes from the side of the eye?

A. Peripheral vision

B. Tunnel vision

C. Perceptive vision

D. Sensation

E. Detection

63. Which of the following correctly lists Piaget's stages of cognitive development?

    A. Sensorimotor, concrete operational, preoperational, formal operational

    B. Preoperational, formal operational, concrete operational, sensorimotor

    C. Formal operational, concrete operational, preoperational, sensorimotor

    D. Concrete operational, preoperational, sensorimotor, formal operational

    E. Sensorimotor, preoperational, concrete operational, formal operational

64. Which of the following therapies is considered a last resort method of treating depression when all other therapies have failed?

    A. Antidepressant medication

    B. Psychoanalytic therapy

    C. Cognitive-behavioral therapy

    D. Electroconvulsive shock therapy

    E. Group therapy

65. Which of the following best describes a cross-sectional study?

   A. A researcher follows the same participants over a period of time.

   B. A researcher examines different groups of people who share one or more similar characteristics.

   C. A researcher brings people into a lab and has them complete a task.

   D. A researcher observes people in their homes.

   E. A researcher surveys observes people in public.

66. Psychology researchers use which of the following terms to describe thinking, reasoning, and solving problems?

   A. Emotion

   B. Intuition

   C. Perception

   D. Sensation

   E. Cognition

67. Lawrence Kohlberg is known for his research in the area of _____ development.

   A. Cognitive

   B. Moral

   C. Personality

   D. Emotional

   E. Physical

68. Which of the following statements about antidepressants do most psychology researchers and practitioners consider true?

   A. Antidepressants are helpful in treating some forms of depression.

   B. For many patients, antidepressants are less helpful than individual therapy in treating depression.

   C. Antidepressants alone are not enough to successfully treat depression in many patients.

   D. All of the above

   E. None of the above

69. Which of the following therapies helps people work through problems by interacting with one or more therapists as well as other individuals experiencing similar struggles?

    A. Individual therapy

    B. Drug therapy

    C. Group therapy

    D. Psychoanalytic therapy

    E. Social-Emotional therapy

70. According to Kübler-Ross, the correct order of the stages of grief are:

    A. denial, anger, bargaining, depression, acceptance.

    B. anger, denial, depression, bargaining, acceptance.

    C. denial, depression, anger, acceptance, bargaining.

    D. depression, denial, anger, bargaining, acceptance.

    E. acceptance, denial, anger, bargaining, depression.

71. Which of the following correctly describes the difference between depression and grief?

   A. Grief often entails a sense of worthlessness whereas depression does not.

   B. Grief involves excessive guilt and depression does not.

   C. Grief lasts longer than major depression.

   D. Grief subsides after a period of time whereas depression often persists for extended periods of time.

   E. Grief is a clinical condition whereas depression is a normal, healthy emotion.

72. Cara describes herself as outgoing, funny and friendly. These characteristics are part of her

   A. self-esteem.

   B. motivation.

   C. self-concept.

   D. group identity.

   E. physique.

73. In personality research, which of the following describes personal characteristics that are biologically determined?

   A. Nature

   B. Environment

   C. State

   D. Trait

   E. Ego

74. Which of the following is not a standard method used to assess personality?

A. Self-reports

B. Observer-reports

C. Test data

D. Projective measures

E. Laboratory study

75. The Big Five personality traits are:

A. Humor, openness, extraversion, agreeableness, neuroticism.

B. Extraversion, agreeableness, enlightenment, openness, neuroticism

C. Openness, conscientiousness, extraversion, agreeableness, neuroticism.

D. Extraversion, introversion, humor, neuroticism, openness

E. Happiness, neuroticism, shyness, openness, extraversion

76. _____ refers to the pattern of thoughts, feelings, social adjustments and behaviors consistently exhibited over time.

A. Preferences

B. Self-esteem

C. Construct

D. Personality

E. Extraversion

77. Conscientiousness refers to one's

A. tendency to be creative, curious, and open to new ideas.

B. tendency to be organized and self-disciplined.

C. tendency to experience unpleasant emotions easily.

D. tendency to be compassionate and cooperative towards others.

E. tendency to exhibit to seek stimulation in the company of others.

78. Which of the following types of psychologists believe that one's personality consists of learned patterns?

    A. Emotional psychologists

    B. Humanists

    C. Behavioral psychologists

    D. Psychoanalytic theorists

    E. Cognitive psychologists

79. Kim lives in Alaska and says that a 60-degree day is warm. Steve lives in Arizona and thinks 60-degree weather is cold. Their perceptions differ because of

    A. their frame of reference

    B. where they place their attention

    C. perceptual constancy

    D. their personalities

    E. their top-down processing

80. Which of the following terms explains why roads appear to converge in the distance?

    A. Light and shadow

    B. Continuing patterns

    C. Texture gradient

    D. Linear perspective

    E. None of the above

81. Anything that can be perceived with one of the five senses is considered _____ stimulus, whereas _____ stimulus refers to the specific object upon which one is focused.

    A. Attended, environmental

    B. Image, recognition

    C. Environmental, attended

    D. Neural, retinal

    E. Neural, image

82. An image on the retina of the eye is transformed into electrical signals in a process known as which of the following?

   A. Transcendence

   B. Abduction

   C. Transformation

   D. Intensification

   E. Transduction

83. Which of the following is true of secondary reinforcers?

   A. They are learned.

   B. They are ineffective.

   C. They are more effective than primary reinforcers.

   D. They are innate.

   E. They are natural.

84. The analysis of information starting with features and building into a complete perception is known as which of the following?

   A. Perceptual constancy

   B. Top-down processing

   C. Bottom-up processing

   D. Chunking

   E. Linking

85. Which of the following allows humans to perceive the world in three dimensions?

   A. Depth perception

   B. Sensation

   C. Disparity

   D. Convergence

   E. Accommodation

86. Neurons are made up of which of the following?

A. Anterior cell, posterior cell, axon

B. Dendrite, soma, axon

C. Cell body, cell wall, nucleus

D. Myelin, dendrite, cell wall

E. None of the above

87. Which of the following describes the main function of myelin?

A. Myelin forms a protective coating over nerve axons.

B. Myelin decreases the speed with which information travels from nerve cell to nerve cell.

C. Myelin blocks reception of acetylcholine.

D. Myelin slows down nerve degeneration.

E. Myelin aids in the transference of neurotransmitters.

88. Neurotransmitters are released at which part of a cell?

A. Dendrite

B. Axon terminal

C. Nucleus

D. Soma

E. Myelin

89. Communication within a neuron is a(n) _____ process, while communication between neurons is a(n) _____ process.

A. Chemical; mechanical

B. Electrical; mechanical

C. Chemical; electrical

D. Electrical; chemical

E. Mechanical; electrical

90. Human behavior is influenced by genetic processes as well their environments and experiences. In psychology, this is known as which of the following?

    A. Genes versus experience

    B. Heredity versus environment.

    C. Climate versus science

    D. Nature versus nurture

    E. Genes versus personality

91. Which of the following is the main link between the brain and the glandular system in the human body?

    A. Hypothalamus

    B. Prefrontal cortex

    C. Central nervous system

    D. Sympathetic nervous system

    E. Parasympathetic nervous system

92. The endocrine system is responsible for which of the following functions?

    A. It pumps blood throughout the body.

    B. It brings oxygen into the body.

    C. It secretes hormones into the blood stream for communication between cells.

    D. It processes sensory information from the eyes and ears.

    E. None of the above.

93. An EEG records which of the following?

    A. The electrical rhythm of the heart.

    B. Electrical impulses from the brain.

    C. Hormone secretion in the bloodstream.

    D. Electrical currents in the body.

    E. The number of neurons in the brain.

94. In Pavlov's famous experiment, the dog's salivation over food was considered which of the following?

    A. Conditioned response

    B. Conditioned stimulus

    C. Automatic stimulus

    D. Unconditioned response

    E. Unconditioned stimulus

95. Which of the following scientists is known for studying operant conditioning?

    A. Pavlov

    B. Freud

    C. Maslow

    D. Piaget

    E. Skinner

ANSWER KEY

Question Number	Correct Answer	Your Answer	Question Number	Correct Answer	Your Answer	Question Number	Correct Answer	Your Answer
1	A		33	D		65	B	
2	C		34	C		66	E	
3	C		35	C		67	B	
4	B		36	E		68	D	
5	D		37	A		69	C	
6	B		38	B		70	A	
7	E		39	D		71	D	
8	E		40	A		72	C	
9	C		41	B		73	D	
10	A		42	D		74	E	
11	B		43	E		75	C	
12	C		44	A		76	D	
13	C		45	D		77	B	
14	C		46	A		78	C	
15	A		47	A		79	A	
16	D		48	B		80	D	
17	A		49	E		81	C	
18	D		50	C		82	E	
19	B		51	D		83	A	
20	D		52	E		84	C	
21	C		53	C		85	A	
22	A		54	C		86	B	
23	B		55	A		87	A	
24	D		56	D		88	B	
25	A		57	C		89	D	
26	E		58	C		90	D	
27	B		59	C		91	A	
28	A		60	A		92	C	
29	D		61	B		93	B	
30	D		62	A		94	D	
31	A		63	E		95	E	
32	B		64	D				

357

RATIONALES

1. Which of the following describes an expression of favor or disfavor for a person, place, thing, or event?

    A. Attitude

    B. Belief

    C. Cognition

    D. Drive

    E. Behavior

The answer is A.
The definition of an attitude is "an expression of favor or disfavor for a person, place, thing, or event."

2. Which of the following is a theory by Ajzen and Fishbein that outlines a model for the prediction of behavioral intention?

    A. Cognitive Dissonance Theory

    B. Social Judgment Theory

    C. Theory of Reasoned Action

    D. Information Integration Theory

    E. Congruity Theory

The answer is C.
Ajzen and Fishbein are known for developing the Theory of Reasoned Action, which outlines a model for the prediction of behavioral intention.

3. According to Petty and Cacioppo's Elaboration Likelihood Model, when a person is persuaded by the likeability of a speaker, he or she is using which processing route?

    A. Central

    B. Heuristic

    C. Peripheral

    D. Systemic

    E. None of the above

The answer is C.
Petty and Cacioppo's Elaboration Likelihood Model suggests that people process persuasive messages using one of two processing routes: the central route and the peripheral route. When a person is persuaded by thinking about the *content* of the message, such as the quality of the arguments and evidence presented, he or she is using the *central* route. When a person is persuaded by factors *other than the content of the message*, such as the likeability of the speaker, he or she is using the *peripheral* route.

4. Which of the following psychologists coined the term *group dynamics* to describe the positive and negative forces within groups of people?

    A. Maslow

    B. Lewin

    C. Freud

    D. Pavlov

    E. Skinner

The answer is B.
Kurt Lewin is known as the founder of Social Psychology. He was one of the first to study *group dynamics*, a term he coined himself. Maslow is known for his Hierarchy of Needs model. Freud is known for his psychodynamic theory. Pavlov is known for his work on classical conditioning.

5.   Which of the following "deals with how the social perceiver uses information to arrive at causal explanations for events?"

A.   Cognitive Dissonance Theory

B.   Classical conditioning

C.   Psychoanalysis

D.   Attribution Theory

E.   Frequency Theory

The answer is D.
The question provides the definition of Attribution Theory, which "deals with how the social perceiver uses information to arrive at causal explanations for events." Cognitive Dissonance Theory focuses on how humans strive for internal consistency (having one's attitudes match his or her behaviors). Classical Conditioning is a type of learning. Psychoanalysis is a branch of psychology founded by Sigmund Freud. Frequency Theory is related to the study of hearing.

6.   Which of the following describes obedience?

A.   The act of changing one's beliefs and attitudes to match those of other members of a social group

B.   The act of following orders without question because they come from a legitimate authority

C.   The act of adapting one's actions to another's wishes or rules

D.   The act of influencing another's attitudes, beliefs, or behaviors

E.   The act of establishing credibility and authority

The answer is B.
Obedience is "the act of following orders without question because they come from a legitimate authority."

7. Paul is driving to work when another driver cuts him off in traffic. Paul begins shouting and pounding on the steering wheel. Paul is exhibiting _____.

    A. passive aggression

    B. passivity

    C. instrumental aggression

    D. dissociative rage

    E. impulsive aggression

The answer is E.

Paul is clearly exhibiting aggressive behavior, but it does not go as far as dissociative rage. Impulsive aggression is marked by strong anger, emotional outbursts, and possible harm to another person. This is also known as hostile aggression. You can see impulsive aggression in Paul's behavior, as he is shouting and pounding the steering wheel. Instrumental aggression harms another person as a means to achieve an end goal (e.g., mugging someone or tackling someone in football). Passive aggression involves indirect expressions of hostility, such as through procrastination, sullenness, or repeated failure to accomplish tasks for which one is responsible.

8.   According to Maslow's Hierarchy of Needs, humans must satisfy
     their physiological needs before they will desire to satisfy which
     other category of needs?

     A.   Safety

     B.   Belonging

     C.   Esteem

     D.   Self-actualization

     E.   All of the above

The answer is E.
In Maslow's Hierarchy of Needs model, he suggests that humans must satisfy
their physiological needs, such as for food, clothing, and shelter, before they
will desire to satisfy any other needs, including all of the other needs listed
here.

9.   Which of the following is considered a prosocial emotion?

     A.   Anger

     B.   Sadness

     C.   Shame

     D.   Happiness

     E.   Awe

The answer is C.
Prosocial emotions are emotions that drive us to behave in ways that benefit
others and society. Shame is a prosocial emotion because it lets people know
when they have broken social and/or moral norms. Shame drives people to
correct their behavior to meet societal norms for appropriate and moral
behavior.

10. **Which of the following statements is true of long-term memory?**

    A. Long-term memory has nearly infinite storage capacity.

    B. Long-term memory is also known as working memory.

    C. Long-term memory allows people to temporarily store and manipulate visual images.

    D. Long-term memory has a shorter duration than working memory.

    E. None of the above statements are true of long-term memory.

The answer is A.
This is the only statement in this set that is true of long-term memory.

11. **The term *chunking* refers to**

    A. transferring memories from short-term to long-term

    B. combining small bits of information into larger, familiar pieces

    C. sensory memory

    D. repeating information over and over to increase the duration of time in which it stays in short-term memory

    E. an organizational process for cataloguing memories

The answer B.
Chunking refers to the process of combining small bits of information into larger, familiar pieces. For example, someone might look at a bunch of broccoli, carrots, and cauliflower and think of them collectively as "vegetables."

12. **The smallest units of speech are called**

    A. vowels

    B. syllables

    C. phonemes

    D. semantic

    E. syntax

The answer is C.
The smallest units of speech are called *phonemes*. The other words are related to language, but they do not describe the smallest units of speech.

13. **Which of the following terms describes the process by which memories fade over time?**

    A. Memory loss

    B. Memory fade

    C. Memory decay

    D. Memory delay

    E. Memory recall

The answer is C.
The process by which memories fade over time is called *memory decay*. The other options are distractions.

14. The study of psychology began in _____ and was established by _____.

    A. The United States; Freud

    B. Germany; Freud

    C. Germany; Ebbinghaus

    D. The United States; Skinner

    E. France; Piaget

The answer is C.
The study of psychology began in Germany in the 1870s. Hermann Ebbinghaus is considered a founding father of the field.

15. Conduction aphasia is caused by which of the following?

    A. Disruptions in the connection between the Wernicke's and Broca's areas

    B. Disruptions in the ability to consolidate information at a neural level

    C. Short-term memory loss due to retrograde amnesia

    D. Blockage of neural circuits in working memory

    E. Damage to the cerebellum

The answer is A.
Conduction aphasia is a specific (and rare) type of aphasia. It is a disconnection between the areas of the brain responsible for speech comprehension (Wernicke's area) and speech production (Broca's area).

365

16. An experiment that produces identical results each time is considered which of the following?

   A. Valid, but not reliable

   B. Reliable, but not valid

   C. Valid and reliable

   D. Reliable with questionable validity

   E. Valid with questionable reliability

The answer is D.
In terms of research methodology and results, *reliability* is the degree to which an assessment tool or experiment produces stable and consistent results. An experiment that produces identical results is reliable. *Validity* refers to the degree to which a test measures what it is intended to measure. In this case, we know that the experiment produces reliable results, but we do not know anything about its validity.

17. The assumption that maladaptive thought patterns and behaviors are learned is associated with which of the following?

   A. Behavioral therapy

   B. Cognitive therapy

   C. Psychoanalytic therapy

   D. Rogerian therapy

   E. Group therapy

The answer is A.
Behavioral therapy assumes that maladaptive thought patterns and behaviors are learned and, thus, they can be replaced with new learned thoughts and behaviors. Therefore, a goal of behavioral therapy is to help patients learn new ways of thinking and behaving that offer better coping and functioning.

18. You have conducted two experiments in which you failed to get the same result although the conditions under which both experiments are identical. It is clear that the measurement lacks which of the following?

    A. Face validity

    B. Construct validity

    C. Inter-rater reliability

    D. Reliability

    E. Internal validity

The answer is D.
Reliability is the degree to which an assessment tool or experiment produces stable and consistent results. If you're conducting identical experiments, they should yield similar results. If they do not, the measurements are not reliable.

19. When is punishment most effective is changing or suppressing behavior?

    A. Punishment is most effective when it is delayed, inconsistent, and mild.

    B. Punishment is most effective when it is immediate, consistent, and intense.

    C. Punishment is most effective when it is explained.

    D. Punishment is most effective when it is immediate, consistent, and mild.

    E. Punishment is most effective when it is vague.

The answer is B.
Research on operant conditioning demonstrates that punishments are most effective in modifying behavior when they are immediate, consistent, and intense. In other words, punishments must occur immediately after the indiscretion. Punishments must also be administered consistently. Finally, to be most effective, punishments should be intense.

20. A psychologist administers the same IQ test three times to the same subject and receives identical or similar results each time. However, many scholars argue that IQ tests do not measure intelligence, but rather measure one's test-taking ability. This suggests that IQ tests are which of the following?

   A. Valid but not reliable

   B. Both valid and reliable

   C. Neither valid nor reliable

   D. Reliable but not valid

   E. Lacking internal reliability

The answer is D.
Reliability is the degree to which an assessment tool or experiment produces stable and consistent results. Validity refers to the degree to which a test measures what it is intended to measure. The prompt in this question is suggesting that IQ tests are reliable but not valid.

21. Which of the following attempts to establish an unpleasant response to the object that produces an undesired behavior?

   A. Systematic desensitization

   B. Implosion therapy

   C. Aversive classical conditioning

   D. Punishment

   E. Unconditioned stimulus

The answer is C.
Classical conditioning is a process of learning in which a natural response (e.g., salivating) to a potent stimulus (e.g., food) comes to be elicited in response to a previously neutral stimulus (e.g., bell). This happens by repeated pairings of the unconditioned stimulus and the conditioned stimulus. Over time, the conditioned stimulus is able to produce the same response (i.e., conditioned response) as the unconditioned stimulus. Aversive classical conditioning is a type of behavior modification that seeks to reduce a undesired behavior by establishing an unpleasant response to that behavior.

22. The ability to imitate the behavior of others and perform the same behavior under the same or similar conditions describes which of the following?

   A. Modeling

   B. Shaping

   C. Imitation

   D. Reinforcement

   E. Play

The answer is A.
The definition of modeling is "the ability to imitate the behavior of others and perform the same behavior under the same or similar conditions." The other choices are distractions from the correct term for this definition.

23. **Which approach to psychology suggests that people are controlled by their environments?**

   A. Humanism

   B. Behaviorism

   C. Psychodynamic

   D. Cognitive

   E. Biological

The answer is B.
The behaviorist approach suggests that people are controlled by their environments. The humanist approach considers the entire person and emphasizes humans' drive for self-actualization. The psychodynamic approach looks at the forces that drive human behavior and emotion. Cognitive psychology examines mental processes, such as attention, thinking, memory, language, and learning. The biological approach studies the physiological, developmental, and genetic mechanisms that drive behavior.

24. **Which of the following statements best describes the evolutionary perspective of psychology?**

   A. The evolutionary approach explains human behavior in terms of classical and operational conditioning.

   B. The evolutionary approach studies the effects of genes on human behavior.

   C. The evolutionary approach seeks to understand the function of different mental processes.

   D. The evolutionary approach explains human behavior in terms of the selective pressures that shape behavior.

   E. The evolutionary approach seeks to study the whole person.

The answer is D.
Choice A is describing behaviorism. Choice B is describing biological psychology. Choice C is describing cognitive psychology. Choice E is describing humanism.

25. Which of the following psychologist founded the psychodynamic perspective of psychology?

   A. Sigmund Freud

   B. Ivan Pavlov

   C. B. F. Skinner

   D. Abraham Maslow

   E. Carl Rogers

The answer is A.
Pavlov and Skinner were behaviorists. Maslow and Rogers were humanists.

26. Jane's experiment did not produce significant results and she is afraid that her paper will not get published. She decides to change some of the numbers in her data to get the outcome she desired. Jane has violated which general principle of ethics, according to the APA?

   A. Beneficence

   B. Fidelity

   C. Responsibility

   D. Justice

   E. Integrity

The answer is E.
The integrity principle of ethics, according to the APA, requires researchers to report their findings accurately and honestly.

27.   With which of the following research methods does the observer have direct contact with the group he or she is observing?

   A.   Field experiment

   B.   Participant observation

   C.   Laboratory experiment

   D.   Natural observation

   E.   Controlled observation

The answer is B.
The participant observer study design allows researchers to blend in with the group of people they are studying.

28.   The requirement that researchers explain to potential participants the purpose and nature of a study, as well as any possible risks associated with participation, is known as

   A.   informed consent

   B.   integrity

   C.   researcher responsibility

   D.   liability

   E.   confidentiality

The answer is A.
Informed consent tells potential participants the purpose and nature of a study, as well as any potential risks, before they engage in it.

29. **Which of the following topics do cognitive psychologists study?**

    A. Behavior

    B. Emotion

    C. Self-actualization

    D. Memory and learning

    E. Genes and DNA

The answer is D.
Cognitive psychologists study mental processes such as thought, memory, learning, language, and attention.

30. **Which of the following psychologists can be categorized as a humanist?**

    A. Sigmund Freud

    B. Ivan Pavlov

    C. B. F. Skinner

    D. Abraham Maslow

    E. Wilhelm Wundt

The answer is D.
Abraham Maslow is the only humanist among these choices.

31.   Which of the following prevents a person from moving while experiencing dreams?

A.   REM atonia

B.   NREM sleep

C.   Muscle relaxers

D.   Beta waves

E.   Alpha waves

The answer is A.
Dreams most often occur during REM sleep. REM atonia keeps people from moving while experiencing dreams.

32.   During the beginning of sleep, when a person is still relatively awake, the brain produces

A.   Rapid Eye Movement

B.   Beta Waves

C.   Alpha waves

D.   Hallucinations

E.   None of the above

The answer is B.
Beta waves are those associated with wakefulness.

33.   **Dreaming most often occurs during which phase of sleep?**

   A.   Stage 1 (theta waves)

   B.   Stage 2 (sleep spindles)

   C.   Stage 3 (delta waves)

   D.   Stage 4 (REM)

   E.   Dreaming occurs in all of the above stages

The answer is D.
Dreams most often occur during REM sleep (Stage 4).

34.   **Which of the following is NOT considered a benefit of meditation?**

   A.   Greater capacity for empathy

   B.   Decreased stress

   C.   Increased anxiety

   D.   Increased gray matter in the brain

   E.   Improved sleep

The answer is C.
Meditation offers a host of benefits and it is especially helpful in reducing
anxiety. It is not known to *increase* anxiety.

35. Research on sleep provides evidence to support the ideas that

A. sleep is not necessary in the production of brain proteins

B. all individuals require at least 8 hours of sleep each night for optimal functioning

C. low-quality sleep and sleep deprivation negatively impact mood

D. sleep does not impact learning

E. sleep is not essential to well-being

The answer is C.
The other statements are inaccurate.

36. A dog learns that when it rings a bell, its owner will let it outside. This is an example of which kind of learning?

A. Modeling

B. Classical conditioning

C. Instrumental conditioning

D. Stimulus control

E. Operant conditioning

The answer is E.
Operant conditioning is sometimes called *instrumental learning*. It involves learning through trial and consequences. Reinforcements and punishments are core tools through which operant behavior modification occurs. In this case, the dog learns that the behavior of ringing a bell is rewarded by its owner opening the door.

37. **Which of the following types of learning involves reinforcement and punishment?**

    A. Operant conditioning

    B. Classical conditioning

    C. Habituation

    D. Instrumental conditioning

    E. Modeling

The answer is A.

Operant conditioning is sometimes called *instrumental learning*. It involves learning through trial and consequences, as well as rewards and punishments.

38. **Which of the following types of learning involves a stimulus and response?**

    A. Operant conditioning

    B. Classical conditioning

    C. Habituation

    D. Instrumental conditioning

    E. Modeling

The answer is B.

Classical conditioning is a process of learning in which a natural response (e.g., salivating) to a potent stimulus (e.g., food) comes to be elicited in response to a previously neutral stimulus (e.g., bell). This happens by repeated pairings of the unconditioned stimulus and the conditioned stimulus. Over time, the conditioned stimulus is able to produce the same response (i.e., conditioned response) as the unconditioned stimulus.

39. Which of the following depicts Freud's stages of psychosexual development in the correct order?

   A. Oral, phallic, anal, latent, genital

   B. Genital, phallic, anal, latent, oral

   C. Phallic, oral, anal, genital, latent

   D. Oral, anal, phallic, latent, genital

   E. Anal, oral, latent, phallic, genital

The answer is D.
The correct order of the stages of psychosexual development are: oral, anal, phallic, latent, and genital.

40. According to Piaget, the sensorimotor stage occurs between which ages?

   A. 0-2 years

   B. 2-7 years

   C. 7-11 years

   D. 11-15 years

   E. 15+ years

The answer is A.
The sensorimotor stage occurs between ages 0 and 2.

41.　Piaget's theory of cognitive development is concerned with which population?

A.　Newborn babies

B.　Children of all ages

C.　Young adults

D.　Mature adults

E.　Elderly adults

The answer is B.

Piaget's theory of cognitive development is concerned with children of all ages.

42.　Which theory explains how parent-child relationships emerge and influence subsequent development?

A.　Psychoanalytic theory

B.　Social learning theory

C.　Cognitive development

D.　Attachment theory

E.　None of the above

The answer is D.

Attachment theory examines the influence that parent-child relationships have on future relational and personal development.

43. **Developmental psychologists often prefer which type of research design?**

    A. Experimental

    B. Participant observation

    C. Case study

    D. Cross-sectional

    E. Longitudinal

The answer is E.
Longitudinal designs allow researchers because these to study the same people repeatedly over long periods of time, which increases the accuracy of any observed changes.

44. **On which level of Kohlberg's moral stages is a child whose morality is based on rules and punishments?**

    A. Level I. Pre-conventional/premoral

    B. Level II: Conventional/Role conformity

    C. Level III: Post-conventional/Self-accepted moral principles

    D. Level IV: Fully moral

    E. None of the above

The answer is A.
On Level I of Kohlnerg's moral stages (the pre-conventional/premoral stage), children's sense of morality is based on the rules they are given as well as punishments that are doled out for breaking those rules.

45. Which of the following disorders is characterized by hallucinations and delusions such as hearing voices?

    A. Depression

    B. Obsessive compulsive disorder

    C. Bipolar disorder

    D. Schizophrenia

    E. Mania

The answer is D.
Schizophrenia is the only one of the listed disorders that is characterized by hallucinations and delusions.

46. Which of the following drugs has stimulant and hallucinogenic effects?

    A. Molly

    B. Adderall

    C. Marijuana

    D. Cocaine

    E. Pain killers

The answer is A.
Molly is a powder form of the drug MDMA. It is the only drug listed in this series that has both stimulant and hallucinogenic effects.

47. Jimmy is experiencing recurring negative thoughts, a loss of interest in activities that used to excite him, trouble sleeping, and a loss of appetite. From which of the following disorders is Jimmy most likely suffering?

    A. Depression

    B. Obsessive compulsive disorder

    C. Bipolar disorder

    D. Schizophrenia

    E. Mania

The answer is A.
The symptoms listed are classic symptoms of depression.

48. Which of the following anxiety disorders is characterized by a fear of losing control, being trapped, or panicking in public places?

    A. Acrophrobia

    B. Agoraphobia

    C. Generalized anxiety disorder

    D. Post-traumatic stress disorder

    E. General panic attack

The answer is B.
Agoraphobia is characterized by a fear of losing control, being trapped, or panicking in public places. People with this disorder are often afraid to leave their homes.

49. **Antidepressants are often associated with which of the following side effects?**

    A. Insomnia

    B. Dry mouth

    C. An increase in suicidal thoughts

    D. Decreased sexual drive and function

    E. All of the above

The answer is E.
All of the side effects listed are associated with antidepressants.

50. **Which of the following types of disorders is characterized by real physical symptoms that cannot be fully explained by a medical condition, the effects of a drug, or another mental disorder?**

    A. Personality disorders

    B. Anxiety disorders

    C. Somatoform disorders

    D. Affective disorders

    E. Dissociative disorders

The answer is C.
People with somatoform disorders experience real symptoms that cannot be fully explained by a medical condition, mental disorder, or drug. Hypochondria is a type of somatoform disorder. People with hypochondria believe they have an illness when there are no objective signs of that illness present. They often diagnose themselves with illnesses and do not believe doctors who disagree with their diagnoses.

51. Which of the following personality disorders is characterized by an exaggerate sense of self- importance, a strong desire to be admired, and a lack of empathy?

    A. Borderline personality disorder

    B. Histrionic personality disorder

    C. Avoidant personality disorder

    D. Narcissistic personality disorder

    E. Antisocial personality disorder

The answer is D.
The only one of the listed disorders that is characterized by an exaggerated sense of self, a strong desire to be admired, and a lack of empathy is the narcissistic personality disorder.

52. People with which of the following personality disorders often lack empathy and remorse, and exhibit aggressive, impulsive, reckless, or irresponsible behavior?

    A. Borderline personality disorder

    B. Histrionic personality disorder

    C. Avoidant personality disorder

    D. Narcissistic personality disorder

    E. Antisocial personality disorder

The answer is E.
Antisocial personality disorder is marked by a lack of empathy and remorse, as well as aggressive, impulsive, reckless, or irresponsible behavior.

53.   A person who experiences depressive and manic episodes may have
       which of the following disorders?

       A.   Depression

       B.   Obsessive compulsive disorder

       C.   Bipolar disorder

       D.   Schizophrenia

       E.   Mania

The answer is C.

Bipolar disorder is characterized by episodes of depression as well as manic
episodes. Sufferers of bipolar disorder are sometimes referred to as *manic-
depressives* for this reason.

54.   Hypochondria is an example of which of the following types of
       disorders?

       A.   Personality disorders

       B.   Anxiety disorders

       C.   Somatoform disorders

       D.   Affective disorders

       E.   Dissociative disorders

The answer is C.

Hypochondria is a type of somatoform disorder. People with somatoform
disorders experience real symptoms that cannot be fully explained by a
medical condition, mental disorder, or drug. People with hypochondria
believe they have an illness when there are no objective signs of that illness
present. They often diagnose themselves with illnesses and do not believe
doctors who disagree with their diagnoses.

55. The _____ nervous system prepares the body for action, while the _____ nervous system keeps the body still.

   A. Sympathetic, parasympathetic

   B. Autonomic, sympathetic

   C. Parasympathetic, autonomic

   D. Sympathetic, autonomic

   E. Parasympathetic, sympathetic

The answer is A.
The sympathetic nervous system prepares the body for action, while the parasympathetic nervous system keeps the body still. These systems together make up the autonomic nervous system.

56. Which of the following theories of emotion suggests that people experience emotions because they perceive physiological changes in their bodies?

   A. Cognitive appraisal

   B. Schachter and Singer's Two-Factor Theory

   C. Evolutionary Theory

   D. James-Lange Theory

   E. Cannon-Bard Theory

The answer is D.
The James-Lange Theory suggests that people experience emotions because they perceive physiological changes in their bodies. In other words, humans feel changes in their bodies and then their brains react to those changes. Reactions to the physiological changes constitute emotions.

57. Which of the following terms describes a theoretical construct that is used to explain the reasons for people's actions, desires, and needs?

    A. Emotion

    B. Empathy

    C. Motivation

    D. Hunger

    E. Thirst

The answer is C.
The term *motivation* is used to describe the reasons for people's actions, desires, and needs, including hunger and thirst. The other answers are distractions.

58. Which of the following is an example of intrinsic motivation?

    A. Money

    B. Receiving an award

    C. Feeling a sense of accomplishment

    D. Winning a prize

    E. A cheering crowd

The answer is C.
Intrinsic motivation comes from within a person. Examples of intrinsic motivation include autonomy, a sense of accomplishment, mastery of a skill, and curiosity. Extrinsic motivation is external to the person, such as external rewards like trophies, awards, money, or prizes.

59.   Which of the following drugs is commonly abused by college students because its stimulant effects can aid in studying?

A.   Cocaine

B.   Marijuana

C.   Adderall

D.   Alcohol

E.   All of the above

The answer is C.
Adderall is prescribed to treat ADHD. It contains a combination of amphetamine and dextroamphetamine, which are stimulants that affect the chemicals in the brain that contribute to hyperactivity and impulse control.

60.   Which of the following theories suggests that we are motivated to take action based on our biological needs?

A.   Drive reduction theory

B.   Arousal theory

C.   Instinct theory

D.   Maslow's Hierarchy of Needs

E.   Goal-setting theory

The answer is A.
Drive reduction theory states that humans are motivated to take action to satisfy biological or physical needs.

61. Which of the following theories of emotion argues that one's experience of emotion depends on their physiological arousal and cognitive interpretation of that arousal?

    A. Cognitive appraisal

    B. Schachter and Singer's Two-Factor Theory

    C. Evolutionary Theory

    D. James-Lange Theory

    E. Cannon-Bard Theory

The answer is B.
Schacter and Singer's Two-Factor Theory says that one's emotional experience is based on two factors: physiological arousal and a label of that arousal. In other words, people's emotional experiences come from physiological feelings (i.e., changes in the body such as increased heart rate, shallow breathing, and sweating) and the labels we assign to those feelings (i.e., sadness, fear, anger).

62. Which of the following is the correct term for vision that comes from the side of the eye?

    A. Peripheral vision

    B. Tunnel vision

    C. Perceptive vision

    D. Sensation

    E. Detection

The answer is A.
Peripheral vision is a part of vision that occurs outside the center of one's gaze. Peripheral sight comes from the outer sides of the field of vision.

63. **Which of the following correctly lists Piaget's stages of cognitive development?**

   A. Sensorimotor, concrete operational, preoperational, formal operational

   B. Preoperational, formal operational, concrete operational. sensorimotor

   C. Formal operational, concrete operational, preoperational, sensorimotor

   D. Concrete operational, preoperational, sensorimotor, formal operational

   E. Sensorimotor, preoperational, concrete operational, formal operational

The answer is E.
The correct order of Piaget's stages of cognitive development is: Sensorimotor, preoperational, concrete operational, formal operational.

64. **Which of the following therapies is considered a last resort method of treating depression when all other therapies have failed?**

   A. Antidepressant medication

   B. Psychoanalytic therapy

   C. Cognitive-behavioral therapy

   D. Electroconvulsive shock therapy

   E. Group therapy

The answer is D.
Electroconvulsive shock therapy is considered a last resort method of treating aggressive clinical depression. Psychoanalytic theory is not widely practiced, nor is it commonly prescribed for the treatment of depression. Common treatments for depression include group therapy, cognitive-behavioral therapy, and antidepressant medication.

65. **Which of the following best describes a cross-sectional study?**

   A. A researcher follows the same participants over a period of time.

   B. A researcher examines different groups of people who share one or more similar characteristics.

   C. A researcher brings people into a lab and has them complete a task.

   D. A researcher observes people in their homes.

   E. A researcher surveys observes people in public.

The answer is B.
A cross-sectional study is one where a researcher examines different groups of people who share one or more similar characteristics, such as age, IQ, or geographical location.

66. **Psychology researchers use which of the following terms to describe thinking, reasoning, and solving problems?**

   A. Emotion

   B. Intuition

   C. Perception

   D. Sensation

   E. Cognition

The answer is E.
Cognition is the mental process of acquiring knowledge and understanding through thought, experience, and the senses. Cognition includes mental processes such as thinking, reasoning, and problem-solving.

67.   Lawrence Kohlberg is known for his research in the area of
_____ development.

    A.   Cognitive

    B.   Moral

    C.   Personality

    D.   Emotional

    E.   Physical

The answer is B.
Lawrence Kohlberg is known for his research in the area of moral
development.

68.   **Which of the following statements about antidepressants do most
psychology researchers and practitioners consider true?**

    A.   Antidepressants are helpful in treating some forms of depression.

    B.   For many patients, antidepressants are less helpful than
individual therapy in treating depression.

    C.   Antidepressants alone are not enough to successfully treat
depression in many patients.

    D.   All of the above

    E.   None of the above

The answer is D.
Choices A, B, and C are all statements about antidepressants that most
psychology researchers and practitioners would consider true.

69. Which of the following therapies helps people work through problems by interacting with one or more therapists as well as other individuals experiencing similar struggles?

   A. Individual therapy

   B. Drug therapy

   C. Group therapy

   D. Psychoanalytic therapy

   E. Social-Emotional therapy

The answer is C.

Group therapy brings together one or more therapists with multiple individuals who are experiencing similar struggles. None of the other theories listed here are conducted in a group setting.

70. According to Kübler-Ross, the correct order of the stages of grief are:

   A. denial, anger, bargaining, depression, acceptance.

   B. anger, denial, depression, bargaining, acceptance.

   C. denial, depression, anger, acceptance, bargaining.

   D. depression, denial, anger, bargaining, acceptance.

   E. acceptance, denial, anger, bargaining, depression.

The answer is A.

According to Kübler-Ross, the stages of grief (in order) are: denial, anger, bargaining, depression, and acceptance.

71. **Which of the following correctly describes the difference between depression and grief?**

   A. Grief often entails a sense of worthlessness whereas depression does not.

   B. Grief involves excessive guilt and depression does not.

   C. Grief lasts longer than major depression.

   D. Grief subsides after a period of time whereas depression often persists for extended periods of time.

   E. Grief is a clinical condition whereas depression is a normal, healthy emotion.

The answer is D.
Grief is a normal, healthy emotion. Depression is a clinical illness. When processed in a normal, healthy way, grief lasts for a period of time and subsides on its own. However, prolonged grief can lead to depression, which is an ongoing mental illness. Depression persists for extended periods of time whereas grief is shorter-lived.

72. **Cara describes herself as outgoing, funny and friendly. These characteristics are part of her**

   A. self-esteem.

   B. motivation.

   C. self-concept.

   D. group identity.

   E. physique.

The answer is C.
Self-concept is a collection of one's beliefs about him or herself. It includes beliefs about one's personality, gender and sexual identities, academic performance, and racial identity, among other characteristics.

73.   In personality research, which of the following describes personal
       characteristics that are biologically determined?

    A.   Nature

    B.   Environment

    C.   State

    D.   Trait

    E.   Ego

The answer is D.
Personal characteristics that are determined by biology are called traits.

74.   Which of the following is not a standard method used to assess
       personality?

    A.   Self-reports

    B.   Observer-reports

    C.   Test data

    D.   Projective measures

    E.   Laboratory study

The answer is E.
Laboratory studies are not commonly used to assess personality. All of the
other research methods listed here are frequently used to assess personality.

75. **The Big Five personality traits are:**

   A.   Humor, openness, extraversion, agreeableness, neuroticism.

   B.   Extraversion, agreeableness, enlightenment, openness, neuroticism

   C.   Openness, conscientiousness, extraversion, agreeableness, neuroticism.

   D.   Extraversion, introversion, humor, neuroticism, openness

   E.   Happiness, neuroticism, shyness, openness, extraversion

The answer is C.
The Big Five personality Traits are: Openness, conscientiousness, extraversion, agreeableness, and neuroticism.

76. **_____ refers to the pattern of thoughts, feelings, social adjustments and behaviors consistently exhibited over time.**

   A.   Preferences

   B.   Self-esteem

   C.   Construct

   D.   Personality

   E.   Extraversion

The answer is D.
The definition of personality is the pattern of thoughts, feelings, social adjustments and behaviors consistently exhibited over time.

77.   **Conscientiousness refers to one's**

     A.   tendency to be creative, curious, and open to new ideas.

     B.   tendency to be organized and self-disciplined.

     C.   tendency to experience unpleasant emotions easily.

     D.   tendency to be compassionate and cooperative towards others.

     E.   tendency to exhibit to seek stimulation in the company of others.

The answer is B.
Conscientiousness refers to one's tendency be organized and self-disciplined.

78.   **Which of the following types of psychologists believe that one's personality consists of learned patterns**

     A.   Emotional psychologists

     B.   Humanists

     C.   Behavioral psychologists

     D.   Psychoanalytic theorists

     E.   Cognitive psychologists

The answer is C.
Behavioral psychologists believe that one's personality consists of learned patterns.

79.   Kim lives in Alaska and says that a 60-degree day is warm. Steve
      lives in Arizona and thinks 60-degree weather is cold. Their
      perceptions differ because of

      A.   their frame of reference

      B.   where they place their attention

      C.   perceptual constancy

      D.   their personalities

      E.   their top-down processing

The answer is A.
Kim and Steve have differing frames of reference, which account for their
different opinions about how cold or warm 60-degree weather is.

80.   Which of the following terms explains why roads appear to converge
      in the distance?

      A.   Light and shadow

      B.   Continuing patterns

      C.   Texture gradient

      D.   Linear perspective

      E.   None of the above

The answer is D.
In linear perspective, parallel lines that recede into the distance appear to get
closer together. This explains why roads appear to converge in the distance.

81. Anything that can be perceived with one of the five senses is considered _____ stimulus, whereas _____ stimulus refers to the specific object upon which one is focused.

    A. Attended, environmental

    B. Image, recognition

    C. Environmental, attended

    D. Neural, retinal

    E. Neural, image

The answer is C.

Environmental stimuli are anything that can be perceived with the five senses. The specific object upon which one's attention is focused is called *attended stimuli*.

82. An image on the retina of the eye is transformed into electrical signals in a process known as which of the following?

    A. Transcendence

    B. Abduction

    C. Transformation

    D. Intensification

    E. Transduction

The answer is E.

Transduction is the process by which our eyes turn light into neural impulses that our brains can understand. Transduction takes an image on the retina of the eye and transforms it into electrical signals that the brain can process.

83. Which of the following is true of secondary reinforcers?

    A. They are learned.

    B. They are ineffective.

    C. They are more effective than primary reinforcers.

    D. They are innate.

    E. They are natural.

The answer is A.
Primary reinforcers occur naturally and do not need to be learned; they have biological and evolutionary bases. Examples of primary reinforcers include food, air, water, sleep, and sex. Secondary reinforcers involve stimuli that are rewarding because they have been paired with another, naturally-occurring reinforcer. Secondary reinforcers are learned.

84. The analysis of information starting with features and building into a complete perception is known as which of the following?

    A. Perceptual constancy

    B. Top-down processing

    C. Bottom-up processing

    D. Chunking

    E. Linking

The answer is C.
Bottom-up processing starts with features and builds up into a complete perception. Top-down processing starts with a perception (i.e., cognition) and then moves down to the senses, or specific features.

85. Which of the following allows humans to perceive the world in three dimensions?

    A. Depth perception

    B. Sensation

    C. Disparity

    D. Convergence

    E. Accommodation

The answer is A.
Depth perception allows humans to see in three dimensions. The other choices are distractions.

86. Neurons are made up of which of the following?

    A. Anterior cell, posterior cell, axon

    B. Dendrite, soma, axon

    C. Cell body, cell wall, nucleus

    D. Myelin, dendrite, cell wall

    E. None of the above

The answer is B.
Neurons are made up of dendrites, a soma, and axon. Dendrites are the treelike structures that receive signals from other nerve cells. The cell body, or soma, produces all of the proteins that make up all of the parts of the neuron. The axon is the main conducting component of the neuron; it transmits electrical signals throughout the nervous system.

87.   Which of the following describes the main function of myelin?

A.   Myelin forms a protective coating over nerve axons.

B.   Myelin decreases the speed with which information travels from nerve cell to nerve cell.

C.   Myelin blocks reception of acetylcholine.

D.   Myelin slows down nerve degeneration.

E.   Myelin aids in the transference of neurotransmitters.

The answer is A.
The function of myelin is to protect the nerve axons. Myelin forms a protective coating over nerve axons.

88.   Neurotransmitters are released at which part of a cell?

A.   Dendrite

B.   Axon terminal

C.   Nucleus

D.   Soma

E.   Myelin

The answer is B.
Neurotransmitters are released at the axon terminal.

89. Communication within a neuron is a(n) _____ process, while communication between neurons is a(n) _____ process.

   A. Chemical; mechanical

   B. Electrical; mechanical

   C. Chemical; electrical

   D. Electrical; chemical

   E. Mechanical; electrical

The answer is D.
Communication within a neuron is an electrical process, while communication between neurons is a chemical process.

90. **Human behavior is influenced by genetic processes as well their environments and experiences. In psychology, this is known as which of the following?**

   A. Genes versus experience

   B. Heredity versus environment

   C. Climate versus science

   D. Nature versus nurture

   E. Genes versus personality

The answer is D.
Psychologists use the phrase *nature versus nurture* to describe how human behavior is influenced by genetic characteristics as well as people's environments and experiences.

91.   Which of the following is the main link between the brain and the glandular system in the human body?

  A. Hypothalamus

  B. Prefrontal cortex

  C. Central nervous system

  D. Sympathetic nervous system

  E. Parasympathetic nervous system

The answer is A.
The hypothalamus is the main link between the brain and the glandular system in the human body. The hypothalamus is responsible for activities of the autonomic nervous system.

92.   The endocrine system is responsible for which of the following functions?

  A. It pumps blood throughout the body.

  B. It brings oxygen into the body.

  C. It secretes hormones into the blood stream for communication between cells.

  D. It processes sensory information from the eyes and ears.

  E. None of the above.

The answer is C.
The endocrine system is responsible for producing and regulating hormones. The endocrine system secretes hormones into the blood system for communication between cells.

93.   An EEG records which of the following?

   A.   The electrical rhythm of the heart.

   B.   Electrical impulses from the brain.

   C.   Hormone secretion in the bloodstream.

   D.   Electrical currents in the body.

   E.   The number of neurons in the brain.

The answer is B.
EEG stands for electroencephalogram, which is a test that detects electrical activity in the brain.

94.   In Pavlov's famous experiment, the dog's salivation over food was considered which of the following?

   A.   Conditioned response

   B.   Conditioned stimulus

   C.   Automatic stimulus

   D.   Unconditioned response

   E.   Unconditioned stimulus

The answer is D.
Dogs naturally salivate in response to food. They do not need to learn this response. Salivating is an unconditioned response to food (an unconditioned stimulus).

95.   Which of the following scientists is known for studying operant
       conditioning?

   A.   Pavlov

   B.   Freud

   C.   Maslow

   D.   Piaget

   E.   Skinner

The answer is E.

B. F. Skinner is known for his work on operant conditioning. Operant
conditioning is sometimes called *instrumental learning*. It involves learning
through trial and consequences. Reinforcements and punishments are core
tools through which behavior modification occurs.

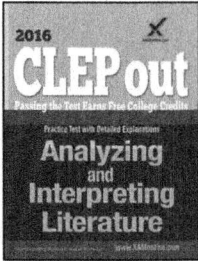

XAMonline

CLEP

Full Study Guides

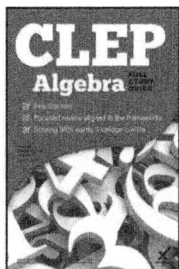

CLEP College Algebra
ISBN: 9781607875598
Price: $34.95

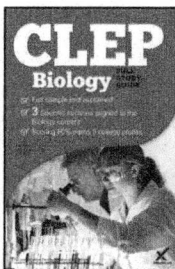

CLEP Biology
ISBN: 9781607875314
Price: $34.95

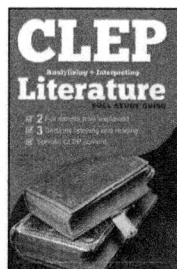

CLEP Analyzing and
Interpreting Literature
ISBN: 9781607875260
Price: $34.95

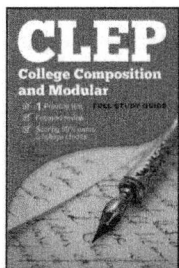

CLEP College Composition
and Modular
ISBN: 9781607875277
Price: $19.99

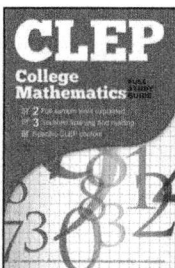

CLEP College Mathematics
ISBN: 9781607875321
Price: $34.95

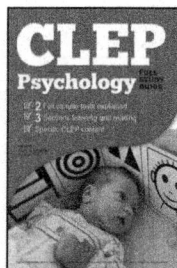

CLEP Psychology
ISBN: 9781607875291
Price: $34.95

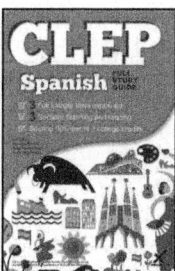

CLEP Spanish
ISBN: 9781607875284
Price: $34.95

XAMonline
CLEP Subject Series
Collection by Topic
Sample Test Approach

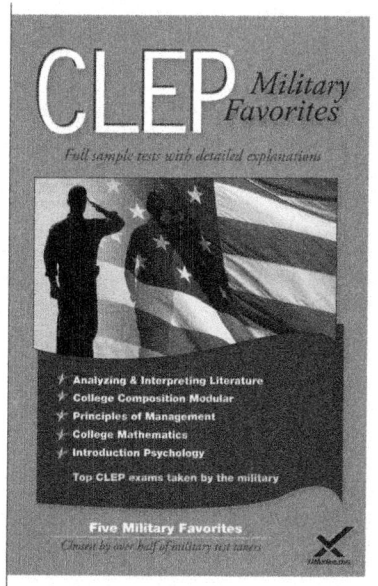

CPSIA information can be obtained
at www.ICGtesting.com
Printed in the USA
BVOW06s0240120917
494630BV00010B/69/P

9 781607 875512